Study Guide

Introduction to Business Statistics: A Microsoft® Excel Integrated Approach

Sixth Edition

Alan H. Kvanli
University of North Texas

Robert J. Pavur
University of North Texas

Kellie B. Keeling
Virginia Polytechnic Institute and State University

Prepared by

P. S. Sundararaghavan
The University of Toledo

THOMSON
SOUTH-WESTERN

Australia · Canada · Mexico · Singapore · Spain · United Kingdom · United States

Study Guide to accompany ***Introduction to Business Statistics: A Microsoft® Excel Integrated Approach, 6e***

Alan H. Kvanli, Robert J. Pavur, and Kellie B. Keeling

Vice President and Team Director:
Melissa Acuña

Senior Acquisitions Editor:
Charles McCormick, Jr.

Senior Developmental Editor:
Alice Denny

Marketing Manager:
Larry Qualls

Production Editor:
Chris Hudson

Manufacturing Coordinator:
Diane Lohman

Printer:
Globus Printing
Minster, Ohio

ISBN: 0-324-15751-7

Printed in the United States of America
1 2 3 4 5 05 04 03 02

For more information contact South-Western, 5191 Natorp Boulevard, Mason, Ohio 45040.
Or you can visit our Internet site at: http://www.swcollege.com

Table of Contents

1. A First Look at Statistics and Data Collection
2. Data Presentation using Descriptive Graphs
3. Data Summary using Descriptive Measures
4. Probability Concepts
5. Discrete Probability Distributions
6. Continuous Probability Distributions
7. Statistical Inference and Sampling
8. Hypothesis Testing for the Mean and Variance of a Population
9. Inference Procedures for Two Populations
10. Estimation and Testing for Population Proportions
11. Analysis of Variance
12. Quality Improvement
13. Applications of the Chi-Square Statistic
14. Correlation and Simple Linear Regression
15. Multiple Linear Regression
16. Time Series Analysis and Index Numbers
17. Quantitative Business Forecasting
18. Nonparametric Statistics

CHAPTER 1
A FIRST LOOK AT STATISTICS AND DATA COLLECTION

Chapter Summary and Learning Objectives

The purpose of this chapter is to establish the frame of reference for the study of statistics. It introduces the student to many of the key terms used throughout the text as well as introducing them to types of data, data sources and methods of data collection.
At the completion of this chapter, the student should be able to answer the following questions:

1. What is "statistics" and why is the study of statistics important to a business manager?
2. What is meant by the term "descriptive statistics"? "Inferential statistics"?
3. What is a population? A sample? A census?
4. What are the types of data? (Discrete/continuous)
5. What are the strengths of data? (Nominal, ordinal, interval, ratio)
6. What distinguishes qualitative data from quantitative data?
7. When should one use primary/secondary data as a data source?
8. What is a random sample and when is it appropriate to use a convenience sample?
9. What should one keep in mind when designing and coding a questionnaire?

Chapter Outline

1.1 Using the Computer
1.2 Use of Statistics in Business
1.3 Some Basic Definitions
1.4 Discrete and Continuous Numerical Data
1.5 Level of Measurement for Numcrical Data
1.6 Sources of Data
1.7 Self-Test Problems
1.8 Glossary
1.9 Solutions to Self-Test Problems

1.1 Introduction and use of computers

Statistics is a science comprising of rules and procedures for collecting, describing, analyzing and interpreting numerical data. (Loosely speaking: Statistics is the art and science of approximating and converting numerical data into meaningful words for decision making.)
Businesses, Government, scientific researchers, medical; researchers, political scientists and many others use statistics. As business students:

1. You might use statistics to interpret reports
2. You might statistics to articulate your request for information to consultants
3. You might make decision based on correct understanding of reports generated by statisticians/computer software

Computer software, specifically EXCEL, is very useful in doing all of these.

1.2 Uses of Statistics in Business

Important business applications:

1. Quality management
2. Forecasting
3. Market research
4. Analysis of financial reports
5. Analysis of human resource issues: performance appraisal, discrimination claims, etc.

1.3 Some Basic Definitions

Simple random sample: similar to drawing from a hat. (Technically speaking) In a random sampling procedure, all elements of the population have an equal chance of getting selected. Similarly, if you take a random sample of size n from a population of size N, all samples have the same chance of being selected. Some examples of population and samples follow.

Population	Sample
All rolls of a pair of dies	50 rolls of the dies
All students at the University of Jamesville	A random sample of 50 students
All potato chips bags manufactured and to be manufactured	A sample of 50 bags collected at the rate 5 on the hour for 10 hours
All consumers of a product	A sample of customers who were surveyed
All brakes fixed by Midas	A sample of customers who filled out a survey of customer satisfaction
All new car buyers in 2002	A sample of customers who filled out consumer report survey
All goods and prices in the market	A sample of prices used by Labor bureau to calculate consumer price index

Table 1.3.1. Examples of Populations and Samples

1.4 Discrete and Continuous Numerical Data

Discrete data: Consists of only whole numbers or a finite set of fractional numbers as possible candidate values. Example: Employees in a firm, amount of candies sold in a store, which only sells it in multiples of half pounds. Number of employees in a firm where each employee could be either full-time or half-time and half-time employees are counted as 0.5 employee. This is still discrete data.

Continuous Data: Weights, heights, age, calories consumed in a typical day, etc. All of these can be measured in continuous data. Time elapsed between the arrivals of two consecutive customers in a Burger King, height of students where height is measured accurately

1.5 Level of Measurement for Numerical data

Nominal data: Categorized data. Examples are: male and female; employees with 5 or less years of experience and employees with more than 5 years of experience, Cars of different colors, homes with pool and home without pool. Another way to look at it is to say, these represent different labels. Assigning a number/label for convenience. Male = 1 and female = 2, or General motors = 1, Chrysler = 2, Ford = 3, Toyota = 4, etc.

Ordinal data: Data can be ordered, that is, there is a natural ranking. Examples: student feed back on courses: (excellent, very good, good, fair, poor), grades in a course, But the distance between the ranks is not necessarily equal. Another example of ordinal measurement would be giving ranks at the end of each exam rather than scores. The difference in the score of 1st and 2nd rank need not be the same as that of difference between 2nd and 3rd. Ranks.

Interval Scale: The differences in values are meaningful, can be averaged, and totaled. Temperature is an interval scale. Many tests require at least interval level of measurement. IQ scores may be an example. A person with 150 IQ is not necessarily 50% smarter than a person with 100 IQ.

Ratio Scale: It has a natural zero point. This represents nothing exists. Foe example score in a test: Nothing is you got zero. Amount of money is your pocket: Nothing means your pocket is empty. If twice the value means twice the strength, it is ratio scale. For example, the amount of money in your pocket.

1.6 Sources of Data

Primary Data:

- Comes from original sources
- Collected for specific research
- Expensive
- Requires more effort
- Addresses your specific research question
- Examples include market research by firms, polls by politicians, satisfaction surveys by companies, student feedback by schools.

Secondary Data:

- Previously recorded data
- Represents usually many years of data
- Difficult to verify appropriateness of collection methods
- *Statistical Abstract of the United States, Canadian Business and Current Affairs Fulltext Business, United Nations Statistical Yearbook.* Business periodicals: *Business Week, Wall Street Journal, and Fortune.*

Sampling:

- Random sampling: All items in the population have equal probability of being selected
- Non random sampling:
    - Convenience sampling: e.g. Instructor sampling his/her class and treating it as a sample of the student population
    - Judgment Sampling: Picking specific people like those who did well and those who did poorly in the last test to find out about their opinion of this test
    - Quota sampling: making a deliberate attempt to get the entire population , like if the class had 30 % boys, sampling 30% from boys and 70% from girls

How to select a set of 50 random samples from 1000 students? Easiest method would be to assign a student identification (ID) number to all 1000 students first. You may do this by first listing all students in alphabetical order and associating number 0 to 999 with the students from the alphabetical list. Then, choose a three digit random numbers, and pick the student with the same student ID as the number picked. If a number repeats, throw it out and pick another number from the table in its place and continue till 50 students have been chose. Random number s in the random number table have two important properties: (a) Uniformity: Probability that any number in the interval 0 to 9 shows up in a cell of the random number table is 0.1. (There is an equal chance for all the whole numbers 0 to 9). (b) Independence: Given any information about a sequence of numbers in a random number table, the probability for 0 to 9 is still uniform and each is equal to 0.1. These two properties together ensure that the sample chosen is indeed random. We can also generate random number through Data Analysis program of Excel.

1.7 Self-Test Problems

Multiple Choice Questions

1. Using Statistics your answer to a question may only be correct most of the time but not all the time. Hence, there is no use in studying Statistics
    a. True
    b. False
2. Statistics is an approximate science to exactly report on inferences, approximations and estimates.
    a. True
    b. False
3. Important statistical applications are found in
    a. Finance
    b. Marketing
    c. (a) and (b)
    d. None of the above
4. Data may be measured in ordinal or interval scale, though ordinal is more accurate way to measure than interval scale.
    a. True
    b. False
5. Ordinal data may be multiplied to get meaningful information
    a. True
    b. False
6. In random sampling, all members of the population have an equal chance of getting selected.
    a. True
    b. False
7. In quota sampling, there is a minimum number that must be sampled from each group regardless of how many members are in that group in the population.
    a. True
    b. False
8. In discrete data, the data must always be whole numbers
    a. True
    b. False
9. Statistics is an exact science for approximating, inferring and estimating using data.
    a. True
    b. False
10. Data may be measured in nominal or ordinal scale, though ordinal has more information than nominal.

    a. True
    b. False

11. In ratio scale 20 units is twice as big as 10 units.
    a. True
    b. False
12. In random sampling, all members of the population have an unequal chance of getting selected.
    a. True
    b. False
13. A closed-end question in a survey allows the subject (person completing the survey) document his/her opinion.
    a. True
    b. False
14. A statistic
    a. is a special way of referring to the science of Statistics
    b. is road-kill
    c. is a value describing a sample
    d. is an average
    e. None of the above
15. In a survey questionnaire, the question asking the subject for his or her opinion is an example of an open-ended question
    a. True
    b. False
16. The CIA-Country data in the CIA website (www. cia.gov/cia/publications/factbook) is an example of primary data because Central Intelligence Agency is charged with the primary responsibility for this project.
    a. True
    b. False

1.8 Glossary

census
A sample that contains the entire population, such as the sample obtained by performing 100% inspection of an incoming batch of material.

closed ended question
A question with a pre-determined number of possible responses.

continuous data
Data that can assume any value over some continuous range.

convenience sample
A sample in which the individuals are selected for their ready availability and presumed resemblance to the population of interest.

data coding
Preparing questionnaire data for computer input.

descriptive statistics
The process of collecting and describing sample data.

discrete data
Data that have limited, specific possible values, characterized by gaps in the possible values.

designed experiment
A source of primary data that examines the effect of changes to a process.

inferential statistics
The process of drawing conclusions about a population based on the results of a statistical sample.

interval data
Data for which both the order of the data and the difference between any two data values is meaningful. However, the value 0 (zero) is not indicative of the absence of whatever is being measured; that is, there is no "zero point".

judgment sample
A sample deliberately selected because of their supposed knowledge of the population.

Likert scale question
A question containing scaled (ranked) responses, generally ranging from "strongly disagree" to "strongly agree."

nominal data
Categorical data that may be numeric codes. This coding is not necessary, since nominal data can also consist of words (such as, MALE and FEMALE).

nonrandom samples
Samples selected in a convenient or deliberate manner with little or no attention paid to randomization.

open-ended question
A question requiring a written response.

ordinal data
Data for which the order of the values is meaningful, but not the distance between them.

parameter
A value that describes a population, such as the average height or the percentage of defective components.

population
The set of all possible measurements that are of interest.
primary data
Data from an original (primary) source designed to gain insight into a specific research question.

quota sample
A sample deliberately selected to be a miniature of the population.

ratio data
Data having all the properties of interval data and also containing a definite zero point.

sample
The portion of the population selected for observation.

sample size
The number of items in a sample, generally written as "n".

secondary data
Previously recorded data, generally collected as part of a regularly scheduled data collection procedure (such as an annual government report or annual company financial statement).

simple random sample
A sample for which every sample of size n has the same chance of being selected.

statistic
A value that describes a sample, such as the average of 200 sample heights or the percentage of defective components in a sample of 500.

qualitative data
Nominal or ordinal data.

quantitative data
Interval or ratio data.

1.9 Answers to Self-Test Problems

Answers to Multiple Choice Questions

Question #	Answer	Question #	Answer	Question #	Answer	Question #	Answer
1	b	5	b	9	a	13	b
2	b	6	a	10	a	14	c
3	c	7	b	11	a	15	a
4	b	8	b	12	b	16	b

CHAPTER 2
DATA PRESENTATION USING DESCRIPTIVE GRAPHS

Chapter Overview and Learning Objectives

Graphical presentation has always been one of the best ways to transmit statistical information. A statistical graph allows you to summarize and describe a set of values from a sample or population. Because of the ease with which many microcomputers can create and print graphs, this usage is growing.
At the completion of this chapter, the student should be able to answer the following questions:

1. What is a frequency distribution, and how would you construct a frequency distribution from a set of data?
2. How does one construct (and when is it appropriate to use) each of the following graphs:
   a. Histogram
   b. Frequency polygon
   c. Ogive
   d. Bar chart
   e. Pie chart
   f. Stem-and-leaf diagram
3. What are some of the ways in which a seemingly accurate graph can be drawn in a misleading and deceptive manner?

Chapter Outline

2.1 Frequency Distributions
2.2 Histograms and Stem and Leaf Diagrams
2.3 Frequency Polygons
2.4 Cumulative Frequencies (Ogives)
2.5 Bar Charts
2.6 Pie Charts
2.7 Deceptive Graphs
2.8 Using Computer Graphics
2.9 Self-Test Problems
2.10 Glossary
2.11 Solutions to Self-Test Problems

2.1 Frequency Distributions

Suppose that you wanted to get an idea of the summer earnings of 30 sophomores in her class in The University of Jamesville, you can collect the data methodically from the 30 sophomores. But to make good sense out of the data, (especially if you had a large set of data) you have to organize it in some way. Frequency distribution is one way of organizing it.

Review Problem 2.1.1

Table 2.1.1. presents details of the summer earnings rounded to the nearest dollar of 30 sophomores of the University of Jamesville. Organize it in a frequency distribution. Give the frequency and relative frequency.

3618	799	1962	4414	274	4733
1971	4208	1570	2496	405	3589
1748	2737	4999	1001	3080	4691
2562	1272	545	4836	4914	0
1604	4162	195	595	2175	1006

Table 2.1.1. Data on Summer Earnings of 30 Sophomores.

First step is to order the data as shown in Table 2.1.1.

0	595	1570	2175	3589	4691
195	799	1604	2496	3618	4733
274	1001	1748	2562	4162	4836
405	1006	1962	2737	4208	4914
545	1272	1971	3080	4414	4999

Table 2.1.2 Data on Summer Earnings of 30 Sophomores in Ascending Order.

Look for the largest value and the smallest value in the table. The smallest value is 0 and the largest value is 4999. Range = Highest value – lowest value = 4999 - 0= 4999. The next question is how many classes are needed? Let us say 5. The width of each interval = 4999/5 = 999.2, Round it to the nearest number which makes sense, say 1000. We need 5 class intervals, starting from 0, and of width 1000, and then grouped in class intervals. by putting a check mark for each number in the interval which leads to Table 2.1.3 called frequency distribution. Relative frequency is obtained by dividing the frequency by the total frequency.

Class interval	Frequency		Relative frequency
0 to under 1000	𝍸 ||	7	7/30 = 0.233
1000 to under 2000	𝍸 |||	8	8/30 = 0.266
2000 to under 3000	||||	4	4/30 = 0.133
3000 to under 4000	|||	3	3/30 = 0.100
4000 to under 5000	𝍸 |||	8	8/30 = 0.266
Total frequency		30	1.0

Table 2.1.3. Frequency Distribution.

Open ended classes: Some class intervals at the top or bottom may be open ended. (e.g. 4000 and above or under 1000.

Outliers: In some data, there may be one or two pieces of data at the upper or lower end , sort of away from the rest of the data. In this case, it may not be a good idea to make many class intervals, which will tend to have very low if not 0 frequency. These outliers may be grouped into some open interval at the top or bottom.

2.2 Histograms and Stem and Leaf Diagrams

Histogram: Graphical representation of frequency distribution:
Relative frequency histogram: Histogram constructed with relative frequencies.

Review Problem 2.2.1.

Construct a Histogram for the data given in Review Problem 2.1.1.

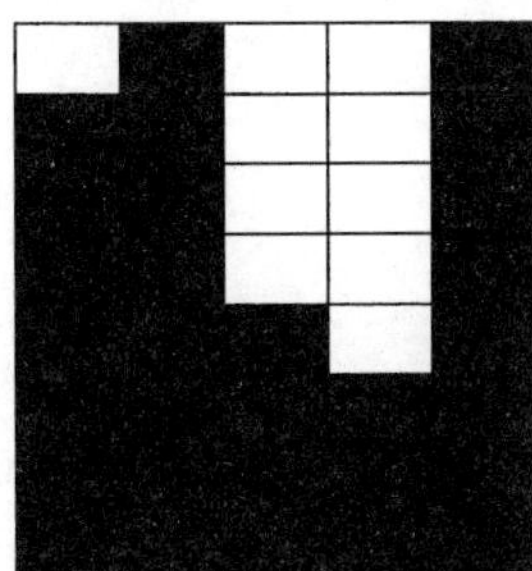

Figure 2.2.1 Histogram (bar chart) for Review Problem 2.2.1.

Histogram is simply a bar diagram with class intervals on the horizontal axis and frequencies on the vertical axis. Table 2.1.3. gives the data required to do the bar chart. and the bar chart/histogram is presented in Figure 2.2.1.

2.3 Frequency Polygon

Review Problem 2.3.1.
A graphical representation of a frequency distribution consisting of dots at the top center of each histogram box along with connecting lines.
Draw a frequency polygon for the data of Review Problem 2.1.1.

The X-axis is used for the earnings and the Y-axis is used for the frequencies. Table 2.3.1 gives the midpoint of class intervals and frequency, including one class interval below the smallest midpoint in the original data with a frequency of 0, and one midpoint above the original class intervals with frequency 0. Figure 2.3.1 gives the frequency polygon.

Midpoint of Class Interval	Frequency
-500	0
500	7
1500	8
2500	4
3500	3
4500	8
5500	0

Table 2.3.1. Midpoint of class interval and Frequency

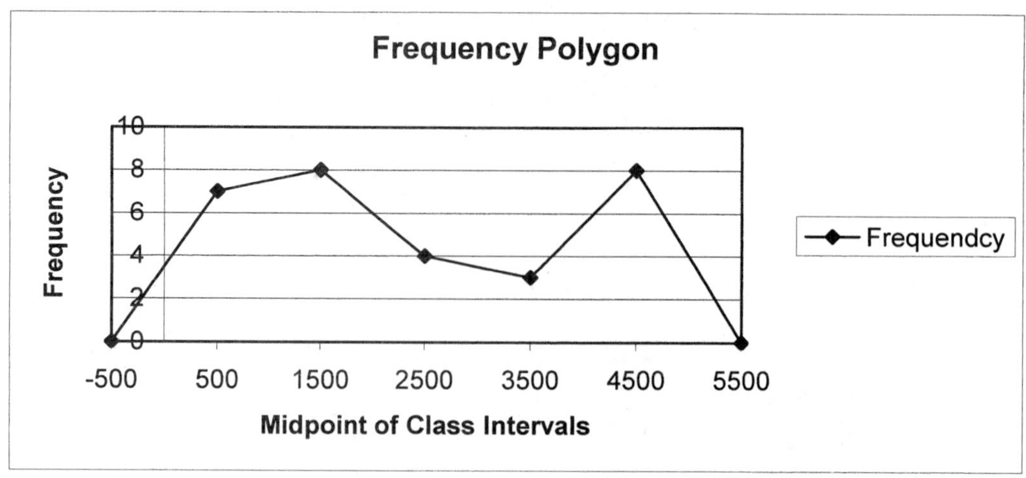

Figure 2.3.1. Frequency Polygon based on Data in Table 2.3.1

Note that the frequency polygon is drawn with midpoint of class intervals as the X-coordinate values, against frequency on the Y-axis. Use a 0 frequency for the midpoint of imaginary intervals to the left and right of the lower and upper intervals respectively to complete the polygon. Vertical axis begins at 0.

2.4 Cumulative Frequencies (Ogives)

Cumulative frequency polygon is the sum of the class frequencies for a particular class and all preceding classes
It represents the number of data values that are less than the upper class limit of the class. It is also called an ogive.

Review Problem 2.4.1.
Construct a cumulative frequency polygon or less than ogive for the data of Review Problem 2.1.1. Data is presented in appropriate format in Table 2.2.3, which gives the upper limit of the class interval and the cumulative frequency up to the upper limit of the class interval in the original data. The graph is presented in Figure 2.4.1.

Upper limit	Cumulative Frequency
< 0	0
< 1000	7
< 2000	15
< 3000	19
< 4000	22
< 5000	30

Table 2.4.1 Data for Cumulative Frequency Polygon (Less-than Ogive)

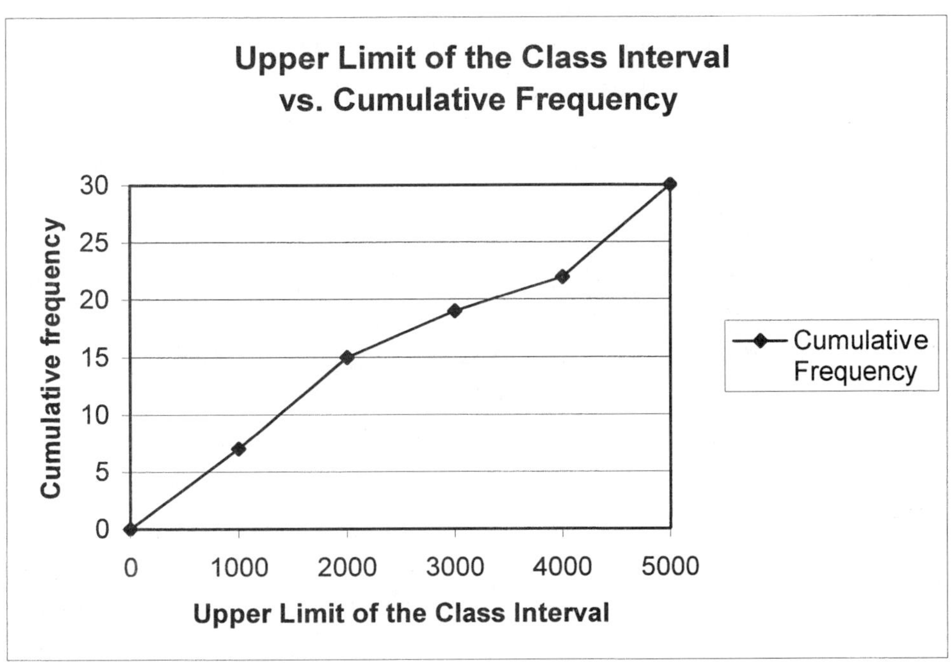

Figure 2.4.1. Cumulative Frequency Polygon (Less-than Ogive) for Data of Table 2.4.1.

Note some differences between frequency polygon and cumulative frequency polygon:

Frequency Polygon	Cumulative Frequency Polygon
X-axis: midpoint of class interval.	X-axis: Upper limit of class interval.
Starts at the midpoint of the imaginary class interval below the lowest class interval with a frequency of 0.	Starts at the first class interval's lower limit with a frequency of 0.
Ends at the midpoint of the imaginary class interval above the largest class interval with a frequency of 0.	Ends with the upper limit of the largest class interval with a frequency equal to the total frequency.

Table 2.4.2. Differences between Frequency Polygon and Cumulative Frequency Polygon.

2.5 Bar Charts

A statistical graph consisting of noncontiguous boxes useful for summarizing nominal or ordinal data.

Review Problem 2.5.1.
Construct a bar chart for the data of Review Problem 2.1.1.
It is usually constructed using the income intervals on the X-axis and frequency on the Y-axis. Data analysis tool of Excel is a general tool to do this. It can also be done using graph paper and drawing like drawing a graph.

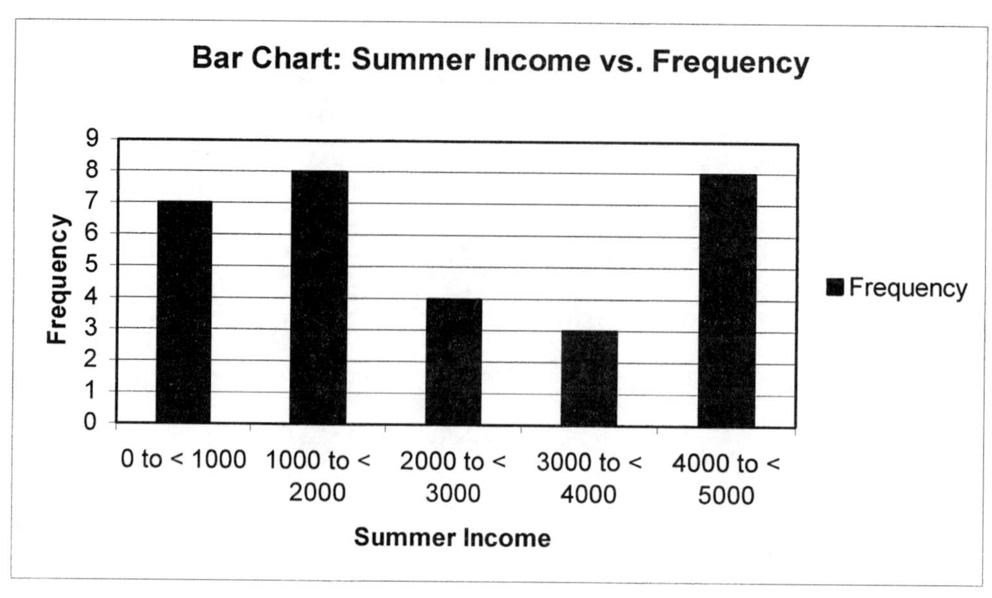

2.6 Pie Charts

Pie chart is a statistical graph useful for presenting a percentage breakdown of a particular quantity. Procedure for constructing a pie chart: Find the relative frequency for each class interval, and multiply the relative frequency by 360 (the number of degrees around a point) to get the number of degrees to be used to represent each class interval.

Review Problem 2.6.1.
Construct a Pie chart for the data of Review Problem 2.1.1.

The degree details are given in Table 2.6.1. and the Pie chart is given in Figure 2.6.1.

Class Interval	Frequency	Relative Frequency	Degrees for the Pie Chart
0 to < 1000	7	0.233333333	84
1000 to < 2000	8	0.266666667	96
2000 to < 3000	4	0.133333333	48
3000 to < 4000	3	0.1	36
4000 to < 5000	8	0.266666667	96

Table 2.6.1. Data for Pie Chart

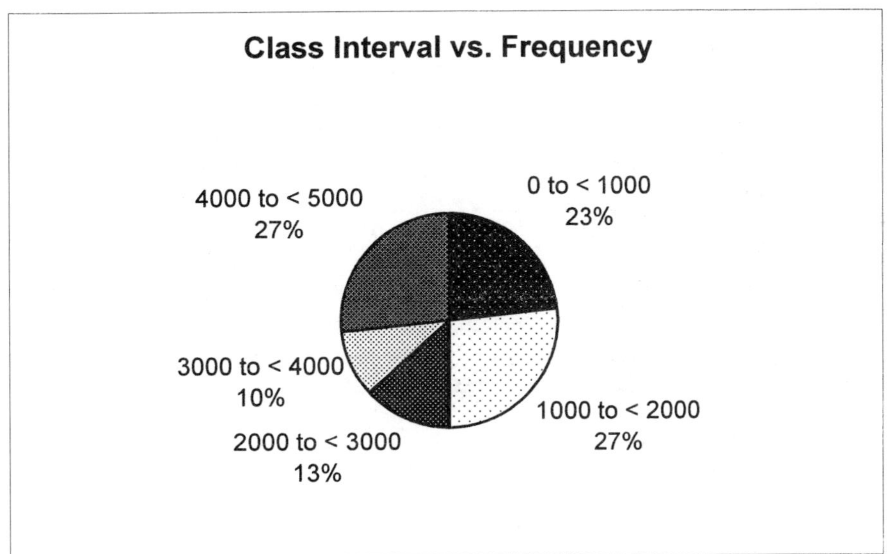

Figure 2.6.1. Pie Chart for Review Problem 2.6.1.

2.7 Deceptive Charts

Misleading impressions may be created when graphs do not start at the origin (especially vertical coordinate), or cut-out of graphs are not properly represented, or using three dimensional graphs. There are many other ways to misrepresent data to a statistically vulnerable or challenged population. One should be aware of these and take precautions while using statistics to get a point across or while questioning a person who is using statistics to get a point across.

2.8 Using Computer Graphics

Data Analysis tool of Excel, which comes with the regular Excel is the most useful generally available tool for statistical analysis. If upon clicking Tool menu in Excel, you do not see data analysis, you would have get your original disk and put it in the CD drive and click Tools -> Add-ins and follow the instructions. The textbook gibes many examples of computer usage and it is not repeated in the Study Guide.

2.9 Self-Test Problems

Self-Test Problem 2.9.1.

Incomes from part-time employment during the academic year for 55 sophomores at The University of Jamesville are given in Table 2.9.1. Do the following:

a. Pick an appropriate set of class intervals to classify the data set.
b. Draw a histogram
c. Draw a frequency polygon
d. Draw a cumulative frequency polygon (less than ogive)
e. Draw a Bar chart
f. Draw a Pie chart

19800	12500	8300	12500	8700
2500	13400	13300	18700	15400
15400	9700	19500	14600	2600
18200	600	500	2200	7600
14900	12300	8600	9900	400
1400	18100	18100	11800	19300
12500	7100	7900	16100	5600
13000	5800	1100	7100	17100
15900	5800	2400	9700	3700
12600	4800	12800	19900	5200
4200	14400	3500	12500	8700

Table 2.9.1. Data on Part-Time Income During The Academic Year For 55 Sophomores at The University of Jamesville

Self-test Multiple Choice

1. For classifying a set of data into frequency distribution, you look at the range and depending on how many intervals you need, you multiply the range by the number of interval to get the width of each interval.
   a. True
   b. False
2. The bar chart is useful for nominal or ordinal data while histogram will be useful for interval or ration data.
   a. True
   b. False
3. Frequency polygon is obtained by connecting the midpoints of the class intervals against the frequency and extending it suitably to cover 0 frequency.
   a. True
   b. False

54	51	41	49	35	44	45	17	25	32
54	40	26	20	15	58	53	36	42	37

Table 2.9.2. Data for Questions 4 – 7

4. Using the data in Table 2.9.2. and using 5 equal-sized class intervals (starting at 10 and ending at 60 : 1st interval : 10 to <20) what is the relative frequency for the second-class interval from the lowest?
   a. 3
   b. 2
   c. .15
   d. .25
   e. None of the above

5. Using the data in Table 2.9.2, using 5 equal-sized class intervals (starting at 10 and ending at 60, 1st interval: 10 to <20) what is the cumulative frequency up to the 3rd interval from the lowest?
   a. 10
   b. 9
   c. .45
   d. .5
   e. None of the above
6. If you draw a stem-and-leaf-diagram for the data of Table 2.9.2. with tens in the stem and ones in the leaf, the number of leaves for the stem 30 would be
   a. 0
   b. 1
   c. 2
   d. 4
   e. None of these
7. Are there any outliers in the data of Table 2.9.2.?
   a. Yes
   b. No
8. In order to find the angles for the pie chart, you must multiply the ___________ by 360.
   a. Frequency
   b. Cumulative frequency
   c. Relative frequency
   d. Sum of the relative frequencies
9. A frequency polygon and cumulative frequency polygon, if drawn on the same graph, will end at the same point.
   a. True
   b. False
10. A cumulative pie chart is an extension of a pie chart, just as cumulative frequency polygon is an extension of a frequency polygon.
   a. True
   b. False

2.10 Glossary

bar chart
A statistical graph consisting of noncontiguous boxes useful for summarizing nominal or ordinal data.

class
A data grouping in a frequency distribution, such as "10 and under 15".

class frequency
The number of data values contained within a particular class. For example, if 27 data values are between 10 and 15 (not including 15), the class frequency for this class is 27.

class limits
The endpoints of each class. For example, for the class "10 and under 15," the value 10 is the lower class limit and 15 is the upper class limit.

class midpoint
The center of each class. For example, 12.5 is the class midpoint for the class "10 and under 15."

class width
The distance between adjacent lower class limits.

cumulative frequency
The sum of the class frequencies for a particular class and all preceding classes
It represents the number of data values that are less than the upper class limit of the class.

frequency distribution
A data summary consisting of classes, frequencies and/or relative frequencies.

frequency polygon
A graphical representation of a frequency distribution consisting of dots at the top center of each histogram box along with connecting lines.

histogram
A graphical representation of a frequency distribution consisting of contiguous boxes
It can be constructed using class frequencies (a frequency histogram) or relative class frequencies (a relative frequency histogram).

ogive
A statistical graph summarizing "less-than" percentages or frequencies.

open ended class
A class that is open on one end, such as "less than 10" or "greater than or equal to 80."

outlier
A data value that is unusually large or small.

ordered array
Data that have been arranged in order from smallest to largest.

pie chart
A statistical graph useful for presenting a percentage breakdown of a particular quantity.

raw data
The original form of the sample data, usually in the order in which the values were obtained.

relative frequency
The frequency of a class divided by the total sample size.

specification limit
A term used in quality control to specify the acceptable range for a particular quality measurement.

stem-and-leaf diagram
A statistical graph that illustrates the shape of the sample data with no loss of information since it is a graphical representation of each sample element; that is, the entire sample.

2.11 Solution to Self-Test Problems

Solution to Self-test Problem 2.9.1.

a. The first order of business is to rearrange the data in Table 2.9.1. in to a set of numbers in increasing order (as shown in Table 2.11.2.) and to find the minimum, maximum, range, number of intervals desired, lower and upper limit of each interval.

400	4200	8600	12500	15900
500	4800	8700	12600	16100
600	5200	8700	12800	17100
1100	5600	9700	13000	18100
1400	5800	9700	13300	18100
2200	5800	9900	13400	18200
2400	7100	11800	14400	18700
2500	7100	12300	14600	19300
2600	7600	12500	14900	19500
3500	7900	12500	15400	19800
3700	8300	12500	15400	19900

Table 2.11.1. Sorted presentation of the raw data

Look for the largest value and the smallest value in the table. The smallest value is 400 and the largest value is 19,900. Range = Highest value - lowest value = 19900-4000 = 19500. The next question is how many classes are needed? Let us say 8. The width of each interval = 19500/8 = 2437.5. Round it to the nearest number, which makes good sense, say 2500. We need 8 class intervals, starting from 0, and of width 2500, and then grouped in class intervals. Putting a check mark for each number in the interval, which leads to Table 2.11.2. is called a frequency distribution. Relative frequency is obtained by dividing the class frequency by the total frequency. The angles required for the pie chart are obtained by multiplying the relative frequency by 360, as shown in Table 2.11.2.

Class interval	Frequency	Relative Frequency	Degrees for Pie chart = relative frequency × 360
0 to under 2500	卌 || 7	7/55 = 0.127	45.7
2500 to under 5000	卌 | 6	6/55 = 0.109	39.2
5000 to under 7500	卌 | 6	6/55 = 0.109	39.2
7500 to under 10000	卌 |||| 9	9/55 = 0.164	59.0
10000 to under 12500	|| 2	2/55 = 0.036	13.0
12500 to under 15000	卌 卌 || 12	12/55 = 0.218	78.5
15000 to under 17500	卌 5	5/55 = 0.091	32.8
17500 to under 20000	卌 ||| 8	8/55 = 0.146	52.6
Total frequency	55	1.0	360.0

Table 2.11.2. Frequency distribution and data for Pie Chart

b. Histogram:

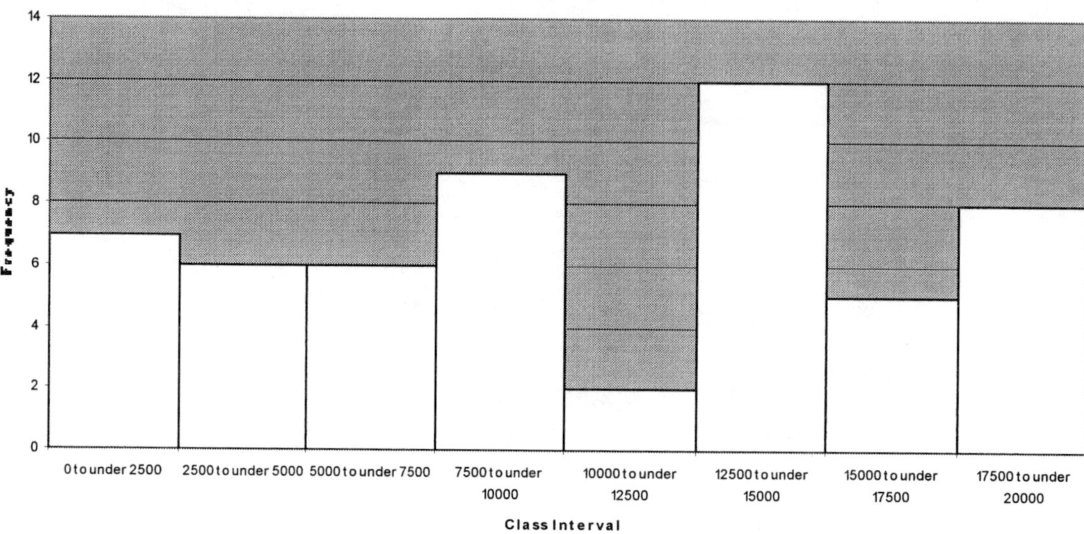

Figure 2.11.1. Histogram for Self-test Problem 2.9.1.

c. Frequency polygon

Midpoint of Class Interval	Frequency
-1250	0
1250	7
3750	6
6250	6
8750	9
11250	2
13750	12
16250	5
18750	8
21250	0

Table. 2.11.3. Data for Frequency Polygon.

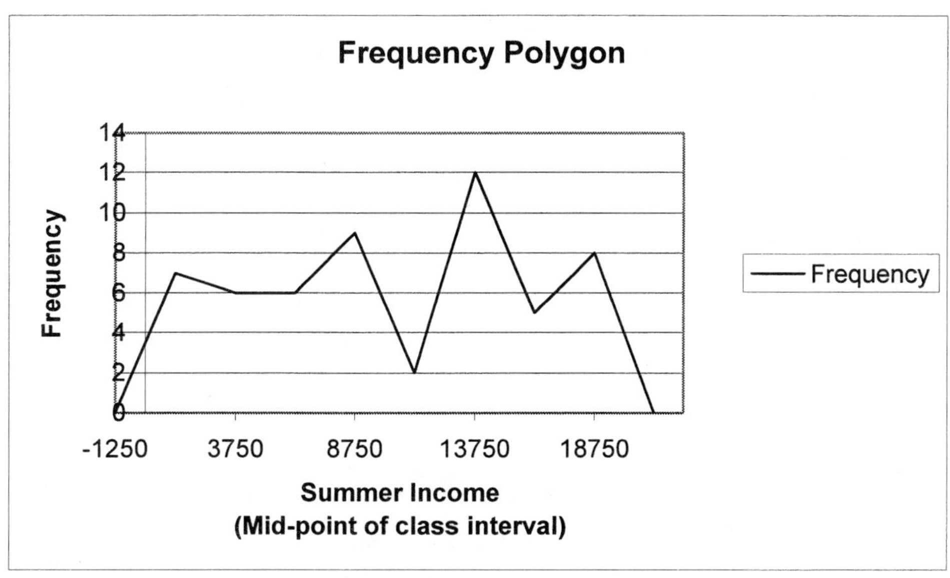

Figure 2.11.2. Frequency Polygon.

d. Cumulative frequency polygon

Upper limit Of class interval	Frequency
0	0
2500	7
5000	13
7500	19
10000	28
12500	30
15000	42
17500	47
20000	55

Table 2.11.4 Data for cumulative frequency polygon.

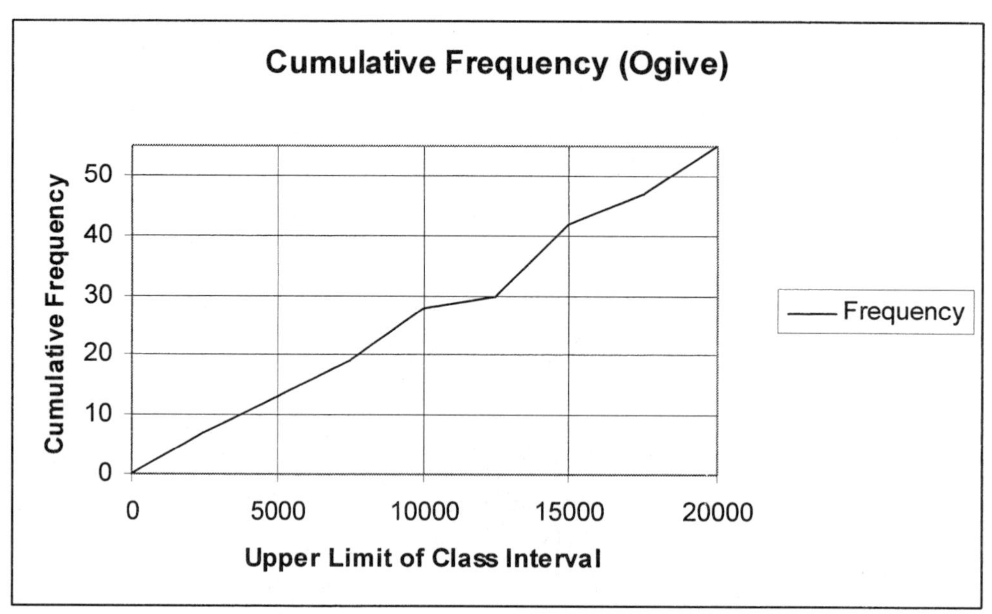

Figure 2.11.3. Cumulative frequency polygon (ogive)

e. Bar chart

The data to be used is in Table 2.11.2

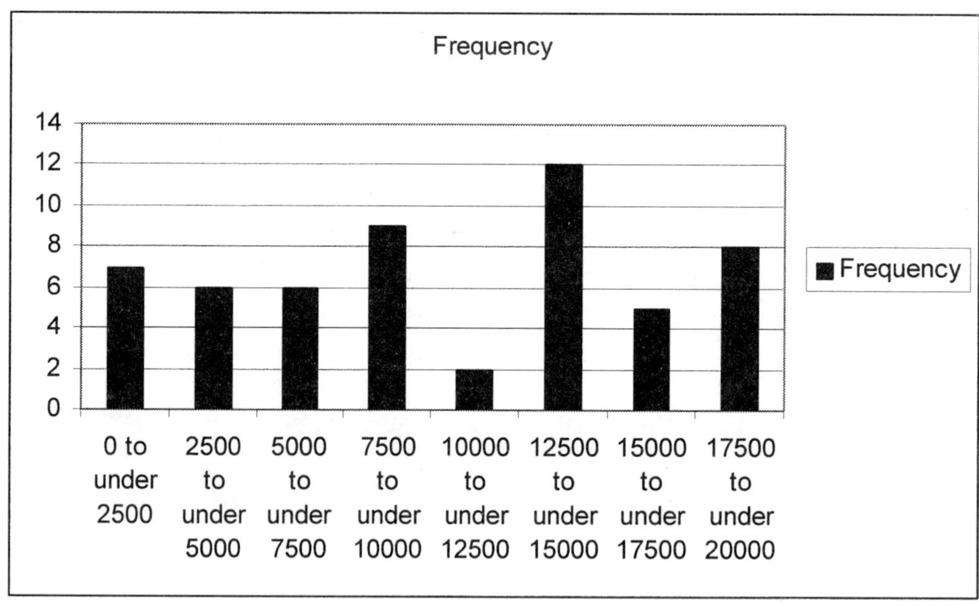

Figure 2.11.4. Bar chart

f. Pie chart
Data for the pie chart is given in Table 2.11.2.

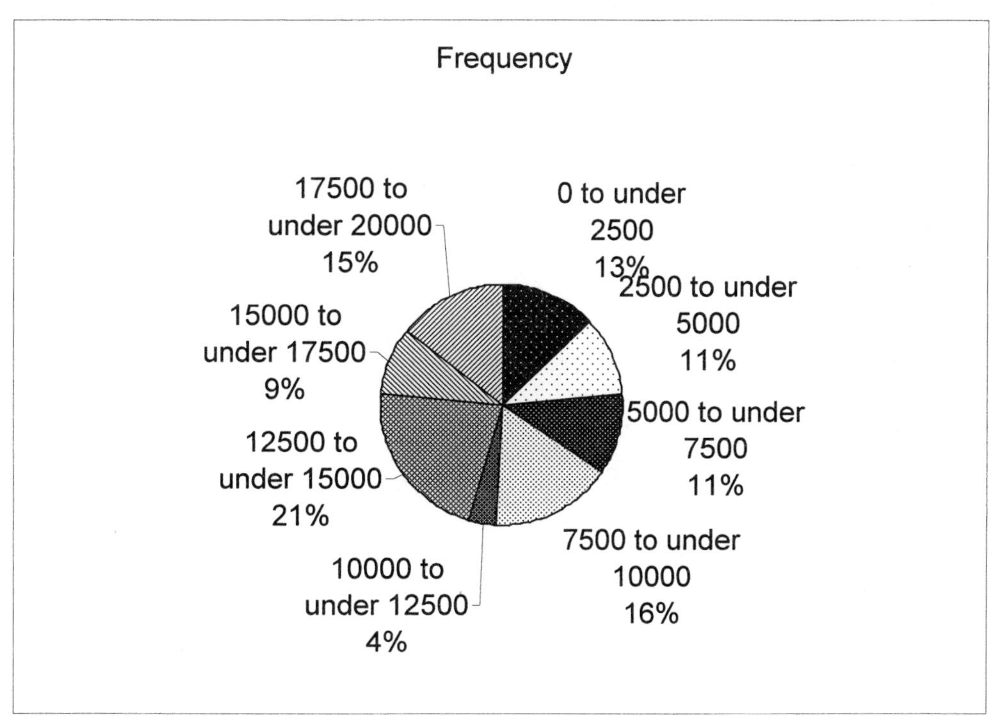

Figure 2.11.5. Pie Chart

Answers to Multiple-Choice Questions

Question #	Answer	Question #	Answer	Question #	Answer
1	b	5	b	9	b
2	a	6	d	10	b
3	a	7	b		
4	c	8	c		

CHAPTER 3
DATA SUMMARY USING DESCRIPTIVE MEASURES

Chapter Overview and Learning Objectives

The purpose of this chapter is to introduce techniques for describing a set of data using one or more numerical measures. By the end of the chapter the student must be able to:

1. Measures of Central Tendency: Mean, Median, Mode and Midrange.
2. Measures of Variation: Range, Standard Deviation, Variance, and Coefficient of Variation.
3. Measures of Position: Percentiles, Quartiles, and *z*-scores.
4. Measures of Shape: Skewness and Kurtosis.
5. Techniques for handling frequency distributions (grouped data).
6. Construction of box plots.

Chapter Outline

3.1 Various Types of Descriptive Measures
3.2 Measures of Central Tendency
3.3 Measures of Variation
3.4 Measures of Position
3.5 Measures of Shape
3.6 Interpreting $\bar{x}$ and s
3.7 Grouped Data
3.8 Box Plots
3.9 Self-Test Problems
3.10 Glossary
3.11 Solution to Self-Test Problems

3.1 Various Types of Descriptive Measures

A descriptive measure is single number computed from the sample data that provides some information about the data:

Measure	Description	Examples
Measure of central tendency	Middle of the data?	Mean, Median, Mode, Midrange
Measure of variation	How dispersed or spread out is the data	Variance, Range, Standard deviation, Coefficient of variation
Measure of position	How does my score compares with others	Percentiles, Quartiles
Measure of shape	Symmetric? Skewed?	Skewness, Kurtosis

Table 3.1.1. Descriptive Measures and Examples

3.2 Measures of Central Tendency

Mean: It is the average of the data. Add all the data elements and divide by the number of data elements. If there are n sample values, $x_1, x_2, x_3, \ldots x_n$, then sample mean $\bar{x}$ is given by

$$\bar{x} = \frac{x_1 + x_2 + \ldots + x_n}{n} = \frac{\sum_{i=1}^{i=n} x_i}{n}$$

and population mean μ is given by

$$\mu = \frac{x_1 + x_2 + \ldots + x_N}{N} = \frac{\sum_{i=1}^{i=N} x_i}{N}$$

Median (*Md*) is the center of the data values when they are arranged from smallest to largest order. If n is odd, median *Md* is the (n + 1)/2 ordered value and if n is even, *Md* is the average of the two center values of the ordered set.

Mode (*Mo*) is the value that occurs more than once and most frequently. *Mo* may not occur at the center and hence sometimes may not be a measure of central tendency. There may be no mode (no number occurs more than once), multiple modes (if two or more sets of numbers occur with maximum frequency).

Midrange (*Mr*) is the average of the highest (*H*) and the lowest (*L*) value.
Mr = (*H* + *L*)/2.

Intuitive Understanding: Table 3.2.1. gives some intuition, which would help you to understand these measures well.

Action	Effect on the Measures of Central Tendency			
	Mean	Median	Mode	Midrange
Add a new data point higher than *H*	Will increase	May change	Will not change	Will change
Add a new data point lower than *L*	Will decrease	May change	Will not change	Will change
Delete a data point from inside the set of data. (not *H* or *L*)	May change (will not change if the item deleted equals the mean)	May change	May change. May become bimodal or may not have mode at all	Will not change
Add a data point whose value equals the mean.	Will not change.	May change	May change	Will not change

Table 3.2.1. Effect of changes in the data on measures of central tendency.

Review Problem 3.2.1.

Weekly overtime hours worked by 15 randomly selected custodial staff of The University of Jamesville in the last week of August 2002 is: 35, 20, 15, 10, 30, 25, 23, 28, 37, 40, 32, 37, 50, 45, 78. Find the (a) mean, (b) median, (c) mode, and (d) midrange of the data.

Solution

a. Mean = (35 + 20 + 15 + 10 + 30 + 25 + 23 + 28 + 37 + 40 + 32 + 37 + 50 + 45 + 78)/15
   = 33.667

b. Median: As a first step, arrange the numbers in ascending order as shown in Table 3.2.2. Since there are an odd number of data points, the median is: (15+1)/2 = 8th data value, which is 32.

10	15	20	23	25	28	30	32	35	37	37	40	45	50	78

Table 3.2.2. Overtime Hours of Custodial Staff of The University of Jamesville during the last week of August 2002.

c. Mode: The most frequently occurring value is 37. Since it occurs more than once, it qualifies as mode.

d. Midrange = (78 + 10)/2 = 44.

3.3 Measures of Variation

Variation is a measure of how dispersed the data values are. Population size is denoted by N and sample size is denoted by n. In general, we use English letters to refer to sample parameters and Greek letters to refer to population parameters.

Range is the difference between the highest (*H*) and the lowest value (*L*).
Sample variance (s^2) defined as:

$$s^2 = \frac{\sum_{i=1}^{i=n} (x_i - \bar{x})^2}{n-1}$$

and **sample standard deviation (*s*)** is defined as

$$s = \sqrt{\frac{\sum_{i=1}^{i=n} (x_i - \bar{x})^2}{n-1}}$$

Population variance (σ^2) is defined as

$$\sigma^2 = \frac{\sum_{i=1}^{i=N} (x_i - \mu)^2}{N}$$

and **Population standard deviation (σ)** is defined as

$$\sigma = \sqrt{\frac{\sum_{i=1}^{i=N} (x_i - \mu)^2}{N}}$$

Coefficient of Variation (CV) is a measure of how big the standard deviation of a sample is as compared to the mean.

$$CV = \frac{s}{\bar{x}} \cdot 100$$

Intuitive Understanding: Table 3.3.1. gives you some intuitive understanding of the effects of changes on the measures studied in this section.

Action	Effect on the Measures of Variation			
	Range	Variance and standard deviation of a sample	Variance and standard deviation of a population	Coefficient of variation
Add a new data point higher than *H*	Will increase	Will increase	Will increase	May change
Add a new data point lower than *L*	Will decrease	Will increase	Will increase	May change
Delete a data point from inside the set of data. (not *H* or *L*)	Will not change	May change	May change.	May change
Add or subtract a constant from all the data items	Will not change.	Will not change	Will not change	Will decrease
Multiply all data items by a positive constant (like changing the unit of measurement from dollars to cents.)	Will get multiplied by the same constant	Variance will be multiplied by the square of the constant and the standard deviation will be multiplied by the constant	Variance will be multiplied by the square of the constant and the standard deviation will be multiplied by the constant	Will not change

Table 3.3.1. Effects of Changes on the Measures of Variation Studied in this section.

Review Problem 3.3.1.

Weekly overtime hours worked by 15 randomly selected custodial staff of The University of Jamesville in the last week of August, 2002 is: 35,20, 15, 10, 30, 25, 23, 28, 37, 40, 32, 37, 50, 45, 78. Find the (a) variance (b) standard deviation (c) coefficient of variation of the data set.

Solution

At first the calculations are shown in the Table 3.3.2.

Overtime Hours (x_i)	$(x_i - \bar{x})$	$(x_i - \bar{x})^2$
10	-23.6667	560.1111
15	-18.6667	348.4444
20	-13.6667	186.7778
23	-10.6667	113.7778
25	-8.66667	75.11111
28	-5.66667	32.11111
30	-3.66667	13.44444
32	-1.66667	2.777778
35	1.333333	1.777778
37	3.333333	11.11111
37	3.333333	11.11111
40	6.333333	40.11111
45	11.33333	128.4444
50	16.33333	266.7778
78	44.33333	1965.444
	Total	3757.333

Table 3.3.2. Details of the Variance calculations

a. Sample variance = 3757.333/(15 - 1) = 268.381
b. Sample standard deviation = 16.382
c. Coefficient of variation = (16.382/33.667) • 100 = 48.66

3.4 Measures of Position

Measures of position are indicators of how a particular value fits with all other data values. Percentiles and *Z*-scores are two commonly used measures of position.

For example: 90th percentile (denoted as P_{90}) is a value such that at most 90% of the data values are less than P_{90} and at most 10% of the data values are more than P_{90}. To calculate P_{90}, first find $n\left(\frac{90}{100}\right)$ and if it is an integer, then let *r* be that integer. P_{90} is the average of the *r*th and the (*r* + 1)th value in the original data set ordered in ascending order. If that is not an integer, **round up** that number to the next integer. Let *r* be that rounded up integer. P_{90} is the *r*th value in the original data set ordered in ascending order.

Median is the 50th percentile and it will satisfy the above definition.

Q_1, Q_2, and Q_3 are respectively first, second and third quartiles. Second quartile is the same as median.

Inter-quartile range (*IQR*) = $Q_3 - Q_1$ (*IQR* can be considered as a measure of variation.)

Z-Score: If a data set has a mean $\bar{x}$ and standard deviation σ, then $z = \frac{x - \bar{x}}{s}$ is a measure of how far an individual value is away from the mean, measured in terms of the standard deviation of the data set. The process is called standardization and the values are called standardized values.

Review Problem 3.4.1.

Weekly overtime hours worked by 15 randomly selected custodial staff of The University of Jamesville in the last week of August, 2002 is: 35, 20, 15, 10, 30, 25, 23, 28, 37, 40, 32, 37, 50, 45, 78. Find the (a) 40th percentile (b) 90th percentile (c) first quartile Q_1 (d) Third quartile (e) *IQR* and *z*-Score corresponding to $x = 23$.

Solution

First we reproduce the table with ordered values of overtime hours.

10	15	20	23	25	28	30	32	35	37	37	40	45	50	78

Table 3.4.1. Overtime Hours of Custodial Staff of The University of Jamesville during the last week of August, 2002.

a. Calculate (for 40th percentile): $n\left(\frac{40}{100}\right) = 15\left(\frac{40}{100}\right) = 6$

   Since it is a whole number, we can meet the requirements of 40th percentile (at most no 40% below and 60% above) by averaging the 6th and 7th ascending order ranked data. That is, average of 28 and 30 = 29.

b. Calculate (for 90th percentile): $n\left(\frac{90}{100}\right) = 15\left(\frac{90}{100}\right) = 13.5$

   Since it is not a whole number, we can meet the requirements of 90th percentile (at most no 90% below and 10% above) by averaging going for the rounded up (14th) ascending order ranked data. That is, 50.

c. Q_1 Calculate (for 25th percentile): $n\left(\frac{25}{100}\right) = 15\left(\frac{25}{100}\right) = 3.75$

   Since it is not a whole number, we round up. That is 4th ascending order ranked data, 23.

d. Q_3 Calculate (for 75th percentile): $n\left(\frac{75}{100}\right) = 15\left(\frac{75}{100}\right) = 11.25$

   Since it is not a whole number, we roundup, that is 12th ascending order ranked data. That is, 40.

e. $IQR = Q_3 - Q_1 = 40 - 23 = 17$.

   From Review Problem 3.2.1., we know that Mean = 33.667. From Review Problem 3.3.1. we know that $s = 16.382$. $z = \frac{23 - 33.667}{16.382} = -0.651$

3.5 Measures of Shape

Skewness: If the data set had a very high values (compared to its mean), the data set is said to be positively skewed (or skewed to the right) or the graph of the frequency Vs. midpoint of class interval has a right tail. On the other hand, if the data set had a few very low values (compared to its mean), the data set is said to be negatively skewed (or skewed to the left) or the graph of the frequency vs. midpoint of class interval has a left tail.. One measure of skewness is the Pearson coefficient of skewness, *Sk* defined as

$$Sk = \frac{3(\bar{x} - Md)}{s}$$

$Sk = 0$ (rare), the data is symmetric, $Sk < 0$, the data is negatively skewed and $Sk > 0$, the data is positively skewed.

Kurtosis: Measures the peakedness of your distribution. Calculation of kurtosis is cumbersome and hence omitted. The value is large if there is a high frequency of observations near the mean and in the tails of the distribution.

Review Problem 3.5.1.

Calculate the Pearson coefficient of skewness, Sk for the data in Table 3.4.1.

Solution

From our solution to Review Problem 3.2.1 and 3.3.1, we know that

$\bar{x} = 33.667, Md = 32$ and $s = 16.382$

$$Sk = \frac{3(\overline{X} - Md)}{s} = \frac{3(33.667 - 32)}{16.382} = 0.3052$$

3.6 Interpreting $\bar{x}$ and s

The standard deviation places a specific limit on the spread of values about the mean in any dataset. Using well-know theorems such as Chebyshev's inequality or Normal rule, we can estimate how many observations from a dataset will fall outside specific intervals such as $\bar{x} \pm 1s,\ \bar{x} \pm 2s,\ \bar{x} \pm 3s,$ or any specific interval.

Chebyshev's inequality: At least (1 - ($1/k^2$)).100% of your data lie between

$\bar{x} - ks$ and $\bar{x} + ks$.

Table 3.6.1 gives the rules about Chebyshev's inequality and Normal rule.

Range of the Standard Deviation	% of Data Contained within the Range	
	Chebyshev's Inequality	Normal Rule (empirical rule)
$\bar{x} - s$ and $\bar{x} + s$	At least 0	About 68
$\bar{x} - 2s$ and $\bar{x} + 2s$	At least 75	About 95
$\bar{x} - 3s$ and $\bar{x} + 3s$	At least 88.88	About 99.7
$\bar{x} - ks$ and $\bar{x} + ks$	At least (1 - (1/k^2)) for any $k > 1$	No general rule. Must refer to the Normal table. (To be covered in a later chapter)

Table 3.6.1 Guidance for Chebyshev's Inequality And Normal Rule (Empirical Rule).

Review Problem 3.6.1.

A sample of experienced data processors (Call them GROUP A) have a mean typing speed of 90 words per minute and a standard deviation of 5. The median speed is 80.

a. According to the normal rule what % of typists from Group A will have a speed between 80 and 100 words per minute? Explain in one line how you found the answer.
b. According to Chebyshev's inequality, what % of typists from Group A will have a speed between 80 and 100 words per minute?
c. Another group of data processors has a typing speed of 100 with a standard deviation of 10. (Call them GROUP B) You would like to recruit 10 data processors randomly from *one of the two* groups. All of them from A or all from B. Your goal is to have 10 employees whose speed is as close to each other possible, without regard to the actual speed. From which group would you recruit?
d. Why? Explain.

Solution

a. Number of standard deviations from the mean = (90 - 80)/5 = 2 and (70 - 80)/5 = -2. According to Normal rule, ±2 standard deviations from the mean contains about 95% of the population.
b. 80 is 2 standard deviations below the mean and 100 is 2 standard deviations above the mean. The % of typists within ±2 (standard deviations) from the mean, according to Chebyshev's inequality is at least (1 - (1/(2 × 2))) = 0.75
c. From Group A.
d. Since they have a smaller standard deviation they are, therefore, more likely to have closer typing speeds.

3.7 Grouped Data

When data is grouped, the formulas for all the measures can be extended.

Intuitive reasoning behind formulas for grouped data:
In most formulas involving grouped data, it is assumed that given a class interval and a frequency, the data is equivalent to an ungrouped data set having a number of data points equal to the frequency with data value equal to the mid point of the class interval. For example, if in a grouped data, for a class interval of 10 to <20, the corresponding frequency is 6, for the purpose

of grouped data formulas, it is as if the data set contained 6 (equal to the frequency) data points of value 15 (mid point of the class interval). In some formulas, it is as if the 6 data points are uniformly spread out in the class interval 10 to < 20.

Mean of grouped data:

$$\bar{x} = \frac{\Sigma mf}{n}; \quad \text{where} \quad m = \text{midpoint of the class interval.}$$

Median of grouped data:

$$\text{Lower limit of med. class} + \frac{\text{((total freq./2)-cum. freq. up to the med. class)}}{\text{frequency of the median class}}\text{(width of the med. class)}$$

Variance of grouped data:

$$s^2 = \frac{\Sigma f \bullet (m - \bar{x})^2}{n-1} \text{..., where } n = \text{total frequency}$$

Standard deviation of grouped data = $\sqrt{Variance}$

Review Problem 3.7.1

Find the mean and median for the following data on the number of bagels sold in the first hour in the Best Bagel Bargain (BBB). *(Note that class intervals are not of equal width.)* Find the (a) Mean, (b) Median and (c) Standard deviation of the data set.

Class Interval	Frequency	Midpoint of Class Interval • Frequency	Cumulative Frequency
10 up to 20	7	15 × 7 = 105	7
20 up to 40	22	660	29
40 up to 60	35	1750	64
60 up to 70	10	650	74

Table 3.7.1 Data for Review Problem 3.7.1

Solution

a. Mean = Sum (Column 3) /total freq. = 3165/74 = 42.77
b. Median class (class interval containing 74/2 = 37th ordered data or the class interval containing the 37th cum frequency) = 40 to 60.
   Median = 40 + ((37 - 29)/35) × (60 - 40) = 44.57
c. Standard deviation

Midpoint of Class Interval	Frequency	Frequency × (Midpoint of class interval - Mean)
15	7	5398.21
30	22	3587.604
50	35	1829.552
65	10	4941.729
	Total	15757.09

Standard deviation = sqrt(15757.09/(74 - 1)) = 14.69

3.8 Box Plots

Box plots are graphical/visual representations of data and it gives an easy way of recognizing outliers. First the formulas are presented.
Lower inner fence = Q_1 - 1.5 × IQR, Upper inner fence = Q_3 + 1.5 × IQR
Lower outer fence = Q_1 - 3.0 × IQR, Upper outer fence = Q_3 + 3.0 × IQR

Review Problem 3.8.1

Weekly overtime hours worked by 15 randomly selected custodial staff of The University of Jamesville in the last week of August, 2002 is: 35, 20, 15, 10, 30, 25, 23, 28, 37, 40, 32, 37, 50, 45, 78. Prepare a box plot.

Solution

Lowest value (L) =10
Q_1 = 23 (using the formulas shown on p102 of your textbook, with P = 0.25 for Q_1 and P = 0.75 for Q_3.)
Q_3 = 40
Median = 32
Highest value = 78
Lower inner fence = 23 - 1.5(17) = -2.5
Upper inner fence = 40 + 1.5(17) = 65.5
Lower outer fence = 23 - 3.0(17) = -28.0
Upper outer fence = 40 + 3.0(17) = 91.0

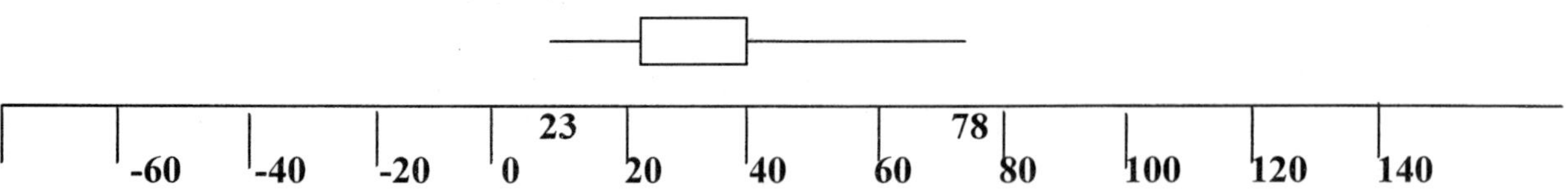

3.9 Self-Test Problems

Self-Test Problem 3.9.1.

The number of loads of wash started in the student laundry in The University of Jamesville during each one hour of a 24-hour period is given in Table 3.9.1. Find the (a) mean, (b) median, (c) mode, and (d) midrange of the data.

9	4	46
21	17	38
28	29	23
3	8	7
47	34	10
13	26	34
2	20	51
37	17	28

Table 3.9.1 Data for Self-Test Problems 3.9.1. through 3.9.4

Self-Test Problem 3.9.2.

The number of loads of wash started in the student laundry in The University of Jamesville during each one hour of a 24-hour period is given in Table 3.9.1. Find the (a) variance (b) standard deviation (c) coefficient of variation of the data set.

Self-Test Problem 3.9.3.

The number of loads of wash started in the student laundry in The University of Jamesville during each one hour of a 24-hour period is given in Table 3.9.1. Find the (a) 40th percentile (b) 90th percentile (c) first quartile (d) third quartile (e) *IQR* and z –Score corresponding to $x = 33$.

Self-Test Problem 3.9.4.

The number of loads of wash started in the student laundry in The University of Jamesville during each one hour of a 24-hour period is given in Table 3.9.1.

a. According to the normal rule what percent of time, will the load be –6.14 (in reality it will be 0 since we cannot have negative number of loads) and 52.14
b. According to Chebyshev's inequality, what percent of time will the load be between –6.14 (in reality it will be 0 since we cannot have negative number of loads) and 52.14?

Self-Test Problem 3.9.5.

Find the (a) mean, (b) median and (c) standard deviation for the following data on the number of pancakes sold in the first hour in the Best Pancake Bargain (BPB).

Class Interval	Frequency
0 to 10	10
10 to 30	20
30 to 60	40
60 to 80	20

Table 3.9.2. Pancakes Sold in The First Hour of The Best Pancake Bargain

Using the mean and standard deviation found and the Chebyshev's theorem, (d) find the minimum probability for number of bagels with in ± 25 of the mean. (Hint: find how many standard deviations is 25 and then apply the theorem.)

Self-Test Multiple Choice Questions

1. Average score of a group of 20 students in Quiz I is 80. John, who was not a member, joined this group. The average for the now 21-member group is 81. John's score must be
   a. higher than 80
   b. lower than 80
   c. 101
   d. (a) and (c) are true
   e. None of the above
2. Average score of a group of 20 students in Quiz I is 80. John, who was not a member, joined this group. The average for the now 21-member group is 70. Assuming that nobody got less than 0, is it possible for the new group to have this low an average?
   a. Possible but not likely
   b. impossible
   c. for this to be true, John's score must be –130
   d. (b) and (c)
   e. none of the above
3. Standard deviation of scores in Quiz I for a group of 20 students is 10. John, who was not a member, joined this group. The standard deviation for the new group of 21 turned out to be the same as the old group of 20. (i.e. it is still 10). Comment on the statement.
   a. Impossible
   b. Possible, but a rare coincidence
   c. It happens often
4. Standard deviation of scores in Quiz I for a group of 20 students is 10. John, who was not a member, joined this group. The standard deviation for the new group of 21 turned out to be lot higher than 10. The most likely reason is
   a. Calculation mistake
   b. John had a score much higher than the average
   c. John had a score much lower than the average
   d. (b) or (c)
   e. None of the above

18	2	11	13	12	14	10	10	17	1
10	19	12	7	0	14	14	14	5	18

Table 3.9.3. Data for Questions 5 - 9

5. The average of the data set given in Table 1 is
   a. 10
   b. 11
   c. 11.05
   d. 10.05
   e. None of the above
6. The standard deviation of the data set, assuming sample standard deviation. is used for estimating the population standard deviation is
   a. −1.234
   b. 4.123
   c. 5.605
   d. 31.418
   e. none
7. The variance of the data set, assuming sample variance is used for estimating the population variance is
   a. −1.234
   b. 4.123
   c. 5.605
   d. 31.418
8. The median of the dataset
   a. 12
   b. 14
   c. 10
   d. 16
9. The mode of the dataset
   a. 12
   b. 14
   c. 10
   d. 16
10. If an instructor has announced that the quiz I class average was 70 and standard deviation was 5. The class size was 100. According to Chebyshev, what is the minimum percentage of students in the score range 60 to 80?
   a. 95%
   b. 99.7%
   c. 75%
   d. 65%
   e. None

3.10 Glossary

box plot
A diagram that demonstrates the lowest and highest values within that portion of the sample not containing outliers, the three sample quartiles, and any sample values determined to be outliers.

Chebyshev's inequality
A rule stating at least what percentage of the sample values are within 1, 2, and 3 standard deviations of the mean.

coefficient of variation
The sample standard deviation divided by the sample mean and multiplied by 100.

descriptive measure
A statistic that describes the location, variation, or shape of a sample or one that describes the position of an individual value in a sample (such as a percentile).

empirical rule
A rule that states approximately what percentage of the sample values are within 1, 2, and 3 standard deviations of the mean. This rule assumes that the population has a bell-shaped (normal) appearance.

grouped data
Summarized data in the form of a frequency distribution.

interquartile range
The difference between the first and third quartiles (Q_3 - Q_1).

kurtosis
A measure of shape that describes the tendency of a distribution to stretch out in a particular direction.

Mean

The average of the sample data; its symbol is $\bar{x}$

measure
See descriptive measure. Measures consist of measures of central tendency, variation, position, and shape.

measures of central tendency
Measures that describe the location (typical value) of a sample, including the sample mean, median, midrange, and mode.

measures of variation
Measures that describe the variation within a sample; they include the sample range, variance, standard deviation, and coefficient of variation.

measures of position
Measures that indicate the relative position of a sample value, such as percentiles, quartiles, and *z*-scores.

measures of shape
Measures that describe the shape (symmetry and peakedness) of a sample, including measures of skewness (lack of symmetry) and kurtosis (peakedness).

median
The value in the center of the ordered data (if the sample size is an odd number) or the average of the two center values (if the sample size is an even number).

midrange
The average of the lowest and highest values in the sample.

mode
The sample value that occurs more than once and the most often.

outlier
An unusually large or small data value in a sample. Such a value can be illustrated and detected using a box plot and is considered to be an **extreme outlier** if it lies beyond either of the **outer fences.** A **mild outlier** is a sample value that lies beyond either of the **inner fences** but not beyond the corresponding outer fence.

percentile
A measure of position, written P_K, where at most K% of the sample values are less than P_K and at most (100 - K)% of the sample values are greater than P_K.

quartiles
Special percentiles; the 1st quartile = 25th percentile, 2nd quartile = 50th percentile (= median), and 3rd quartile = 75th percentile.

range
The difference between the highest and lowest data values in the sample.

skewness
A measure of shape that describes the degree of symmetry in the sample data.

standard deviation
The square root of the sample variance; its symbol is s.

variance
A measure of variation that is obtained by summing the squared deviations from the sample mean and dividing by one less than the sample size; its symbol is s^2.

***z*-score**
A measure of position for any particular value in a sample. It is obtained by subtracting the mean and dividing by the standard deviation. It tells how many standard deviations to the right or left of the mean this value lies.

3.11 Solutions to Self-Test Problems

Solution to Self-Test Problem 3.9.1.

Data set ordered in ascending order is presented in Table 3.11.1.

2	17	29
3	17	34
4	20	34
7	21	37
8	23	38
9	26	46
10	28	47
13	28	51

Table 3.11.1 Ordered data

a. mean = 552/24 = 23
b. median = (21 + 23)/2 = 22
c. mode = 17, 28 and 34
d. midrange = (51 + 2)/2 = 26.5

Solution to Self-Test Problem 3.9.2.

# of loads	$(x - xbar)^2$
2	441
3	400
4	361
7	256
8	225
9	196
10	169
13	100
17	36
17	36
20	9
21	4
23	0
26	9
28	25
28	25
29	36
34	121
34	121
37	196
38	225
46	529
47	576
51	784
552	4880
Mean = 23	Variance = 212.1739
	Standard deviation = 14.57

Table 3.11.2.

c. Coefficient of variation = (14.56/23) × 100 = 63.30

Solution to Self-Test Problem 3.9.3.

a. Calculate (for 40th percentile): $n\left(\frac{40}{100}\right) = 24\left(\frac{40}{100}\right) = 9.6$

Since it is a fraction, round it up to 10. Answer: 17.

b. Calculate (for 90th percentile): $n\left(\frac{90}{100}\right) = 24\left(\frac{90}{100}\right) = 21.6$

Since it is not a whole number, we round up to 22. Answers: 46.

c. Q_1 Calculate (for 25th percentile): $n\left(\frac{25}{100}\right) = 24\left(\frac{25}{100}\right) = 6$

Since it is a whole number, we have to average 6th and 7th ranked data: (9 + 10)/2 = 9.5

d. Q_3 Calculate (for 75th percentile): $n\left(\frac{75}{100}\right) = 24\left(\frac{75}{100}\right) = 18.0$

Since it is a whole number, we average 18th and 19th ranked data: (34 + 34)/2 = 34.

e. IQR = 34.0 - 9.5 = 24.5.

f. From Self-Test Problem 3.9.1, we know that Mean = 23.0. From Self-Test Problem 3.9.2., we know that s = 14.57. $z = \frac{33.0 - 23.0}{14.57} = 0.686$

Solution to Self-Test Problem 3.9.4.

a. Normal rule: (52.14 - 23)/14.57 = 2.0 and (-6.14 - 23)/14.57 = -2. Using Table 3.6.1, the answer is 95%.
b. Chebyshev's inequality: The number of standard deviations away from the mean are + or - 2. According to Table 3.6.1., the answer is 88.88%.

Solution to Self-Test Problem 3.9.5.

Class Interval	Frequency	fx	fx^2
0 to 10	10	50	250
10 to 30	20	400	8,000
30 to 60	40	1800	81,000
60 to 80	20	1400	98,000
Totals		3650	187,250

Table 3.11.3.

a. Mean = 3650/90 = 40.55
b. Median = 30 + ((45 - 30)/40) • 30 = 41.25
c. Standard deviation = sqrt((187,250 - ((3650)^2/90)))/(90 - 1))
= 20.99 (Using the formula in the textbook.)

Answers to Multiple-choice Questions (Detailed solution is given due to the unconventional nature of some of the questions.)

1. d Total score of all 20 = 80(20) = 1600 based on the fact that average = total/number of the group and hence Total = (average × number in the group). Similarly, the total score of the 21 students = 81(21) = 1701. Since the total has gone up from 1600 to 1701 (up by 1701 - 1600 = 101), John must have had a score of 101. Any time the average goes up by adding one more to the group, it must be true that the added member must have higher score. Hence (d) is the answer.

2. d Total for 20 + 20(80) = 1600. Total for 21 students = 21(70) = 1470. John's score = 1470 - 1600 = -130. Since nobody got less than 0, it impossible. Hence, (d)
3. b The standard deviation is a measure of dispersion. Since adding one more score may change the average and affect all squares of (x - $x$bar). So it is possible to adjust the numbers in such a way as to get same standard deviation, but it is not likely.
4. d The standard deviation can increase if individual scores are much higher or much lower than the mean. See spreadsheet attached.

	Data	$(x - \text{xbar})^2$
	18	48.3025
	2	81.9025
	11	0.0025
	13	3.8025
	12	0.9025
	14	8.7025
	10	1.1025
	10	1.1025
	17	35.4025
	1	101.0025
	10	1.1025
	19	63.2025
	12	0.9025
	7	16.4025
	0	122.1025
	14	8.7025
	14	8.7025
	14	8.7025
	5	36.6025
	18	48.3025
Total	221	596.95
Average	11.05	
Variance		31.4184
Standard	Deviation	5.60521

Table 3.11.4.

Answers for questions 5 - 9 are obtained from the above table or the formulas.

5. c
6. c
7. d
8. a
9. b
10. c

CHAPTER 4 PROBABILITY CONCEPTS

Chapter Overview and Learning Objectives

This chapter presents methods for dealing with events involving uncertainty. Uncertainty is a very real part of the business environment. Any type of forecast involves elements of risk and uncertainty.

1. What is meant by the term "probability?" How would each of these techniques be used to generate a probability: classical approach, relative frequency approach, and subjective probability approach?
2. How are multiple events handled? What is meant by the term joint probability? How do you compute probabilities using the additive rule? The multiplicative rule?
3. What is a Venn diagram? What is a tree diagram? How are they used to determine probabilities?
4. How do you count the number of possible outcomes using permutations and combinations?

Chapter Outline

4.1 Events and Probability
4.2 Basic Concepts
4.3 Going Beyond the Contingency Table
4.4 Applying the Concepts
4.5 Tree Diagram
4.6 Probabilities for More than Two Events
4.7 Counting Rules
4.8 Simple Random Samples
4.9 Self-test Problems
4.10 Glossary
4.11 Solutions to Self-Test Problems

4.1 Events and Probability

An experiment has one or more outcomes, with probability associated with each outcome. Sample space of an experiment is defined as the set of all outcomes. Events (usually denoted by capital letters) are defined over the outcomes, typically one or more outcomes together is defined as an event. Table 4.1.1. gives some examples.

Classical probability definition: (all probabilities are between 0 to 1.0). If an experiment has n equally likely outcomes and event *A* occurs in m of these n outcomes, then, probability of event *A* is denoted as $P(A)$ = m/n.

Experiment	Outcomes	Probability
Tossing a fair coin	Head	0.5
	Tail	0.5
Rolling a fair die	1 shows up	0.1666
	2 shows up	0.1666
	3 shows up	0.1666
	4 shows up	0.1666
	5 shows up	0.1666
	6 shows up	0.1666
Taking a course	Pass	? Depends (use subjective probability)
	Fail	? Depends (use subjective probability)

Table 4.1.1. Examples of Experiments and Outcomes

Table 4.1.2 defines experiments and some selected events and their probabilities.

Experiment	Events	Probability
Tossing a fair coin	Head shows up	0.5
	Tail shows up	0.5
Rolling a fair die	Getting 5 on the top face	1/6 Since there are 6 possible outcomes, all equally likely and one of which belongs to "getting a 5 on the top face", the probability is (1/6).
	Getting an odd number	0.5 Since there are 6 possible outcomes, all equally likely and three of which belong to "getting an odd number", the probability is (3/6).
	Getting a number greater than 4	(2/6) Since there are 6 possible outcomes, all equally likely and two of which belong to "getting a number greater than 4", the probability is (2/6).
Drawing a card from a standard pack of 52 cards	Getting a heart	¼ Since there are 52 possible outcomes, all equally likely and 13 of which belong to "getting a hearts", the probability is (13/52) = ¼.
	Getting a picture card	16/52 Since there are 52 possible outcomes, all equally likely and 16 of which belong to "getting a picture card", the probability is (16/52).

Table 4.1.2. Experiments, Events and Probability.

The relative frequency approach to probability states that, for event *A*, *P(A)* = m/n, where n is the number of outcomes observed and n is the number of outcomes that correspond to event *A*.

Subjective probability is a measure of your belief.

4.2 Basic Concepts

Contingency table or a cross-tab is a tabulation of data in two ways. Table 4.2.1. gives a cross-tab data on moving violations during 1998 and age of drivers in Toledo, based on a randomly sampled set of drivers.

Age	0 ticket	1 ticket	2 or more tickets	Total
16-20	30,000	10,000	12,000	52,000
20-30	25,000	8,000	11,000	44,000
>30	50,000	12,000	15,000	77,000
Total	105,000	30,000	38,000	173,000

Table 4.2.1. Contingency Table of Age and Tickets

Experiment is "Randomly pick one person from this population". (There are 173,000 possible outcomes in this experiment, each with equal probability.) **Event A** is "Pick a person in age range 16-20" and **Event B** is "Picking a person who got 2 or more tickets."

Using Classical probability definition:

P(A) = 52,000/173,000 (since there are 52,000 who are in the age 16-20.)

P(B) = 38,000/173,000 (since there are 38,000 who have 2 or more tickets.)

These are also called marginal probabilities (single events used to define the contingency table such as 0 tickets), since these events count each category completely.

For a complete list of probability definitions, see Table 4.2.2.

Term	Definition	How it applies to events *A* and *B*
Compliment	Compliment of an event is all outcomes that does not correspond to the event	Compliment of *A* is "Picking some one not in the age range 16-20.
Mutually exclusive	Two events are mutually exclusive if they both cannot occur at the same time (during the same outcome). Events *A* and *B* are mutually exclusive if *P(A and B)* = 0.0	*A* and *B* are not mutually exclusive because, we can pick a 16-20 age range and who has 2 or tickets.
Joint probability of *A and B*: *P(A and B)*	Probability that both *A and B* will occur.	*P(A and B)* = 12,000/173,000 (since 12,000 satisfy the condition of 16-20 and having 2 or more tickets)
Conditional probability: *P(A/B)*	Probability event *A* occurs, given that event *B* has already occurred.	Given that you have already picked someone with 2 or more tickets a.k.a. Event *B* has occurred, what is the probability Event *A* will occur = *P(A/B)* = 12,000/38,000.
Independent events	Events *A* and *B* are independent if *P(A)* = *P(A/B)*, or *P(B/A)* = *P(B)*, or *P(A and B)* = *P(A)* × *P(B)*	*P(A)* = 52,000/173,000 and *P(A/B)* = 12,000/38,000 and since the two probabilities are not equal *A* and *B* are not independent. This is the safest test for independence.

Table 4.2.2. Probability definitions and illustration

Review Problem 4.2.1.

Using the data on Table 4.2.1. Answer the following questions; assuming a random record is selected from the data set.

a. Probability of having 2 or more tickets during 1998?
b. Probability of picking a person with one ticket, given that a person aged > 30 has been selected?

c. Are events: “1 ticket” and “age > 30” independent?
d. What is the probability of 1 ticket and any age 20 or more?

Solution

a. 38,000/173,000
b. 12,000/77,000
c. Not independent because, *P*(1 ticket) = 30,000/173,000 is not equal to *P(*1ticket/age>30) = 12,000/77,000.
d. (8000+12,000)/173,000

Review Problem 4.2.2.

Make a set of data, preserving the row and column totals, but such that age and ticket status are independent. We have to make *P(*0 ticket/16-20) = *P(*0 ticket) and all of these other conditional probabilities similarly equal. Now, *P(*0 ticket) equal to: 105,000/173,000. To make the *P(*0 ticket/16-20) equal to 105,000/173,000, we simply multiply by 52,000 which is the total number of 16-20 yr. old. That is, (105,000/173,000) × 52,000 = 31,560. Similarly we can fill up all the rest Table 4.2.3.

Age	0 ticket	1 ticket	2 or more tickets	Total
16-20	31,560	9,017	11,422	52,000
20-30	26,705	7,630	9,664	44,000
>30	46,730	13,352	16,913	77,000
Total	105,000	30,000	38,000	173,000

Table 4.2.3. Solution to Review Problem 4.2.2

4.3 Going Beyond the Contingency Table

Venn Diagram: Representation of events *A* and *B*. A typical Venn diagram is shown in Figure 4.3.1. Events *A* and *B* are shown in a circle inside the rectangle, representing the universe.

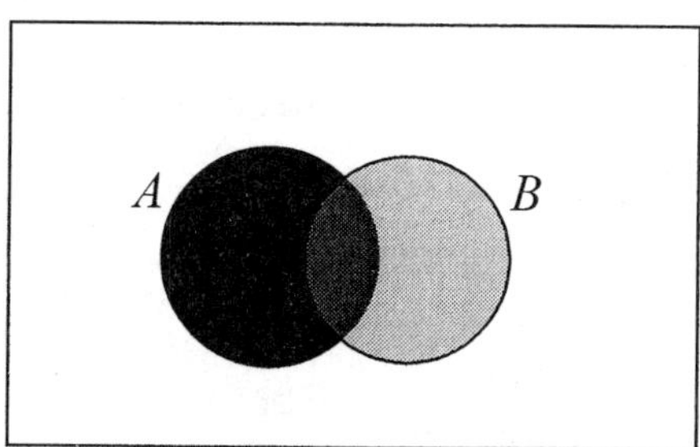

Event *A* is shown in the dark shaded circle; Event *B* is the light shaded circle. The gray shaded area shaped like a lens refers to *A* and *B*, whereas the two circles together, without double counting the intersecting lens-like area, is *A* or *B*. All the formulas needed are given below.

1. *P(A or B) = P(A) + P(B) – P(A and B)*
2. *P(A or B) = P(B or A)*
3. *P(A and B) = P(B and A)*

4. $P(A/B) = \dfrac{P(A \text{ and } B)}{P(B)}$ $P(B) > 0$.

5. $P(B/A) = \dfrac{P(A \text{ and } B)}{P(A)}$ $P(A) > 0$.

6. $P(A \text{ and } B) = P(A/B) \times P(B)$
7. $P(A \text{ and } B) = P(B/A) \times P(A)$
8. $P(A \text{ and } B) + P(A \text{ and } \overline{B}) = P(A)$
9. $P(A) + P(\overline{A}) = 1.0$
10. $P(A/B) + P(\overline{A}/B) = 1.0$

4.4 Applying the Concepts

Review Problem 4.4.1

You pick a card at random from a standard pack of 52 cards.

a. What is the probability that you will get an ace?
b. What is the probability you will get a heart?
c. Given that you got a heart, what is the probability of getting an even-numbered card?
d. Are the events "Getting an ace" and "Getting a heart" independent? Apply the usual test to answer the question.
e. Are events "Getting an ace" and "Getting a heart" mutually exclusive?
f. Describe two events that are mutually exclusive.
g. Describe two independent events.

Solution:

a. There are 4 aces out of a total of 52 cards. So the probability is 4/520 or 1/13.
b. There are 13 hearts out of 52. So the probability is 13/52 or ¼.
c. Given that you got a heart means, you have chosen one of the 13 hearts cards, there are 5 even numbered card among the hearts (2,4,6,8,10). Hence, the probability is 5/13.
d. *P(*heart) = ¼. *P(*ace) = 1/13. *P(*ace/hearts) = 1/13 because there are 13 hearts and exactly one of which is ace. *P(*ace) = *P(*ace/heart), satisfying $P(A/B) = P(A)$, where *A* stands for ace and *B* stands for heart. Hence, ace and heart are independent.
e. *P(*ace and heart) = 1/52 because there is exactly one outcome, namely choosing ace of hears out of the 52 possible outcomes, that satisfies the condition ace and heart. Since *P(*ace and heart) > 0, the events ace and heart are not mutually exclusive.
f. Event *A* is Choosing a heart; Event *B* is Choosing a club. These are mutually exclusive because *P(*heart and club) = 0. There is no card that is both a heart and a club.
g. Event *A*: Pick an ace; Event *B*: Pick a heart. These events are independent, because *P(*ace) = 1/13 and *P(*ace/heart) = 1/13, thus making *P(*ace) = *P(*ace/heart). *P(*ace) = 1/13 and *P(*ace/heart) = 1/13.

4.5. Tree Diagrams:

Suppose in analyzing the performance of Honda-CRV sales force, you find the following probabilities:

*P(*any customer has seen an advertisement for Honda-CRV) = 0.3.
*P(*any customer has not seen an advertisement for Honda-CRV) = 1-0.3=0.7.
*P(*any customer buys a Honda-CRV/seen an advertisement) = 0.6.
*P(*any customer buys a Honda-CRV/not seen an advertisement) = 0.2.

These can be represented by means of a tree diagram as follows:

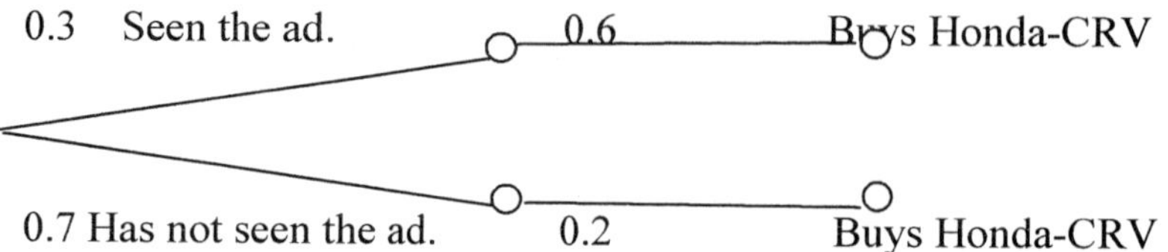

Figure 4.5.1 Tree diagram

Rule #1: *P(*buys a Honda-CRV) = 0.3(0.6) + 0.7(0.2) = 0.32

Rule #2 (Bayes' Rule): *P(*seen the ad/Buys Honda-CRV):

$$\frac{\text{Probability of the first path}}{\text{Probability of sum of the paths}} = \frac{0.18}{0.32} = 0.5625$$

Review Problem 4.5.1.

From long experience, it is known that people default on their credit card with a probability 0.2. Probability of no default on credit card = 1-0.2 = 0.8. A new personality test classifies people as Honest and Slippery. Given all people who default, the probability of Honest is 0.3. Given all people who do not default, probability of Honest is 0.8. What is the

a. Probability (Default Given Honest).
b. Probability (No default given Slippery.)
c. Probability (No Default Given Honest)
d. Probability (Default given Slippery.)

Solution

a. 06/0.70
b. 0.16/0.30
c. 0.64/0.70
d. 0.14/0.30

Table 4.5.1. gives complete details of the calculations.

HONEST					SLIPPERY				
Event	Prior	Conditional	Joint	Revised	Event	Prior	Conditional	Joint	Revised
Default	0.2	0.3	0.06	0.06/.70	Default	0.2	0.7	0.14	0.14/.30
No default	0.8	0.8	0.64	0.64/.70	No default	0.8	0.2	0.16	0.16/.30
		*P(*HONEST)	0.70				*P(*SLIPPERY)	0.30	

Table 4.5.1. Data for Review Problem 4.5.1.

4.6 Probability of More than Two Events

For mutually exclusive events A, B and C: $P(A \text{ or } B \text{ or } C) = P(A) + P(B) + P(C)$

For independent events A, B, and C: $P(A \text{ and } B \text{ and } C) = P(A) \times P(B) \times P(C)$.

If three events are not mutually exclusive, then the $P(A \text{ or } B \text{ or } C)$ is more complicated to calculate. Similarly if three events A, B and C are not independent, then $P(A \text{ and } B \text{ and } C)$ is more complicated to calculate.

4.7 Counting Rules

There are many subtle and intricate differences in this type of problems. It is best to find out what is asked and try to match it precisely to what you know. Table 4.7.1. gives a classification of problems and solutions.

Problem type	Answer	Comments
Filling Slots: You are looking at car models: There are three interior colors, four exterior colors and two roof colors. How many different types of cars are possible?	It is a straight fill problem: 3×4×2 = 24 different combinations for cars.	It is simply a product because there is no duplication or arrangement.
Arrangement: There are 5 students and how many different ways in which 3 of the 5 students can be seated in a row of three seats.	5P3 = 5!/(5-3)! = 5×4×3×2×1/1×2 = 60.	The seats should be a straight line. Even if the same three students are sitting in the seats, the order in which they are seated matters. Each order counts as an arrangement.
Permutations: There are 8 students and 3 of them are to be selected to be members of a committee. How many distinct committees are possible?	8C3 = 8×7×6/1×2×3 = 56	If three are selected, the order of selection does not matter; the committee will be the same.
From a group of 8 students, 1 president, one secretary and one treasurer must be selected. How many different ways in which the officer slots can be filled?	8×7×6 = 336	Just like permutation.

Review Problem 4.7.1.

a. How many different ways in which you can select 5 students from a class of 10 to take part in a project?
b. How many different ways in which you can seat a set of four solo singers on the front bench for a choir performance?
c. How many different ways can 3 students can be selected from a group of 5, and in how many different ways can 3 choir members be seated on the back bench.

Solution

a. 10C5 = 252
b. Factorial (4) = 4×3×2×1 = 24
c. (5C3) and factorial (3) = 60

4.8 Simple Random Samples

Review Problem 4.8.1

The number of samples of size n from a population of size N, without replacement: (An application example would be choosing 5 brake pads from a lot of 60 to test the break strength of the pads. This has to be without replacement because the pads will get destroyed during the test.) will be NCn. If N = 60, n = 5, 60C5 = 5,461,512.

Probability of any one group being selected = 1/NCn = 1/5461512.

The number of samples of size n from a population of size N, with replacement: (An application example would be choosing 5 brake pads from a lot of 60 to test the length, which will not destroy the pad.) will be = 60^5.

4.9 Self-test problems

Self-test Problem 4.9.1.

Assume that you are rolling two square-shaped rods, each of the rods is numbered 1 to 4.

a. What is the sample space (set of all possible outcomes)?
b. What is the probability of getting 4 or more on the top faces added together?
c. What is the probability of getting an odd numbered total?
d. Given that you have a total of 6 or more what is the probability of getting 8?
e. Are events “Getting a total of 7 or more” and “Getting an odd number” independent?
f. Are events “Getting less than 6” and “Getting an odd number” mutually exclusive?
g. Make up two ME events.
h. Make up a set of two independent events.

Self-test Problem 4.9.2.

How many different ways can you

a. Select 3 students from a class of 15 to take part in a project?
b. Seat a set of five solo singers in the front row for a choir performance if there are 5 seats in a row.
c. Select 3 students from a group of 6? and in how many different ways can three choir members can be seated in the back bench.

Self-test Problem 4.9.3.

You pick a card at random from a standard pack of 52 cards.

a. What is the probability that you will get an Ace or Queen?
b. Given that you got Hearts, what is the probability of getting an odd-numbered card?
c. Are the events “Getting a Diamond” and “Getting an Ace" independent? Apply the usual test to answer the question.

d. Are events "Getting an Ace" and "Getting a club" mutually exclusive?
e. Can two events be both mutually exclusive and independent? Explain.

Self-test Problem 4.9.4.

From long experience, it is known that people default on their credit card with a probability 0.3. A new personality test classifies people as Honest and Cheat. Given all people who default, the probability of Honest is 0.4. Given all people who do not default, probability of Honest is 0.7.

a. What is the probability of Default Given Honest
b. Probability (No default given Cheat.).

Self-test Problem 4.9.5.

The following table of number of moving violations during 1999 and age of drivers in Toledo based on a randomly sampled set of drivers.

Age	0 ticket	1 ticket	2 or more tickets	Total
16-20	7,000	4,000		
20-30		2,000	2,000	
>30	5,000		3,000	15,000
Total	15,000		10,000	

Table 4.9.1. Data for Self-test Problem 4.9.5.

a. Fill up any missing numbers logically and answer the questions below. (Be sure to remember to use the correct order in which to fill the missing numbers.)
b. What is the probability that a randomly selected driver from this population of drivers will have 2 or more tickets during 1999?
c. Are 1 ticket and > 30 independent?
d. Probability of 0 ticket and any age 20 or more?

Multiple-choice Questions

Use Table 4.9.2. for questions 1-4

	<25 years of age	25-40 years of age	>40 years of age
Male	6000	2000	1500
Female	5000	3000	2500

Table 4.9.2. Contingency Table Of Gender And Age Distribution Of Stakeholders Of The University Of Jamesville.

1. Probability of randomly picking a male stakeholder is:
   a. 0.6
   b. 0.475
   c. 0.5
   d. 0.55
2. Probability of randomly picking a female stakeholder, given that a stockholder <25 has been picked, is:
   a. 5/11
   b. 5/20
   c. 0.525
   d. 0.55

3. Probability of randomly picking a 25-40 year old given a male has been picked. is:
   a. 1/10
   b. 4/19
   c. 2/5
   d. 5/20
4. Probability of randomly picking a male given a >40 year old has been picked is:
   a. 15/40
   b. 15/100
   c. 4000/20000
   d. 9500/20000

Data for questions 5-10: P(A) = 0.6, P(B) = 0.8, P(A and B) = 0.4

5. *P(A/B)* is
   a. 0.4
   b. 0.5
   c. 0.6666
   d. 1.0
6. *P(B/A)* is
   a. 0.6
   b. 0.8
   c. 0.66666
   d. 0.4
7. *P(A and B-bar)* is
   a. 0.4
   b. 0.6
   c. 0.8
   d. 0.5
   e. 0.2
8. *P(A/B-bar)* is
   a. 0.2
   b. 0.4
   c. 1.0
   d. 0
9. *P(A or B)*
   a. 0.2
   b. 1.0
   c. 0.6
   d. 0.8
10. Are *A* and *B* collectively exhaustive?
    a. yes
    b. no

Use Table 4.9.3 for questions 11-14.

	Total grocery bill		
	< $30.00	$30.00 to $50.00	> $50.00
Male	400	500	200
Female	100	1500	300

Table 4.9.3 Contingency Table of Gender and Purchasing Habits of Customers

11. Probability of randomly picking a male customer and whose bill is in the $30.00 to $50.00 range is:
    a. 0.25
    b. 0.16666
    c. 0.454545
    d. 0.5
12. Probability of randomly picking a female customer or a customer whose bill is > $50.00 is:
    a. 0.8
    b. 0.63333
    c. 0.10
    d. 0.7
13. Probability of randomly picking a customer whose bill is <$30.00, given that a female customer has been picked is:
    a. 0.05263
    b. 0.2
    c. 0.6333
    d. 0.1666
14. Probability of randomly picking a male customer given that a customer whose bill is either $30 to $50 or over $50 has been picked is:
    a. 0.25
    b. 0.8333
    c. 0.28
    d. 0.08

Data for questions 15-20: *P(A)* = 0.4, *P(B)* = 0.7, *P(A and B)* = 0.1

15. *P(A/B)* is
    a. 0.1
    b. 0.7
    c. 0.1428
    d. 0.25
16. *P(B or A)*
    a. 1.1
    b. 0.25
    c. 1.0
    d. 0.1
17. $P(A\ and\,\overline{B})$ is
    a. 0.4
    b. 0.28
    c. 0.3
    d. 0.6
    e. 1.0
18. $P(B/\overline{A})$ is
    a. 0.6666
    b. 0.6
    c. 1.0
    d. d. 0

19. $P(\overline{A})$ is
   a. 0.4
   b. 0.3
   c. 0.6
   d. 0.7
20. *A* and *B* are mutually exclusive.
   a. True
   b. False

4.10 Glossary

additive rule
A rule that determines the probability of event *A* <u>or</u> event *B* occurring.

Bayes' rule
A method of using decision trees to determine posterior probabilities.

classical definition of probability
A method of assigning probabilities where the experimental outcomes are equally likely.

combination
The number of possible outcomes for an experiment when the order of selection is <u>not</u> considered.

complement of an event

The complement of event *A* consists of all outcomes not in *A*. It is written $P(\bar{A})$.

conditional probability
The probability of an event (say, *A*) given that another event (say, *B*) has occurred. It is written $P(A \times B)$.

event
One or more possible outcomes of an experiment.

experiment
An activity for which the outcome is uncertain.

independent events
Two events are independent if the occurrence of one event has no effect on the probability that the other event occurs.

joint probability
The probability of event *A* <u>and</u> event *B* occurring.

marginal probability
The probability of a single event, such as *P(*Male) or *P(*Blue).

multiplicative rule
A rule that determines the probability of event *A* <u>and</u> event *B* occurring.

mutually exclusive events
Two events that can never occur simultaneously.

permutation
The number of possible outcomes for an experiment when the order of selection is considered.

posterior probability
A revised probability based upon additional information.

prior probability
An initial estimate of the probability of an event.

probability
A numeric measure of the likelihood that an event will occur.

relative frequency definition of probability
A method of assigning probabilities by using past information concerning the event.

subjective probability
A method of assigning probabilities that indicates a belief that an event will occur.

tree diagram
A graphical device that structures a probability problem containing multiple steps.

Venn diagram
A graphical method of representing all possible outcomes and events for any experiment.

4.11 Solution to Self-test problems:

Self-test Problem 4.9.1.

a. The numbers below denote the value that may show up on each side.

1,1	1,2	1,3	1,4
2,1	2,2	2,3	2,4
3,1	3,2	3,3	3,4
4,1	4,2	4,3	4,4

b. Exactly 13 of the 16 outcomes add up to 13. So the probability is 13/16.
c. Exactly 8 of the 16 outcomes add up to an odd number. So the probability is 8/16=1/2.
d. There are 6 outcomes, which add up to 6 or more. Out of these, one outcome adds up to 8. So the probability is 1/6.
e. *P(*7 or more) = 3/16. *P(*odd numbered total) = 8/16. *P(*7 or more/odd number) = 2/8 is not equal to *P(*7 or more). So not independent.
f. *P(*less than 6) = 10/16. P (odd number) = 8/16. *P(*less than 6 and odd number) = 6/16. Since it is not 0, "less than 6" and "odd number" are not mutually exclusive.
g. Getting a four and getting a 5
h. Event *A*: Getting a four on the first rod. Event *B*: Getting a 1 in the second rod. *P(A/B)* = ¼. *P(A)* = 4/16 = 1/4. Hence independent.

Self-test Problem 4.9.2.

a. 15C3 = 455
b. 5P0 = 5×4×3×2×1 = 120
c. 6C3 × 3! = (6×5×4/1×2×3) × (3×2×1) = 120

Self-test Problem 4.9.3.

You pick a card at random from a standard pack of 52 cards.

a. There are 4 aces and 4 queens. There are 52 outcomes possible. *P(*ace or queen) = 8/52.
b. There are 13 hearts. Given hearts means we restrict to the 13 heart cards; there are 5 odd-numbered cards among the hearts. *P(*odd/hearts) = 5/13.
c. *P(*diamond) = 13/52. *P(*diamond/ace) = ¼, same as 13/52. Hence the two events are independent.
d. No, since they have a common event "getting ace of hearts."
e. No, since mutually exclusive events are always dependent. *P(A/B)* = 0 which will not be equal to *P(A)*.

Self-test Problem 4.9.4.

From long experience, it is known that people default on their credit card with a probability 0.3. A new personality test classifies people as Honest and Cheat. Given all people who default, the probability of Honest is 0.4. Given all people who do not default, probability of Honest is 0.7.

HONEST					CHEAT				
Event	Prior	Conditional	Joint	Revised	Event	Prior	Conditional	Joint	Revised
Default	0.3	0.4 *P*(H/D)	0.12(*P*(H and D))	0.12/.61	Default	0.3	0.6	0.18	0.18/.39
No default	0.7	0.7(*P*(H/ND)	0.49	0.49/.61	No default	0.7	0.3	0.21	0.21/.39
		*P(*HONEST)	0.61				*P(*CHEAT)	0.39	

Table 4.11.1. Data for Review Problem 4.9.4.

a. *P(*Default given Honest) = 0.12/0.61= 0.197
b. Probability (No default given Cheat.) = 0.21/0.39 = 0.538. Note: In the table *P(*H/D) + *P(C/D)* = 1.0 and similarly *P(H/No D)* + *P(C/No D)* = 1.0

Self-test Problem 4.9.5.

a. Fill up any missing numbers logically and answer the questions below. (You have to remember to use the correct order in which to fill the missing numbers.) First fill out any row or column with only one number missing.

Age	0 Ticket	1 Ticket	2 Or More Tickets	Total
16-20	7,000	4,000	5,000	16,000
20-30	3,000	2,000	2,000	7,000
>30	5,000	7,000	3,000	15,000
Total	15,000	13,000	10,000	38,000

Table 4.11.2. Moving violations during 1999 and age of drivers

b. 10,000/38,000
c. $P($1 ticket$) = 13{,}000/38{,}000$. $P($1 ticket$/{>}30) = 7{,}000/15{,}000$. Since the two figures are not equal, 1 ticket and > 30 are not independent.
d. 8,000/38,000

Answers to Multiple-Choice Questions

Question #	Answer	Question #	Answer	Question #	Answer	Question #	Answer
1	b	6	c	11	b	16	c
2	a	7	e	12	d	17	c
3	b	8	c	13	a	18	c
4	a	9	b	14	c	19	c
5	b	10	a	15	e	20	b

CHAPTER 5 DISCRETE PROBABILITY DISTRIBUTIONS

Chapter Overview and Learning Objectives

This chapter introduces the concept of probability distributions, that is, mathematical distributions that allow a person to more easily compute the probability of various events.

1. What is meant by the term "probability distribution?"
2. What is the formula for the mean and variance of a discrete random variable?
3. When, and how, is the discrete uniform distribution used?
4. When, and how, is the binomial distribution used?
5. When, and how, is the hypergeometric distribution used?
6. When, and how, is the Poisson distribution used?

Chapter Outline

5.1 Random variables
5.2 Representing Probability Distributions for Discrete Random variables
5.3 Mean and Variance of Discrete Random variables
5.4 Binomial random Variables
5.5 The Hypergeometric Distribution
5.6 The Poisson distribution
5.7 Self-Test Problems
5.8 Glossary
5.9 Solutions to Self-Test Problems

5.1 Random variables

Discrete Random Variables:

Random variable is a function that assigns a numerical value to each outcome (sample space) of an experiment. For example, in a coin tossing experiment, define "winnings": as follows: If event H happens, "Win \$100" and Event T happens, "Win \$1". The winning is a random variable defined over the sample space of the coin tossing experiment. In a rolling a die experiment, define a random variable X as follows: "win \$2 × the number (for odd numbers)" and "lose \$1.5 × the number (for even number)", then X is a random variable. If you roll a pair of dice, another random variable X could be "sum of the two numbers on the dice".

Discrete random variables are random variables that can only take on discrete values such as whole numbers, or countable set of fractional values.

Continuous random variables are random variables that can take on any value.

5.2 Representing Probability Distributions for Discrete Random Variables

Probability Mass Function (PMF) of random variable X, is a function that assigns a probability to each value of X, denoted by $P(X)$. Note: $0 \le P(X) \le 1.0$ and

$$\sum P(X) = 1.0$$

Review Problem 5.2.1

Find the Probability Mass Function for the random variable X, where X is the sum of the two numbers that shows up when you roll a pair of dies.

Value of random variable X	Corresponding outcomes (in the sample space)	Probability
2	(1,1)	1/36
3	(1,2), (2,1)	2/36
4	(1,3), (2,2), (3,1)	3/36
5	(1,4), (2,3), (3,2), (4,1)	4/36
6	(1,5), (2,4), (3,3), (4,2), (5,1)	5/36
7	(1,6), (2,5), (3,4), (4,3), (5,2), (6,1)	6/36
8	(2,6), (3,5), (4,4), (5,3), (6,2)	5/36
9	(3,6), (4,5), (5,4), (6,3)	4/36
10	(4,6), (5,5), (6,4)	3/36
11	(5,6), (6,5)	2/36
12	(6,6)	1/36

Table 5.2.1. PMF for a random variable X (sum of two dies.)

Generalization of this probability mass function:

$$P(X) = \frac{X - 1}{36}$$

5.3 Mean and Variance of Discrete random Variables

Mean of a discrete random variable X is defined as:

$$\mu = \sum X \cdot P(X)$$

Variance of a discrete random variable X is defined as:

$$\sigma^2 = \sum (X - \mu)^2 \cdot P(X)$$

Standard deviation of a discrete random variable:

$$\sigma = \sqrt{\sum (X - \mu)^2 \cdot P(X)}$$

Review Problem 5.3.1.

Find the (a.) Mean and (b) Standard deviation of the random variable X defined in Review Problem 5.2.1.

Solution:
This simply involves applying the definition as shown in Table 5.3.1.

Value of x	P(X)	X.P(X)	(X-Bar)^2.P(X)
2	1/36 = 0.0278	0.0556	0.6950
3	2/36 = 0.0556	0.1668	0.8896
4	3/36 = 0.0833	0.3332	0.7497
5	4/36 = 0.1111	0.5555	0.4444
6	5/36 = 0.1389	0.8334	0.1389
7	6/36 = 0.1667	1.1669	0.0000
8	5/36 = 0.1389	1.1112	0.1389
9	4/36 = 0.1111	0.9999	0.4444
10	3/36 = 0.0833	0.8330	0.7497
11	2/36 = 0.0556	0.6116	0.8896
12	1/36 = 0.0278	0.3336	0.6950
		Mean -> 7.0000	5.8352
			Standard deviation-> 2.4156

Table 5.3.1. Calculations for Mean and Standard Deviations (Note that this is slightly different set of calculations as compared to the book. It will result in the same answer.)

5.4 Binomial Random Variables

A special discrete random variable following the properties listed in Table 5.4.1. It is called Binomial random variable and it has a PDF as shown in the formula in the Table.

Description	Value
Name	Binomial distribution
Type of random variable	Discrete
Experiment	Involves repeating a trial (e.g. tossing a coin)
Number of outcomes of the experiment	2
Usual names of the outcome	Success and failure
Probability of success in a single trial	*P*
Probability of failure in a single trial	(1-*p*)
Number of trials	*N*
Nature of trials	Independent from each other
P(x successes in n trials) (PMF)	nCx $p^x(1-p)^{n-x}$
Mean (can calculate using standard formulas)	*Np*
Standard deviation (can calculate using standard formulas)	$\sqrt{n*p*(1-p)}$

Table 5.4.1. Properties of Binomial Distribution

Review Problem 5.4.1

From a general survey, it has been found that there are 70% Optimists and the rest are Pessimists. Suppose that you ask a random sample of 10 persons from this population:

a. On an average, how many optimists will you find?
b. What is the standard deviation of the number of optimists?
c. What is the probability of getting exactly 6 optimists out of 10?
d. What is the probability of getting 2 or fewer optimists?

e. What is the probability of getting 8 or more optimists?
f. What is the probability of getting 2 or more optimists?

Solution:

a. 10(0)(7) = 7
b. Sqrt ((10)(0.7)(1-0.7)) = 1.449
c. $10C6(0.7)^6(1-0.7)^{10-4}$
d. $10C2(0.7)^2(1-0.7)^{10-2} + 10C1(0.7)^1(1-0.7)^{10-1} + 10C0(0.7)^0(1-0.7)^{10-0}$
e. $10C8(0.7)^8(1-0.7)^{10-8} + 10C9(0.7)^9(1-0.7)^{10-9} + 10C10(0.7)^{10}(1-0.7)^{10-10}$
f. 1 - *P*(1 optimist) – *P*(0 optimists) = $1 - 10C1(0.7)^1(1-0.7)^{10-1} - 10C0\,(0.7)^0(1-0.7)^{10-0}$

5.5 Hypergeometric Distribution

Another special discrete random variable following the properties listed in Table 5.5.1. is called Binomial random variable and it has a PDF as shown in the formula in the Table.

Description	Value
Name	Hypergeometric distribution
Type of random variable	Discrete
Experiment	involves repeating a trial (e.g. tossing a coin)
Number of outcomes of the experiment	2
Usual names of the outcome	Success and failure
Probability of success in a single trial	*p*
Probability of failure in a single trial	(1-*p*)
Number of trials	*n*
Nature of trials	Dependent upon the previous trial, because it is sampling without replacement.
Population Size	*N*
Number of successes in the population	*k*
Number of failures in the population	*N-k*
P(*x* successes and *n-x* failures in *n* trials) (PMF)	$\frac{kCx.\ (N-k)Cn-x}{NCn}$
Mean (can be calculated long hand using standard formulas)	$\frac{nk}{N}$
Standard deviation (can be calculated long hand using standard formulas)	$\sqrt{n.\left(\frac{k}{N}\right).\left(1-\frac{k}{N}\right)\left(\frac{N-n}{N-1}\right)}$

Table 5.5.1 Properties of a Hypergeometric Random Variable.

5.6 Poisson Distribution

Another important discrete random variable following the properties listed in Table 5.6.1. is said to follow Poisson distribution.

Description	Value
Name	Poisson distribution
Type of random variable	Discrete
Applications	• Number of defects in a car • Number of blemishes in an auto painting • Number of customers coming into a stores in 1 hour • Number of accidents in a highway per hour • Number of units of car sold in an hour in a dealership
Assumptions	• Number of events occurring in one interval (say 10.00 to 11.00 is unaffected by number of events in another interval, say 2.00 to 3.00 • Expected number of events is proportional to the length of the time interval • Events cannot occur exactly at one and the same time. involves repeating a trial (e.g. tossing a coin)
Random variable	The number of events per unit time
P(X) PDF, *x* is the number of events per unit time	$P(x) = \frac{\mu^x e^{-\mu}}{x!}$; μ is the average rate per unit time
Mean	*M*
Standard deviation	$\sqrt{\mu}$

Table 5.6.1 Properties of a Poisson random variable

Review Problem 5.6.1.

The number of customers walking into a store follows a Poisson distribution with a rate of 3 per minute.

a. What is the probability that 2 or more customers will come during a typical minute?
b. What is the probability of more than 2 customers walking into the store during a typical minute?
c. The probability of exactly 2 customers walking into the store during a typical minute is?
d. The probability of no more than 2 customers walking into the store during a typical minute is?

Solution

a. It is $P(2) + P(3) + P(4) + \ldots$.. (..., means keep on going with $P(5)$, $P(6)$ etc. Note that in theory, there could be any number of customers up to infinity, though the probability for most of the term will be close to 0)

Note that $P(0) + P(1) + P(2) + P(3) + \ldots\ldots = 1.0$
$P(2) + P(3) + P(4) + \ldots.. = 1 - P(0) - P(1)$
$= 1 - e^{-3}3^0/0! - e^{-3}3^1/1!$
$= 1 - 0.0498 - 0.1494;$
$= 0.8008$

b. Because of "the more than 2" in the question, the answers is $P(3) + P(4) + P(5) + ..$
Note that $P(0) + P(1) + P(2) + P(3) + \ldots\ldots = 1.0$
Hence, $P(3) + P(4) + P(5) + \ldots. = 1 - P(0) - P(1) - P(2)$

$= 1 - 0.0498 - 0.1494 - 0.2240$
$= 0.5768$

c. Note that "exactly", $P(2) = e^{-3}\, 3^2 / 2! = 0.2240$
d. "No more than 2" means: 2 or less: $P(2) + P(1) + P(0)$
$= 0.2240 + 0.1494 + 0.0498$
$= 0.4232$

Note: You can also look this up in the table, as long as you have the right values for μ, and you locate the table for the X value in question.

5.7 Self-test Problems

Self-test Problem 5.7.1.

The probability of placing an order for any customer who visits the www.ThingsJamaica.com webite is 0.20.

a. On an afternoon, 10 customers visited this page. What is the probability of getting at least one customer who will order?
b. What is the probability of having no more than three customers who will order?

Self-test Problem 5.7.2

The probability of placing an order for any customer who visits the www.ThingsJamaica.com website is 0.20. Suppose on a whole day, 50 customers visited it. Get numerical answers to the probability of getting 8 to 12 customers both inclusive using Poisson approximation.

Self-test Problem 5.7.3.

From a general survey, it has been found that there are 70% Optimists and the rest are Pessimists. Suppose that you ask a random sample of 10 persons from this population: Are you an Optimist or Pessimist?

a. Using Poisson approximation to Binomial, find the probability that exactly 5 out of 10 people surveyed, would be optimists.
b. Using Poisson approximation to Binomial, find the probability that 2 or less out of 10 people surveyed, would be optimists.
c. Using Poisson approximation to Binomial, find the probability that exactly 9 out of 10 people surveyed, would be pessimists.

Self-test Problem 5.7.4.

A class has 10 IS/OM majors and 15 Accounting majors. A committee of 5 is formed choosing members without replacement (this means use hypergeometric distribution). What is the probability that this committee will have 2 IS/OM and 3 Accounting majors?

Multiple-choice:

1. Estimated probability of any sales call maturing into an actual sale is 0.2. Tim Smith made 7 sales calls this week. What is the probability that exactly one of his calls matures into an actual sale.
   a. $(0.2)^7$
   b. 0.2
   c. $7C1\ (0.2)^1\ .\ (1\text{-}0.2)^{7\text{-}1}$
   d. None of the above
2. Estimated probability of any sales call maturing into an actual sale is 0.2. Tim Smith made 7 sales calls this week. What is the probability that at least one of his calls matures into an actual sale.
   a. $(0.2)^1(1\text{-}0.2)^6$
   b. $7C1(0.2)^1(1\text{-}0.2)^6 + 7C0(0.2)^0(1\text{-}0.2)^7$
   c. $1\text{-}\ 7C0(0.2)^0(1\text{-}0.2)^7$
   d. $1\text{-}\ 7C1(0.2)^1(1\text{-}0.2)^6 - 7C0(0.2)^0(1\text{-}0.2)^7$
3. Estimated probability of any sales call maturing into an actual sale is 0.2. Tim Smith made 7 sales calls this week. What is the probability that no more than one of his calls matures into an actual sale.
   a. $(0.2)^1\ (1\text{-}0.2)^6$
   b. $7C1(0.2)^1(1\text{-}0.2)^6 + 7C0(0.2)^0(1\text{-}0.2)^7$
   c. $1\text{-}\ 7C0(0.2)^0(1\text{-}0.2)^7$
   d. $1\text{-}\ 7C1(0.2)^1(1\text{-}0.2)^6 - 7C0(0.2)^0(1\text{-}0.2)^7$
4. Assume that the probability of getting a defective when I pick one part from a population of parts is 0.2. If I randomly pick 5 parts from this population, (assuming that the probability of finding a defective continues to be 0.2) The probability of finding exactly 1 or less defectives is:
   a. $5C1(0.2)^1(1\text{-}0.2)^{5\text{-}1}$
   b. $(0.2)^5$
   c. $5C0(0.2)^0(1\text{-}0.2)^{5\text{-}0}$
   d. $5C1(0.2)^1(1\text{-}0.2)^{5\text{-}1} + 5C0(0.2)^0(1\text{-}0.2)^{5\text{-}0}$
   e. None of the above
5. Assume that the probability of getting a defective when I pick one part from a population of parts is 0.1. If I randomly pick 5 parts from this population, (assuming that the probability of finding a defective continues to be 0.1) The probability of finding 5 defectives is:
   a. $5C4(0.1)^4(1\text{-}0.1)^{5\text{-}4}$
   b. $5C5(0.1)^5(1\text{-}0.1)^{5\text{-}5}$
   c. $1\ \text{-}\ 5C4(0.1)^4(1\text{-}0.1)^{5\text{-}4}$
   d. $1\ \text{-}\ 5C5(0.1)^5(1\text{-}0.1)^{5\text{-}5}$
   e. $1\ \text{-}\ 5C4(0.1)^4(1\text{-}0.1)^{5\text{-}4}\ \text{-}\ 5C5(0.1)^5(1\text{-}0.1)^{5\text{-}5}$
6. Assume that the probability of getting a defective when I pick one part from a population of parts is 0.1. If I randomly pick 5 parts from this population, (assuming that the probability of finding a defective continues to be 0.1) The probability of finding at least 3 defectives is:
   a. $5C4(0.1)^4\ (1\text{-}0.1)^{5\text{-}4}$
   b. $5C5(0.1)^5\ (1\text{-}0.1)^{5\text{-}5}$
   c. $1\text{-}5C4(0.1)^4(1\text{-}0.1)^{5\text{-}4}$
   d. $1\text{-}5C4(0.1)^4(1\text{-}0.1)^{5\text{-}4}\ \text{-}\ 5C5(0.1)^5(1\text{-}0.1)^{5\text{-}5}$
   e. None of the above
7. Assume that the probability of getting a male student when I pick one student from a class of 40 students is 0.3. I pick 5 students with replacement. (That is the probability remains as 0.3 for each choice) to represent the class. What is the probability of choosing 3 male and 2 females?

a. $5C3(0.3)^3(1-0.3)^{5-3}$
b. $5C3(0.3)^3$
c. $5C3(0.3)^3(1-0.3)^3$
d. $1 - 5C3(0.3)^3(1-0.3)^{5-2}$
e. None

8. The average number of students visiting my office hours is 4 per hour. What is the probability of having 1 student visit me during a typical hour?
   a. $e^{-4} 4^1 /1!$
   b. $e^{-4} 4^4 /4!$
   c. $e^{-4} 4^4 /1!$
   d. None
9. The average number of students visiting my office hours is 4 per hour. What is the probability of having 1 or more students visit me during a typical hour?
   a. $e^{-4} 4^1/1!$
   b. $1 - e^{-4} 4^1/1!$
   c. $1 - e^{-4} 4^0/0!$
   d. None
10. The average number of students visiting my office hours is 4 per hour. What is the probability of having 4 or more students visit me during a typical hour?
    a. $e^{-4} 4^1/1!$
    b. $1 - e^{-4} 4^1/1!$
    c. $1 - e^{-4} 4^0 /0!$
    d. None
11. The number of customers walking into a store follows a Poisson distribution with a rate of 3 per minute. The probability that 2 or more customers will come during a typical minute is:
    a. 0.2240
    b. 0.1494
    c. 0.9502
    d. 0.8008
12. The number of customers walking into a store follows a Poisson distribution with a rate of 3 per minute. The probability of more than 2 customers walking into the store during a typical minute is:
    a. 0.2240
    b. 0.1494
    c. 0.9502
    d. 0.8008
    e. 0.5768
13. The number of customers walking into a store follows a Poisson distribution with a rate of 3 per minute. The probability of exactly 2 customers walking into the store during a typical minute is:
    a. 0.2240
    b. 0.1494
    c. 0.9502
    d. 0.8008
    e. 0.5768

14. The number of customers walking into a store follows a Poisson distribution with a rate of 3 per minute. The probability of no more than 2 customers walking into the store during a typical minute is:
    a. 0.2240
    b. 0.1494
    c. 0.4232
    d. 0.8008
    e. 0.5768
15. A class has 10 IS/OM majors and 15 Accounting majors. A committee of 5 is formed choosing members without replacement (this means use hypergeometric distribution). What is the probability that this committee will have 2 IS/OM and 3 Accounting majors?
    a. $\frac{(10C3)(15C2)}{25C5}$ b. $\frac{(10C2)(15C3)}{25C5}$ c. $\frac{(5C2)(15C3)}{5C5}$ d. $\frac{(10C2)(15C3)}{5C5}$
16. A used car salesperson succeeds in selling a lemon with a probability of 0.2 to a typical customer. If he/she attempts to sell lemons to 10 typical customers, on average how many lemons will he sell?
    a. 1
    b. 2.
    c. 3
    d. 4
    e. 0
17. A used car salesperson succeeds in selling a lemon with a probability of 0.2 to a typical customer. If he/she attempts to sell lemons to 10 typical customers, what is the probability of selling 3 lemons?
    a. 0.201
    b. 0.878
    c. 0.677
    d. 0.323

5.8 Glossary

binomial random variable
A discrete random variable characterized by n independent trials each of which have two possible outcomes (success or failure). The binomial random variable is the number of successes (in the n trials).

continuous random variable
A random variable for which any value is possible over a certain range, such as X = height of adult male.

discrete random variable
A random variable characterized by gaps in the possible values, such as X = total of two dice (possible values are 2, 3, 4, …, 12).

discrete uniform random variable
A discrete random variable having a finite number of outcomes, each equally likely to occur.

hypergeometric random variable

A discrete random variable characterized by n trials, each of which has two possible outcomes (success or failure). The size of the population (*N*), the number of successes in the population (*k*), and the number of failures in the population (*N* - *k*) are known. The hypergeometric random variable is the number of successes (in the *n* trials).

mean of a random variable
The average value of the random variable if observed over an indefinite period of time

Poisson random variable
A discrete random variable useful for describing the number of occurrences of a particular event over a specified period of time or space.

probability distribution
For discrete random variables, a representation of all possible values and corresponding probabilities.

probability mass function (PMF)
A function that assigns a probability to each possible value of a discrete random variable.

5.9 Solutions to Self-test Problems

Self-test Problem 5.7.1.

a. It is a binomial. *P(*success*)* = 0.2, n = 10.
b. *P(*at least one customer*)* = 1 - *P(*0 customers) = $1 - 10C0(0.2)^0(1\text{-}0.2)^{(10-0)}$
c. $P(0) + P(1) + P(2) + P(3) = 10C0(0.2)^0(1\text{-}0.2)^{(10-0)} + 10C0(0.2)^1(1\text{-}0.2)^{(10-1)} + 10C0(0.2)^2 (1\text{-}0.2)^{(10-2)} + 10C0(0.2)^3(1\text{-}0.2)^{(10-3)}$

Self-test Problem 5.7.2.

Poisson approximation:
Mean = np = 50(0.2) = 10.
$P(8) + P(9) + P(10) + P(11) + P(12) = e^{-10}10^8/8! + e^{-10}10^9/9! + e^{-10}10^{10}/10! + e^{-10}10^{11}/11! + e^{-10}10^{12}/12!$

Self-test Problem 5.7.3.

a. Average number of optimists = 10(0.7) = 7. $P(5) = e^{-7}7^5/5!$
b. $e^{-7}7^2/2! + e^{-7}7^1/1! + e^{-7}7^0/0!$
c. Average number of pessimists = 10(0.3) = 3. $P(9) = e^{-3}3^9/9!$

Self-test Problem 5.7.4.

Denominator is the number of ways in which one can pick a committee of 5 from 25 (10 IS/OM and 15 Accounting majors). Numerator is the number of ways in which 2 IS/OM from 10 and 3 Accounting from 15 can be picked.

$$\frac{(10C2)(15C3)}{5C5}$$

Answers to Multiple-Choice Questions

Question #	Answer	Question #	Answer	Question #	Answer
1	c	8	a	15	b
2	c	9	c	16	b
3	b	10	d	17	a
4	d	11	d		
5	b	12	e		
6	e	13	b		
7	a	14	c		

CHAPTER 6 CONTINUOUS PROBABILITY DISTRIBUTIONS

Chapter Overview And Objectives

This chapter presents three continuous distributions: the normal, uniform, and exponential. By the end of the chapter, the student should be able to:

1. Distinguish between a discrete distribution and a continuous distribution.
2. For each of these three distributions: the normal, uniform, and exponential, sketch the distribution, and describe the situations for which each distribution is most appropriate.
3. Be able to work problems involving each of these three continuous distributions.
4. Using Excel, SPSS, or MINITAB, be able to determine areas under any normal curve and determine the value of a normal random variable having a specified area.

Chapter Outline

6.1 Continuous Random Variables
6.2 Normal Random variables
6.3 Determine the Probability for a Normal Random Variable
6.4 Finding Area under Normal Curve
6.5 Applications Where the Area Under the Normal Curve is Provided
6.6 Another Look at Empirical Rule
6.7 Using Excel to Determine Areas and Values Having a Specified Area for Normal Populations
6.8 Normal Approximation to Binomial
6.9 Other Continuous Distribution
6.10 Self-Test Problems
6.11 Glossary
6.12 Solution to Self-Test Problems

6.1 Continuous Random Variables

Continuous random variables can take on any value integer and fractional values. Normal, Uniform and Exponential are the distributions studied in this chapter. The area under the curve of a continuous distribution is equal to 1.0.

6.2 Normal random variables

Table 6.2.1. gives a summary of all the properties of the Normal distribution.

Property	Description
Type of random variable	Continuous
Values the random variable may take	-infinity to +infinity
Shape	Symmetric about its mean
Role of standard deviation on the shape of the distribution	• The smaller the standard deviation, the more peaked is the distribution. • The larger the standard deviation, the more flat is the distribution.
Z-Distribution	Special Normal distribution with mean 0 and standard deviation = 1.0
Relationship between a normal random variable *X* with mean μ and standard deviation σ and *Z*, the standard normal distribution.	$Z = \frac{X - \mu}{\sigma}$
X in terms of *Z*	$X = \mu + Z\sigma$
Probability density function (PDF)	• Bell-shaped, symmetric curve • The equation describing it is very complicated • Areas are tabulted for the *Z* distribution • Areas for any Normal distribution with known mean and standard deviation can be found using the relationship between *Z* and *X*
Normal Rule	• Area beween the mean and + or - one standard deviation is about 68% • Area beween the mean and + or - two standard deviations is about 95% • Area beween the mean and + or - three standard deviations is about 99.7%
Areas of Normal curve	• 90 % area (that is 45% on either side of the mean corresponds to –1.645 to +1.645 • 95 % area (that is 47.5% on either side of the mean corresponds to –1.96 to +1.96 • 99 % area (that is 49.5% on either side of the mean corresponds to –2.58 to +2.58

Table 6.2.1. Properties of Normal Distribution

6.3 Determining a Probability for a Normal Random variable

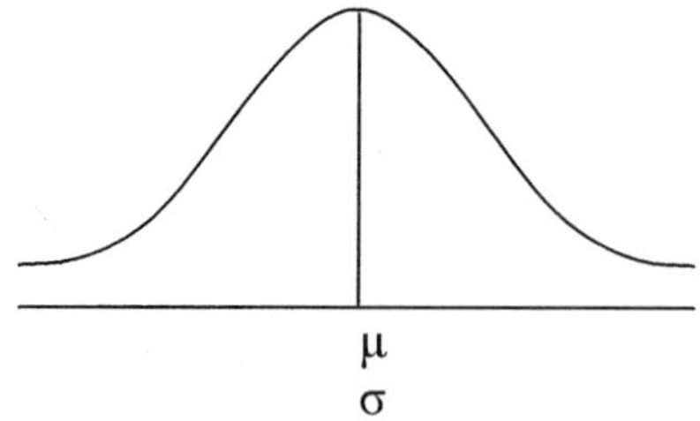

Figure 6.3.1. A typical Normal Distribution with mean μ and standard deviation = σ

- If you want to find the probability that a random value from this distribution will be more than μ, you simply find the ratio of area under the curve to the right of μ to the area under the entire curve. It will be 0.5, because of symmetry.

- If you want to find the probability that a random value from this distribution will be less than μ +100, you simply find the ratio of area under the curve to the left of μ + 100 to the area under the entire curve.

- If you want to find the probability that a random value from this distribution will be between μ –100 to μ + 200, you simply find the ratio of area under the curve between μ –100 to μ + 200 to the area under the entire curve.

In practice, we do not deal with this curve. We transform any Normal distribution with mean μ and standard deviation = σ, into an equivalent *Z* distribution, using the formula

$$Z = \frac{X - \mu}{\sigma}$$

and refer to the Standard normal table to find the exact answer.

6.4 Finding Areas Under the Standard Normal Curve

Looking up areas from the Z-table: The total area under the entire *Z*-distribution (also called standard normal distribution or normal distribution with μ = 0 and σ =1) is equal to 1.0. The *Z*-table is simply a listing of the area under the *Z*-distribution from *Z* = 0 to all necessary positive *Z* values till 5.0. The area from 0 to 5.0 is almost 0.4999997. Area from *Z* = 0 to *Z* = ∞, is only 0.5. That is, beyond *Z* = 5, the area simply does not change appreciably.

Hence for any value of *Z* > 5, the area from 0 to such a *Z* may be assumed as 0.5. Because of symmetry, areas from 0 to negative values are equal to the area from 0 to the corresponding positive values. For example, area from 0 to –2 is the same as area from 0 to 2. Similarly area from *Z* = -1 to *Z* = -2 is the same as area from *Z* =1 to *Z* = 2.

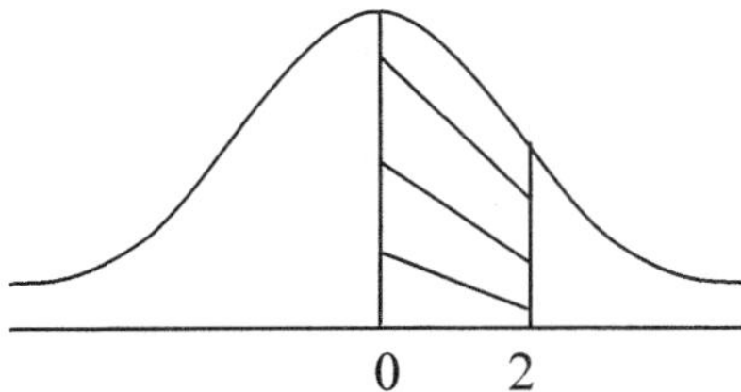

Figure 6.5.1. Standard Normal Distribution (or *Z*-Distribution) with Mean = 0 and Standard Deviation =1

Review Problem 6.4.1.

In Figure 6.5.1., a random variable distributed according to the Standard Normal distribution with Mean = 0 and Standard Deviation = 1 is presented.

a. Find the probability that a random sample from this distribution will fall between 0 and 2, i.e. $P(0 < Z < 2.0)$.
b. Find the probability that a random sample from this distribution will fall between –1 and 2, i.e. $P(-1.0 < Z < 2.0)$.
c. Find the probability that a random sample from this distribution will fall between –1 and –2, i.e. $P(-2.0 < Z < -1.0)$.
d. Find the probability that a random sample from this distribution will fall between 1.2 and +∞, i.e. $P(1.2 < Z < \infty)$.

Solution

a. It is simply the shaded area of Figure 6.5.1. It can be found by looking up the *Z*-table, for a *Z* value of 2.0, i.e. $P(0 < Z < 2.0) = 0.4772$.

b. $P(-1.0 < Z < 2.0)$. This is the shaded area of Figure 6.4.2.

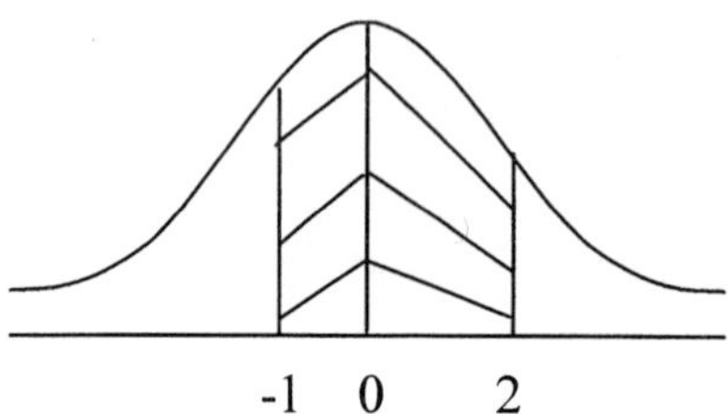

Figure 6.4.2. Shaded Area Corresponding to $P(-1.0 < Z < 2.0)$.

The answer is found in two steps as shown below.

$$\begin{aligned} P(-1.0 < Z < 2.0) &= P(-1.0 < Z < 0) + P(0 < Z < 2.0) \\ &= P(0 < Z < 1.0) + P(0 < Z < 2.0) \\ &= 0.3413 + 0.4772 = 0.8185 \end{aligned}$$

c. $P(-2.0 < Z < -1.0)$ is the shaded area of Figure 6.4.3.

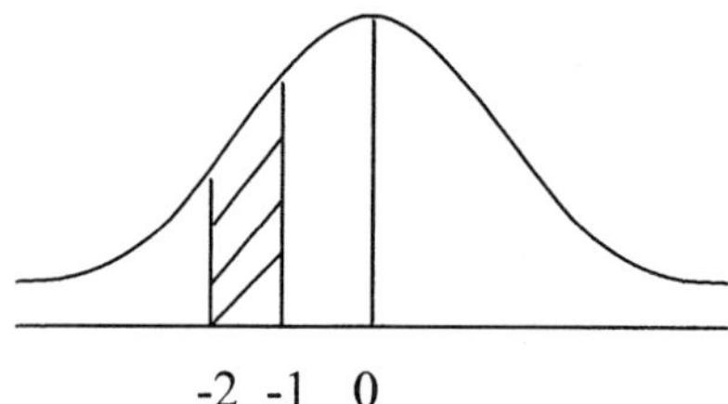

Figure 6.4.3. Shaded area corresponding to $P(-2.0 < Z < -1.0)$.

The answer is found in two steps as shown below.

$$\begin{aligned} P(-2.0 < Z < -1.0) &= P(-2.0 < Z < 0).- P(-1.0 < Z < 0) \\ &= P(0 < Z < 2). - P(0 < Z < 1.0) \\ &= 0.4772 - 0.3413 = 0.1359 \end{aligned}$$

d. $P(1.2 < Z < \infty)$.is the shaded area of Figure 6.4.4..

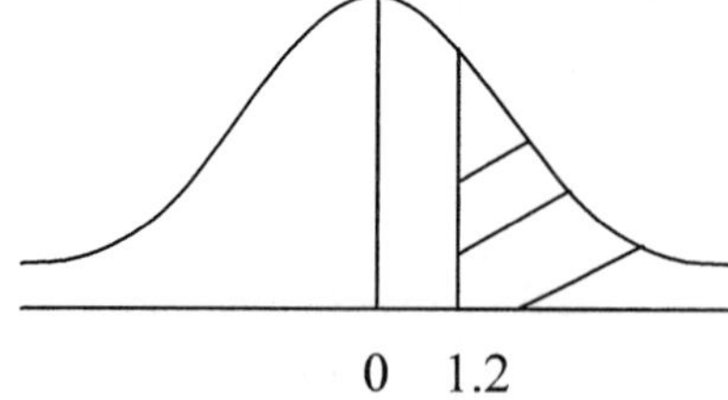

Figure 6.4.4. Shaded Area Corresponding to $P(1.2 < Z < \infty)$.

$$\begin{aligned} P(1.2 < Z < \infty) &= P(0 < Z < \infty).- P(0 < Z < 1.2) \\ &= 0.5 - 0.3849 = 0.1151 \end{aligned}$$

Review Problem 6.4.2.

In Figure 6.5.1., a random variable distributed according to the Standard Normal distribution with $\mu = 0$ and $\sigma = 1$ is presented.

a. Find that *Z*-value that makes the probability that a random sample from *Z*-distribution will be greater than *Z* value with a probability 0.10. If such a *Z*-value is denoted by z, we want to find that z that makes $P(Z>z) = 0.10$.
b. Find that *Z*-value that makes the probability that a random sample from *Z*-distribution will be less than that *Z* value with a probability 0.60. If such a *Z*-value is denoted by z, we want to find that z that makes $P(Z<z) = 0.60$.

Solution

a. Figure 6.4.5. gives the schematic diagram and shows z that makes $P(Z > z) = 0.10$.

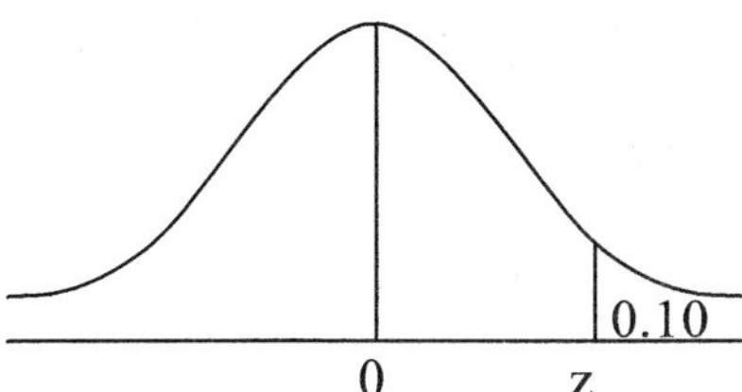

Figure 6.4.5.

Since area from $Z = 0$ to $Z = \infty$ is 0.5, area from $Z = 0$ to $Z = z$ should be equal to 0.5-0.1 = 0.4. Look inside the *Z*-table for the value closest to 0.4. You will find 0.3997. This corresponds to 1.2 on the horizontal side and 0.08 on the vertical side. The corresponding *Z* value is 1.2 + 0.08 = 1.28, which is the answer.

b. Figure 6.4.6. gives the schematic diagram and shows z that makes $P(Z < z) = 0.60$.

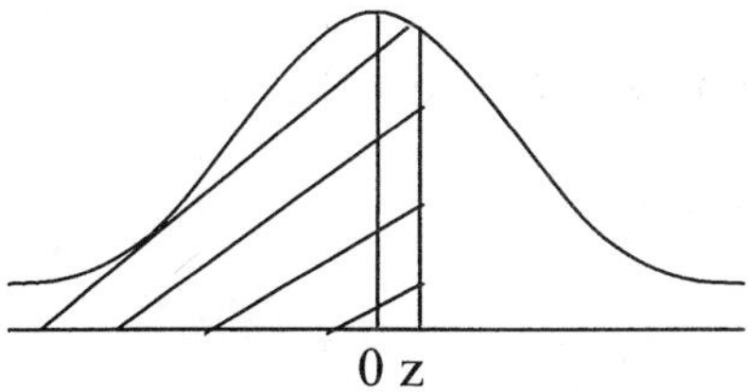

Figure 6.4.6.

Since area from $Z = -\infty$ to $Z = z$ is 0.6 (shaded area), the area from $Z = 0$ to $Z = z$ should be equal to 0.6-0.5 = 0.1. Look inside the *Z*-table for the value closest to 0.1. You will find 0.0987. This corresponds to 0.2 on the horizontal side and 0.05 on the vertical side. The corresponding *Z* value is 0.2 + 0.05 = 0.25, which is the answer.

6.5 Applications Where Area under a Normal Curve is Provided

If *X* is a random variable which is normal with mean 300 and standard deviation = 25, then *X*-300 is normal with mean 0 and standard deviation = 25. (Subtracting a constant from each possible value of *X* shifts the mean by the amount subtracted, just like in a set of numbers, but leaves the standard deviation unchanged.) Divide the (*X*-300) by its standard deviation to obtain

$$Z = \frac{X - 300}{25}$$

Z also normal, with mean 0 and standard deviation = original standard deviation/25 = 1.0. Thus any normal random variable X can be converted to the standard normal random variable Z, by the use of the above formula.

Similarly any standard normal variable Z, can be converted to normal random variable with mean μ and standard deviation = σ, by using the following formula

$$X = \mu + Z\sigma$$

which is just an algebraic rearrangement of the previous formula for Z.

A Normal Random variable with $\mu = 300$ and $\sigma = 25$

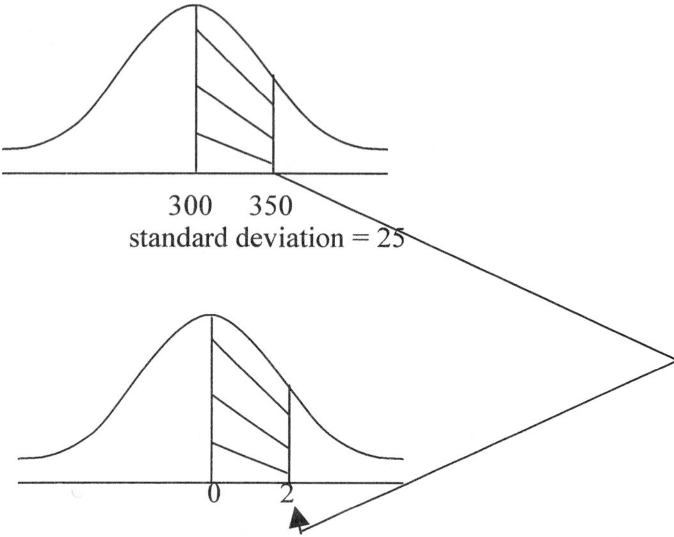

Figure 6.5.1.Corresponding Z random variable with $\mu = 0$ and $\sigma = 1$.

In Figure 6.5.1., a random variable distributed according to the Normal distribution with mean = 300 and standard deviation = 25 is presented. If you want to find the probability that a random sample form this distribution will fall between 300 and 350, is simply the shaded area and it can be found by first finding the corresponding $Z = (350\text{-}300)/25 = 2.0$ and looking up the Z-table, as in Section 6.6. The answer is 0.4772.

Review Problem 6.5.2.

Monthly demand for cars at Jamesville's dealership follows a normal distribution with mean 3000 and standard deviation 100.

a. What is the probability that the demand for a typical month will be between 2700 and 3200?
b. What is the probability that the demand will be more than 3300 for a typical month?
c. If all city dealerships that sell more than the 90th percentile of cars are given an award, what is the minimum number of cars Jamesville would have to sell in order to qualify for the award?
d. Given that the demand for a specific month was at least 3200, what is the probability that the demand was more than 3300?

Solution

a. Just to illustrate, the areas two corresponding distributions are shown in Figure 6.6.1. In order to find the area from 2700 to 3200, split that area into two areas: area to the left of the mean and area to the right of the mean.

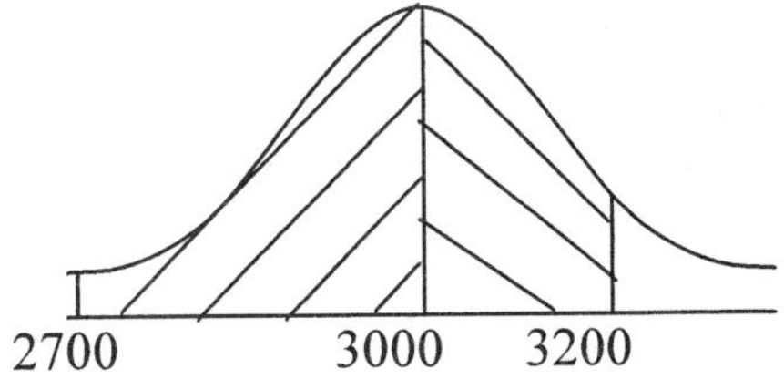

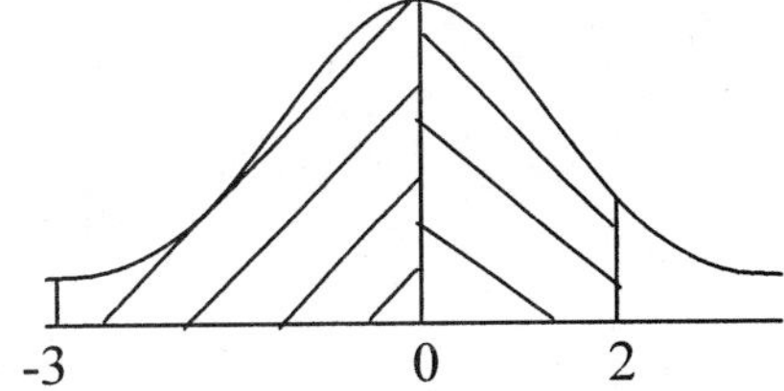

Figure 6.5.2. Normal ($\mu = 300$ and $\sigma = 25$) and the corresponding Z distribution.

Area to the left of the mean:
2700 to 3000
$Z(2700) = (2700\text{-}3000)/100 = -3$; $Z(3000) = (3000\text{-}3000)/100 = 0$.
Area from –3 to 0 is equal to 0.4987

Area to the right of the mean 2:
3000 to 3200
$Z(3000) = 0$, $Z(3200) = (3200\text{-}3000)/100 = 2$;
Area by looking up in the Z-table corresponding to 2.0 is 0.4772.
Answer: 0.4987 + 0.4772 = 0.9759.

b. $Z(3300) = (3300\text{-}3000)/100 = 3$. What is the area beyond 3.0 in the Z-distribution?
0.5-0.4987 = 0.0013

c. Figure 6.5.3 illustrates the solution.

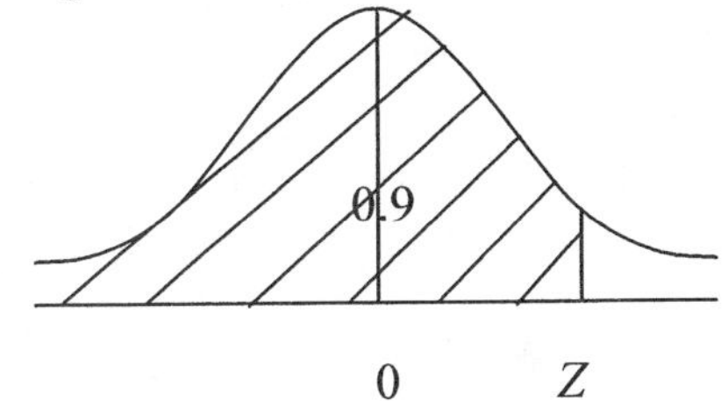

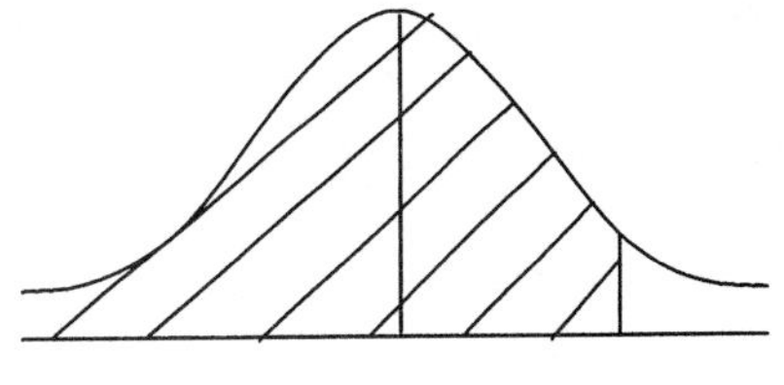

Figure 6.5.3. Z and the Corresponding X Distribution.

We first find Z such that the area to its left is 0.9 or the area from 0 to Z should be 0.9 - 0.5 (the left half) = 0.4.
$Z = 1.28$.
$X = 3000 + 1.28(100) = 3128$ cars.

d. P(at least 3200) = (find $Z(3200)$ and area to the right).
$Z(3200) = (3200 - 3000)/100 = 2.0$. Area from 0 to 2.0, 0.4772.
P(at least 3200) = 0.5-0.4772 = 0.0228.
P(demand > 3300) = Area to the right of $Z(3300)$ = 0.0013 (see part b.)
P(demand > 3300/demand >3200) = 0.0013/0.0228 = 0.057

6.6 Another Look at the Empirical Rule

It is best summarized by means of a table. See Table 6.6.1. for details

Variable X follows Normal distribution with Mean = μ and standard deviation = σ		Variable Z follows Normal distribution with Mean = 0 and standard deviation = 1	
Limits On X	Area Of The Distribution Covered	Limits On Z	Area Of The Distribution Covered
Between μ-1σ to μ-1σ also known as $P(\mu-1\sigma < X < \mu+1\sigma)$	0.68	Between -1 to +1 also known as $P(-1 < Z < 1)$	0.68
Between μ-2σ to μ-2σ also known as $P(\mu-2\sigma < X < \mu+2\sigma)$	0.9544	Between -2 to +2 also known as $P(-2 < Z < 2)$	0.9544
Between μ-3σ to μ-3σ also known as $P(\mu-3\sigma < X < \mu+3\sigma)$	0.9974	Between -3 to +3 also known as $P(-3 < Z < 3)$	0.9974

Table 6.6.1. Normal rule

6.7 Using Excel to Determine Areas and Values Having a Specified Area for the Normal Distribution

We can use Excel to easily find the areas. Since it is easier still to find it using the Z-Table, the Excel method is not detailed here.

6.8 Normal Approximation to the Binomial

Binomial distribution with n trials, p probability of success, and X is the number of successes has $\mu = np$ and

$$\sigma = \sqrt{np(1-p)}$$

In order to use normal distribution to approximate binomial, use

$$Z = \frac{X - np}{\sqrt{np(1-p)}}$$

Review Problem 6.8.1

The probability of any customer who visits the www.ThingsJamaica.com web page placing an order is 0.20. Of 50 people who visit the site what is the probability that 8 to 12 orders will be received?

Solution

Use Normal approximation to binomial for $n = 50$, p = 0.2 and the probability desired is the customer-orders to be between 8 to 12 both inclusive.
Mean of normal distribution = np = 50(0.2) = 10.
Standard deviation of normal distribution = sqrt(np(1-p)) = sqrt(8) = 2.828

Adjusting for continuity, you reduce the 8 to 7.5, since we are interested in the probability of more than 7.5, and adjust the 12 to 12.5 since less than 12.5 is the desired probability.

Z(7.5) = (7.5 - 10)/2.828 = -.884 and Z(12.5) = (12.5 - 10)/2.828 = +0.884
Area from –0.884 to +0.884 = 2 × (area from 0 to 0.884) = 2.0(0.3106) = 0.6212

6.9 Other Continuous Distributions

Uniform Distribution:

Uniform Distribution is another popular distribution whose properties are noted in Table 6.9.1.

Property	Description
Name	Uniform Distribution
Type of random variable	Continuous
Values the random variable may take	*a* to *b* where *a* is the lower limit and *b* is the upper limit.
Shape	Like a rectangle.
Height of the rectangle	1/(*b*-*a*)
Probability density function (PDF)	• Rectangle shaped • The equation describing it: f(x) = 1/(*b*-*a*) • Areas between any two values *x* and *y* is (*y*-x)/(*b*-*a*), where $a \leq x \leq y \leq b$
Mean	$\mu = (a+b)/2$
Standard deviation (standard deviation)	$\sigma = \dfrac{b-a}{\sqrt{12}}$

Table 6.9.1. Properties of Uniform Distribution

Review Problem 6.9.1.

The time to take a quiz for a typical Business Statistics 2000 student is uniform (20,30).

a. What is the probability of completing the quiz between 20 and 23 minutes?
b. What is the probability of taking longer than 26 minutes?
c. What is the probability of taking less than 25 minutes?

Solution

a. (23-20/(30-20) = 0.3
b. (30-26)/(30-20) = 0.4
c. (25-20)/(30-20) = 0.5

Exponential Distribution:

The Exponential Distribution is another popular distribution; its properties are listed in Table 6.9.2., shown on the next page.

Property	Description
Name	Exponential Distribution
Type of random variable	Continuous
Special Property	Memoryless (Any information about how history of events, will not enable us to revise the probability for future.) Normal and uniform have memories.
Values the random variable may take	0 to + ∞
Shape	Starts from its rate and goes down.
Probability density function (PDF): If time between events follows exponential with rate A events per unit time	$P(\text{time between events} < X) = 1\text{-}e^{-Ax}$
Probability density function (PDF): If time between events follows exponential with rate A events per unit time:	$P(\text{time between events} > X) = e^{-Ax}$
Mean	= 1/A
Standard deviation	= 1/A

Table 6.9.1. Properties of Exponential Distribution

Review Problem 6.9.2

Time to take the quiz for a typical IS/OM 2060 student is exponential with A = 3 per hour,

a. What is the probability that the time taken by a student < 30 minutes?
b. What is the probability that the time taken by a student > 25 minutes?

Solution to Review Problem 6.9.2

a. The rate 3 per hour must be converted to 3/60 per minute or 1/20 per minute, because all units must be measured in the same unit. Since 30 minutes is given, minutes are needed.
   Answer: $1- e^{-(1/20)30}$
b. $e^{-(1/20)25}$

6.10 Self-test Problems

Self-test Problem 6.10.1.

a. Monthly demand for a product follows normal distribution with mean 300 and standard deviation 50. What is the probability of the demand during a typical month exceeding 360?
b. Monthly demand for a product follows normal distribution with mean 300 and standard deviation 50. What is the probability of the demand during a typical month is less than 360?
c. Monthly demand for a product follows normal distribution with mean 300 and standard deviation 50. What is the probability of the demand during a typical month is between 240 and 360?

Self-test Problem 6.10.2.

A door-to-door salesman estimates that on every house call, there is a 0.1 chance of making a sale. If he visits 80 households, using normal approximation to binomial, answer the following questions.

a. What is the probability of making 7 or more sales?
b. What is the probability of making between 5 and 7 sales?

c. What is the minimum sales level that will put him in the 80th percentile of salesman? (80th percentile salesman sell more than 80% of salesman.)

Self-test Problem 6.10.3.

Time (minutes) to make a sales presentation is uniform (30,50). Calculate the following.
a. *P*(presentation is finished within 45 minutes?
b. *P*(presentation lasts at least 40 minutes)?
c. *P*(presentation ends between 32 and 40 minutes)?

Self-test Problem 6.10.4.

Time to make a sales presentation is exponential with rate 1.5 per hour. Calculate the following.
a. *P*(presentation is finished within 45 minutes)
b. *P*(presentation lasts at least 40 minutes)?

Multiple Choice Questions:

1. Exponential distribution is a memory-less distribution.
   a. True
   b. False
2. Exponential distribution is a discrete distribution
   a. True
   b. False
3. Mean of the exponential distribution is (using textbook notation):
   a. *A*
   b. 1/*A*
   c. sqrt(1/*A*)
   d. None of these alternatives.
4. Standard deviation of the exponential distribution is (using textbook notation):
   a. *A*
   b. 1/*A*
   c. sqrt(1/*A*)
   d. None of these alternatives.
5. If time to take a quiz for a typical business student is uniform (20,30) then, the average time to take the quiz is:
   a. 20
   b. 30
   c. 25
   d. None of these alternatives.
6. If time to take a quiz for a typical business student is uniform (20,30) then, the standard deviation of the time to take the quiz is:
   a. 20
   b. 10
   c. 10/sqrt(12)
   d. 10/sqrt(10)
   e. None of these alternatives.
7. If time to take the quiz for a typical business student is exponential with $A = 3$ per hour, then **P**(time taken by a student < 30 minutes) is given by: (Hint: The rate 3 per hour must be converted to 3/60 per minute or 1/20 per minute. Because, all units must be measured in the same unit. Since 30 minutes is given this was needed.)

a. $e^{-(3)30}$
b. $1- e^{-(3)30}$
c. $e^{-(1/20)30}$
d. $1- e^{-(1/20)30}$

8. If time to take a quiz for a typical business student is uniform (20,30) then, the probability of completing the quiz between 20 and 23 minutes is:
   a. 0.3
   b. 0.5
   c. 3.0
   d. None of these alternatives.
9. If time to take a quiz for a typical business student is uniform (20,30), then the probability of taking longer than 26 minutes is:
   a. 0.6
   b. 0.4
   c. 3.0
   d. None of these alternatives.
10. If time to take the quiz for a typical business student is exponential with $A = 3$ per hour, then P(time taken by a student < 1 hour) is given by: (hint: There is no need No need to change the unit of measurement, since A and time are in hours.)
   a. $e^{-(3)1}$
   b. $1- e^{-(3)1}$
   c. $e^{-(1/20)10}$
   d. $1- e^{-(1/20)20}$
11. Monthly demand for a product follows normal distribution with mean 300 and standard deviation 50. What is the probability of the demand during a typical month exceeding 360?
   a. 0.3848
   b. 0.6151
   c. 0.1151
   d. –0.1151
   e. 0.7696
12. Monthly demand for a product follows normal distribution with mean 300 and standard deviation 50. What is the probability that the demand during a typical month is less than 360?
   a. 0.8848
   b. 0.6151
   c. 0.1151
   d. –0.1151
   e. 0.7696
13. Monthly demand for a product follows normal distribution with mean 300 and standard deviation 50. What is the probability that the demand during a typical month is between 240 and 360?
   a. 0.3848
   b. 0.6151
   c. 0.1151
   d. –0.1151
   e. 0.7696

6.11 Glossary

adjustment for continuity
An adjustment made to better approximate binomial probabilities using the normal distribution.

continuous random variable
A random variable for which any value is possible over a specified range
Its distribution is described by a smooth curve.

exponential random variable
A continuous random variable, characterized by a steadily decreasing distribution.

mean of a continuous random variable
The average (expected) value of the population described by this random variable.

normal random variable
A continuous random variable characterized by a symmetric, bell-shaped distribution.

parameter
A value that describes a population
A normal population is described using two parameters; the mean and standard deviation

standard deviation of a continuous random variable
A measure of the variability of the population described by this random variable.

standard normal random variable (Z)
A normal random variable with a mean of zero and standard deviation of one.

standardize
To subtract the mean of a normal random variable and divide by its standard deviation
This procedure converts a normal random variable (X) into a standard normal random variable (Z).

uniform random variable
A continuous random variable, characterized by a flat distribution.

variance of a continuous random variable
A measure of the population variability; equal to the square of the standard deviation.

6.12 Solution to Self-test Problems

Solution to Self-test Problem 6.10.1.

a. First find the Z value corresponding to 360, using the formula

$$Z = \frac{X - \mu}{\sigma} = \frac{360 - 300}{50} = 1.2$$

Probability of demand exceeding 360 in Normal (mean 300 and standard deviation 50) is the same as the probability of exceeding 1.2 in the Z distribution.

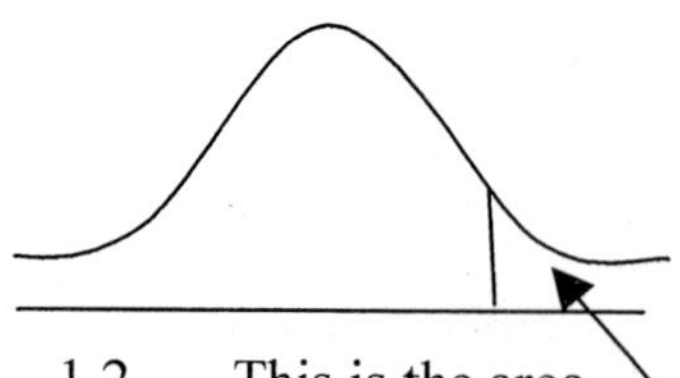

From the Z table, look for 1.2 on the left column and 0.0 on top row to get
Tabulated area is given above pictorially and given below in table form.

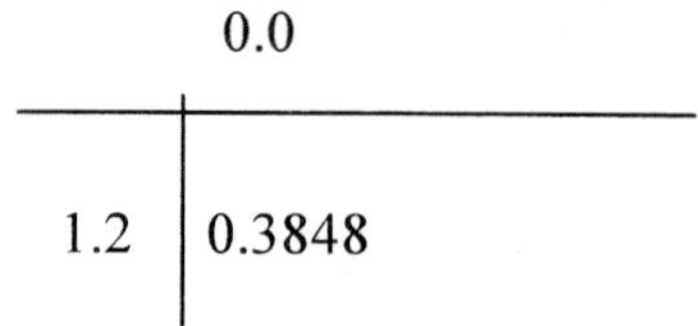

	0.0
1.2	0.3848

Area of interest = 0.5-0.3848 = 0.1152

b.

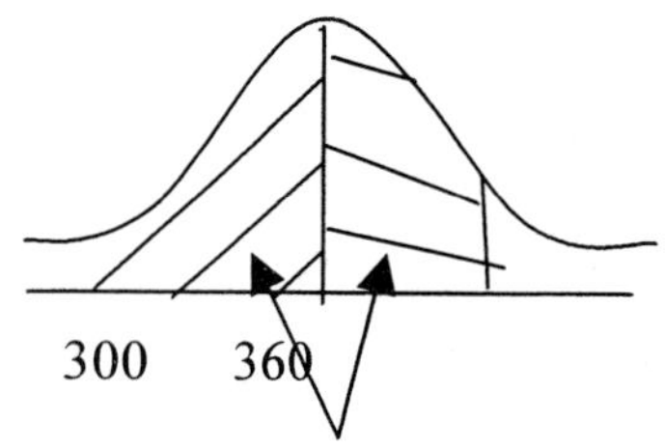

For less than 360, Z value is still 1.2, the area of interest is from $-\infty$ to 1.2 in the Z distribution = 0.5 (for $-\infty$ to 0) + 0.3848 = 0.8848

c. Between 240 and 360, Z = (240-360)/50 = -1.2
The area is -1.2 to 1.2, which is 2(0.3848) = 0.7696

Solution to Self-test Problem 6.10.2.

Mean of the Normal distribution = 80(0.10) = 8
Standard deviation of the normal distribution approximation = sqrt(80(0.10)(1-0.10) = 2.68
Use these for all 3 questions.

a. 7 or more, using continuity correction will be the area from 6.5 to $+\infty$ in a normal distribution with mean 8 and standard deviation 2.68.

$Z_{7.5}$ = (6.5-8)/2.68 = -0.56
Z distribution area from -0.56 to $+\infty$ = Area from Z = - 0.56 to Z = 0 + area from 0 to $+\infty$.
= Area from 0 to 0.56 +area from 0 to $+\infty$
= 0.2123 + 0.5
= 0.7123

b. P(5 < sales < 7): Using continuity correction, = P(4.5 < sales < 7.5)
$Z_{4.5}$ = (4.5-8)/2.68=-1.306
$Z_{7.5}$ = (7.5-8)/2.68=-0.187

Area from -1.306 to 0 = Area from 1.306 to 0 = 0.4131
Area from -0.187 to 0 = Area from 0.187 to 0 = 0.0753
Area from -1.306 to -0.187 = 0.4131-0.0753 = 0.3378

c. 80th percentile means, that Z which makes the area to its left equal to 0.8, or area from $Z = 0$ to the Z-value in question to be 0.8-0.5 = 0.3. Look inside the Z-table to find the nearest value to 0.3, which is 0.2995, which gives a Z-value of 0.84.
The corresponding X value: $x = 8 + 0.84(2.68) = 10.25$
If he sells 10.25 or more, using continuity correction, it may be 10.

Solution to Self-test Problem 6.10.3.

Time (minutes) to make a sales presentation is uniform (30,50).

a. (45-30)/(50-30) = 0.75
b. (50-40)/(50-30) = 0.5
c. (40-32)/(50-30) = 0.4

Solution to Self-test Problem 6.10.4.

Rate in presentations per minute must be calculated first, because the questions use minute as the unit of measurement. A = 1.5/60 = 1/40 per minute.

a. $1-e^{-(1/40).45} = 0.588$
b. $e^{-(1/40).40} = 0.368$

Answers to Multiple Choice Questions

Question #	Answer	Question #	Answer	Question #	Answer
1	a	5	c	9	b
2	b	6	c	10	b
3	b	7	d	11	c
4	b	8	a	12	a
				13	e

CHAPTER 7 STATISTICAL INFERENCE AND SAMPLING

Chapter Overview and Learning Objectives

Chapter 6 introduced several continuous probability distributions, including the very important normal distribution. In this chapter, the use of the normal distribution will be extended to problems involving statistical estimation and statistical inference, that is, the estimation of population characteristics (parameters) on the basis of sample information. By the end of this chapter, the student should be able to:

1. Define and distinguish between sample statistics and population parameters.
2. Discuss the Central Limit Theorem and illustrate its use in statistical inference.
3. Construct confidence intervals using both the normal distribution and the Student *t* distribution.
4. Describe different aspects of sampling and sampling techniques such as: sampling error, finite population correction factor, systematic sampling, stratified sampling, and cluster sampling.

Chapter Outline

7.1 Random Sampling and Distribution of the Sampling Mean
7.2 The central Limit Theorem
7.3 Confidence Interval for the Mean of a Normal Population (σ known)
7.4 Confidence Interval for the Mean of a Normal Population (σ unknown)
7.5 Selecting the Necessary Sample Size
7.6 Self-test Problems
7.7 Glossary
7.8 Solution to Self-test Problems

7.1 Random Sampling and the Distribution of the sample Mean

Distribution of the sample Mean and the Central limit theorem:
Suppose that from a population of size *N*, with mean μ and standard deviation σ, we take all possible samples (sampling with replacement) of size *n*, the mean of the sample means $\mu_{\overline{X}} = \mu$ and standard deviation of the sample means (found using the population standard deviation formula) $\sigma_{\overline{X}} = \frac{\sigma}{\sqrt{n}}$, and if the sample size *n* is large (>30), the distribution of the sample mean $\left(\overline{X}\right)$ will be approximately normal, regardless of the distribution of the population. Further, if the population follows normal distribution, then the sampling distribution of sample mean $\left(\overline{X}\right)$ will be normal distribution regardless of sample size.

Next, Review Problem 7.1.1. illustrates the mean and standard deviation calculation of the sample means using a small population.

Review Problem 7.1.1.

Consider the population of size $(N) = 4$ given in Table 7.1. List all possible samples of size $(n) = 2$ from this population. And illustrate the characteristics of the distribution of sample means.

Solution

Table 7.1.1 gives the population and its mean and standard deviation calculated using the population standard deviation formula. Since there are 4 elements in the population, there are 4^2 = 16 possible samples of size 2. Note that the sampling is with replacement and hence the sample elements could be repeated. Further, 7 & 8 counts as one sample and 8 & 7 counts as another sample. The 16 samples and their means are shown in Table 7.1.2. Finally Table 7.1.3 presents the mean, standard deviation and the attendant calculations, showing that the characteristics hold.

	Original Population
	8
	7
	9
	20
Population Size (*N*)	4
Population Mean	11
Population standard deviation	5.244044

Table 7.1.1 Population

All Possible Samples Of Size 2 (*n*) From This Population								
	Sample 1	Sample 2	Sample 3	Sample 4	Sample 5	Sample 6	Sample 7	Sample 8
	8	8	8	8	7	7	7	7
	8	7	9	20	8	7	9	20
Sample Mean	8	7.5	8.5	14	7.5	7	8	13.5
	Sample 9	Sample 10	Sample 11	Sample 12	Sample 13	Sample 14	Sample 15	Sample 16
	9	9	9	9	20	20	20	20
	8	7	9	20	8	7	9	20
Sample Mean	8.5	8	9	14.5	14	13.5	14.5	20

Table 7.1.2 All possible sample of size (*n*), where $n = 2$.

Sample Mean	$(X - X\text{-bar})^2$
8	9
7.5	12.25
8.5	6.25
14	9
7.5	12.25
7	16
8	9
13.5	6.25
8.5	6.25
8	9
9	4
14.5	12.25

14	9
13.5	6.25
14.5	12.25
20	81
11	
3.71	
3.71	

Table 7.1.3: Population Of Sample Means And Its Parameters As Compared To Population Parameters.

7.2 The Central Limit Theorem

Review Problem 7.2.1.

Sales revenue generated per month by any salesperson in XYZ Inc. is normal with mean \$20,000.00 and standard deviation \$5,000.00.

a. What is the probability that Joe Smith, a sales person of XYZ Inc. will sell more than \$24,000.00 this month?
b. Kathy Sullivan, Vice-President has 10 salespersons under her command. Considering them as a random sample of salespersons, what is the probability that the average sales for this group will be more than \$24,000 this month?
c. Which probability (a) or (b) is higher and why?

Solution

Sales revenue generated per month is Normal as shown below. The shaded area gives the probability of generating more than \$24,000 in sales during this month. In order to find the shaded area, we need to find the corresponding area in the *Z*-distribution.

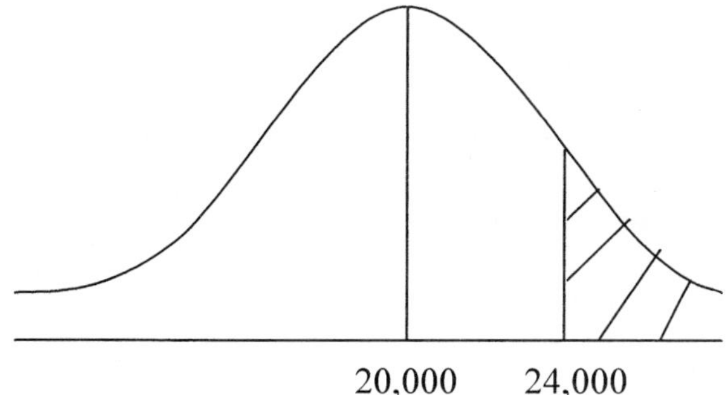

Figure 7.2.1.

a. First find the corresponding $Z = (24000\text{-}20000)/5000 = 0.8$.
   The table gives the area from $Z = 0$ to $Z = 0.8$, which is equal to 0.2881.
   Area from a Z value of 0.8 to $+\infty = 0.5000\text{-}0.2881 = 0.2119$.
   Probability that Joe Smith will sell more than \$24,000.00 this month = 0.2119.

b. The average sale for a group of 10 salespersons will follow the Normal distribution with mean = \$20, 000 and standard deviation will be 5000/sqrt(10) = \$1581.14.
   Probability that the average exceeds \$24,000 is given by the area from \$24,000 to $+\infty$, and this is equal to the corresponding area in the *Z*-distribution.

$Z = (24000\text{-}20000)/1581.11 = 2.53$.
From the Z-table, the area from 0 to 2.53 is 0.4943.
Area from 2.53 to $+\infty = 0.5000\text{-}0.4943 = 0.0047$
Probability that the average sales for this group will be more than \$24,000 = 0.0047

c. The probability that an individual salesperson (Joe Smith) will sell more than \$24000 is lot higher than the average of 10 salesman exceeding \$24000. Since 24000 is higher than the average and we want find the probability of exceeding it, one salesperson is more likely exceed than the average of a group of 10. (Average has smaller standard deviation.)

Distribution Of The Sample Mean When Sampling Without Replacement

Suppose that from a population of size N, with mean μ and standard deviation σ, we take all possible samples (sampling without replacement) of size n, the mean of the sample means $\mu_{\overline{X}} = \mu$ and standard deviation of the sample means (found using the population standard deviation formula) $\sigma_{\overline{X}} = \frac{\sigma}{\sqrt{n}}\left(\sqrt{\frac{(N-n)}{(N-1)}}\right)$, the distribution of the sample mean $\left(\overline{X}\right)$ will be approximately normal.

Review Problem 7.2.2.

A firm has received a special lot of size 200 of an important component for a space shuttle application. 20 of these components go into a knapsack in the shuttle and the average weight of the components should not exceed 41 ounces. If the distribution of the weight of the components in the lot is normal with mean 40 ounces and standard deviation 3 ounces, what is the probability that a random sample of 20 taken without replacement will meet the requirement of the shuttle application?

Solution

The random sample without replacement will have mean = 40 ounces and the

$\sigma_{\overline{X}} = \frac{3}{\sqrt{20}}\left(\sqrt{\frac{(200-20)}{(200-1)}}\right) = 0.6379$. The probability that a random variable which is normal with mean 40 and standard deviation = 0.6379 will exceed 41, is given by the area of the Z-distribution from $-\infty$ to Z, where $Z = (41\text{-}40)/0.6379 = 1.56$. From the Z-table, area from 0 to 1,56 is equal to 0.4406. Area from $-\infty$ to 0 in Z-distribution is 0.500. Hence, the area from $-\infty$ to 1.56 = 0.5000 + 0.4406 = 0.9406.

Probability that a random sample of 20 taken without replacement will meet the requirement of the shuttle application = 0.9406.

7.3 Confidence Interval for the Mean of a Normal Distribution (σ known)

The confidence interval is for the population mean. Here 95% confidence interval means that on an average, if we take 200 samples and construct 200 of these 95% confidence intervals for the population mean, approximately 190 (that is 95% of 200 or 0.95(200) = 190) of these intervals will contain the population mean. In other words, we can have 95% confidence that any one interval will contain the population mean. The 95% is called the confidence level for the interval.

The greater the confidence level, the wider will be the interval. In order to find any confidence interval, we need the confidence level required, the standard error of the distribution of the test statistic, sample mean and the correct formula to be used. For a test statistic following the Z-distribution, (1- α)(100%) confidence interval is given by:

$$\left[\overline{X} - Z_{\alpha/2}\left[\frac{\sigma}{\sqrt{n}}\right]\right] \text{to} \left[\overline{X} + Z_{\alpha/2}\left[\frac{\sigma}{\sqrt{n}}\right]\right]$$

where $Z_{\alpha/2}$ (i.e. Z-value that makes the area to its right in the Z-distribution equal to (α /2).) is to be found using the Z-table, because the underlying test statistic follows Z-distribution. For 95% confidence interval (or for α = 0.05, you want to find that pair of values of Z that contains the central 95% of the Z-distribution. So the tails together must contain 5% of the area. Each tail must have 2.5% of the area. Since Z-distribution is symmetric with mean 0, the area to the right of 0 is always 50%. If the tail is 2.5%, $Z_{0.025}$ is the Z-value that makes the area to the right of this value in the Z-distribution equal to 0.025. That is, the area from 0 to this Z-value will be equal to 47.5% or 0.475. Look in the Z-table for 0.475 or number/s close to it (and are on both sides of 0.475). Such a Z-value is 1.96 which makes the $Z_{\alpha/2}$ for this problem 1.96.

The 95% confidence interval is:

$$\left[\overline{X} - 1.96\left[\frac{\sigma}{\sqrt{n}}\right]\right] \text{to} \left[\overline{X} + 1.96\left[\frac{\sigma}{\sqrt{n}}\right]\right]$$

Review Problem 7.3.1.

It is known that the test score in the Graduate Management Admission Test (GMAT) of graduating seniors of The University of Jamesville follows normal distribution with σ = 100. A random sample of 36 friends and associates of 2002 graduating seniors had a mean score of 545. Find the 96% confidence interval for the population mean of GMAT scores of graduating seniors at The University of Jamesville.

Solution

The 96% confidence interval is obtained by using

$$\left[\overline{X} - Z_{\alpha/2}\left[\frac{\sigma}{\sqrt{n}}\right]\right] \text{to} \left[\overline{X} + Z_{\alpha/2}\left[\frac{\sigma}{\sqrt{n}}\right]\right]$$

Where α = 0.04 (corresponding to 96%, i.e. 1-.96) or α/2 = 0.02. Find $Z_{0.02}$, the Z-value that makes area to its right equal to 0.02, or area from 0 to the Z-value equal to 0.500-0.0.2 = 0.48. Z-value of 2.05 corresponds to an area of 0.4798, and 2.06 corresponds to 0.4803. Assuming that we are interested in at least 96%, choose that Z-value that just crosses 0.48, that is, let $Z = 2.06$.Substituting the known values in the confidence interval formula yields

$$\left[545 - 2.06\left[\frac{100}{\sqrt{36}}\right]\right] \text{to} \left[545 + 2.06\left[\frac{100}{\sqrt{36}}\right]\right]$$

and simplifies to [510.66, 579.33].

Comments about Confidence Interval

1. If you generate fifty 90% confidence intervals for a population mean by taking fifty different sample means, then 90% of the fifty intervals, that is, about 45 of them (does not mean exactly 45 of them) may contain the population mean μ. About 10% of the fifty intervals, that is 5 intervals (does not mean exactly 5 of them) may not contain the μ.
2. No specific comments may be made about whether a specific interval contains it.
3. One can also state that he or she is 90% confident that his or her estimate of μ, which is $\overline{X}$, is within $Z_{\alpha/2}\left[\frac{\sigma}{\sqrt{n}}\right]$ amount of the true μ.
4. The value of $Z_{\alpha/2}\left[\frac{\sigma}{\sqrt{n}}\right]$ is called the margin of error, *E*.
5. Other things remaining the same, larger the sample size *n*, narrower will be the confidence interval
6. Note that the "Probability that a 90% confidence interval contains μ" with a probability of 0.9 is **wrong**. It either contains μ or it does not contain it. So we cannot talk in terms of probability.

7.4 Confidence Intervals for the Mean (μ) of a Normal Population (σ unknown)

Consider the statistic t (defined below) obtained if we substitute σ by s, an estimate of the population standard deviation σ. This also follows a well-known distribution called *t*-distribution, which is a family of distributions unlike the *Z*-distribution, which is a single distribution. The family is defined by its degrees of freedom, which is (*n*-1).

$$t = \frac{\overline{X} - \mu}{s/\sqrt{n}}$$

Properties of *t*-distribution are listed in Table 7.4.1. This can be used to derive a (1-α).100% confidence interval for μ.

$$\left[\overline{X} - t_{\alpha/2,n-1}\left[\frac{s}{\sqrt{n}}\right]\right] \text{to} \left[\overline{X} + t_{\alpha/2,n-1}\left[\frac{s}{\sqrt{n}}\right]\right]$$

where $t_{\alpha/2,(n-1)}$ is the *t*-value to be looked up in the *t*-table with (*n*-1) degrees of freedom and the right tail equal to α/2.

Property	Description
Name	*t*-distribution
Type of random variable	Continuous
Values the random variable may take	-∞ to +∞
Shape	Symmetric about its mean
Family or just one	Family of distributions one for each degree of freedom
Role of degrees of freedom on the shape of the distribution	• Smaller the degrees of freedom, the more flat is the distribution. • Larger the degrees of freedom, the more peaked is the distribution.

Table 7.4.1. Properties of *t*-distribution

Review Problem 7.4.1.

Speedway is interested in estimating the average amount spent in their convenience stores by gas customers. Surveying 20 random customers revealed the average spent by them is $5.90 and the sample standard deviation was 0.70.
Find the 90% confidence interval for the population mean.

Solution

Find t for degrees of freedom = 20-1 = 19.
For 90% confidence interval, α/2 = (1-0.9)/2 = 0.05.
From Table A.5, *t*-value for 19 degrees of freedom and that which makes the right tail = 0.05 is 1.729.The 90% confidence interval is:

$$\left[5.90-1.729\left[\frac{0.70}{\sqrt{20}}\right]\right] to \left[5.90+1.729\left[\frac{0.70}{\sqrt{20}}\right]\right]$$

which simplifies to [5.63, 6.17].

7.5 Selecting the Necessary Sample Size

We can find the confidence interval for any given set of data. However, the width of the interval tells you how good is the confidence interval. If it is very wide, it is not of much use. In some applications, you may want to find an interval, which is within a fairly narrow range. Half the length of the interval is called Error, denoted by E. Decision makers can specify the amount of error they can tolerate. Given the amount of error, we can determine the sample size needed to achieve the specified amount of error. The formula below gives the sample size required.

$$n=\left[\frac{Z_{\alpha}/2\sigma}{E}\right]^2$$

Review Problem 7.5.1.

Average shopper at grocery stores buys 24 cans based on a survey of 49 shoppers. The population standard deviation of purchases was known to be 7 cans. The manager wants have an error of no more than 2 cans, in developing a 99% confidence interval for the population mean of the number of cans purchased by its customers. What is the sample size needed?

Solution

Z corresponding to the right tail of (1-0.99)/2 = 0.005 in the Z distribution is 2.58. If the Kroger Sales Manager wants to know the true mean of the population with an accuracy of +-2 cans, with a 99% confidence level, how many customers should be surveyed?

$$n = \left[\frac{2.58(7)}{2}\right]^2 = 82$$

Simple Random Samples: All elements of the population has an equal chance of getting selected. Similarly, if you take a random sample of size n from a population of size N, all samples have the same chance of being selected.

Sampling with replacement: For example, if you are conducting a study of heights of students, sampling 6 students from a class of 40, $N = 40$, $n = 6$, in sampling with replacement, you will sample one student at a time, find his/her height and put them back in the population, till you get all the 6.

Sampling without replacement: For example, if you are conducting a study of heights of students, sampling 6 students from a class of 40, $N = 40$, $n = 6$, in sampling without replacement, you will sample one student at a time, find his/her height and keep the out of the population until all 6 students are picked.

Number of samples: If we have a population of size $N = 40$, and if we take samples of size $n = 6$ from the population with replacement, there are 40^6 possible samples. If we sample without replacement there will be 40C6 (40 choose 6) possible samples.

Distribution of the sample mean: If we take all possible random samples of size n from a normal population with mean = μ and standard deviation = σ, then we can construct the distribution of the sample means (X-bar), with mean and standard deviation given as follows. (.)

$$\mu_{\overline{X}} = \mu \text{......................(1)}$$

$$\sigma_{\overline{X}} = \frac{\sigma}{\sqrt{n}} \text{................(2)}$$

Again this assumes infinite population or sampling with replacement and that the distribution is normal.

Central limit Theorem: If the population is not normal, the distribution of the sample mean is approximately normal with mean and standard deviation given by (1) and (2) above.

Formula (2) above is modified for cases **without replacement** for finite populations is:

$$\sigma_{\overline{X}} = \frac{\sigma}{\sqrt{n}}\sqrt{\frac{N-n}{N-1}}$$

7.6 Self-test Problems

Self-test Problem 7.6.1:

XYZ Inc. divides its sales force into groups of 9. Joe Cunningham heads one of the groups. Monthly sales by any salesperson follow a normal distribution with mean \$10,000 and standard deviation 2000. A Monthly High Sales Achievement Award is given to any salesperson that exceeds \$11,500 in sales during the month. A Monthly Group High Sales Achievement Award is given to any group that has an average sales exceeding \$11,500 or if the total sales of the group exceeds \$103,500 (\$11,500 × 9).

a. What is the probability that any salesman to get this award?
b. What is the probability that Joe Cunningham's group will get the Group high sales achievement award?
c. A new VP (Sales) changes the structure and reorganizes the sales force into groups of 16. Other award parameters remain unchanged. Has it become more or less difficult to get Monthly high sales achievement award? Has it become more or less difficult to get Monthly Group high sales achievement award?

Self-test Problem 7.6.2.

Sales during the first year of any salesperson for the XYZ Inc. follows a normal distribution with σ = \$15,000. A sample of 64 salespersons had a first year average of \$198,000. Construct a 92% confidence interval for μ, for the population mean.

Self-test Problem 7.6.3

A survey of 50 college professors revealed that 20% of them have never used a webpage in teaching.

a. Develop a 95% confidence interval for the population proportion of professors who have never used a webpage.
b. What is the 90% confidence interval for the population of professors who have used a webpage at least once in teaching?

Multiple Choice Questions:

Name	Years
Ms. Smith	15
Mr. Jones	20
Mr. Robert	18
Ms. Thomas	10

Table 7.6.1 Work Experience at The University of Toledo

1. The work experience of four executives at University of Toledo is given in Table 7.6.1. The number of samples of size 2 without replacement would be:
   a. 5
   b. 2
   c. 6
   d. 16
2. Again using the work experience of the four executives shown in Table 7.6.1., the number of samples of size 2 with replacement would be:
   a. 5
   b. 2
   c. 6
   d. 16
3. Again using the work experience of the four executives shown in Table 7.6.1., the $\mu_{\bar{X}}$ for samples of size 2 with replacement would be:
   a. 17.5
   b. 15.75
   c. 19
   d. Cannot tell because it depends on the sample taken
4. Again using the work experience of the four executives shown in Table 7.6.1., the $\mu_{\bar{X}}$ for samples of size 2 without replacement would be:
   a. 17.5
   b. 15.75
   c. 19
   d. Cannot tell because it depends on the sample taken
5. Again using the work experience of the four executives shown in Table 7.6.1., the σ of the population (using population σ formula)
   a. 4.3493
   b. 3.7663
   c. 2.38
   d. Cannot tell because it depends on the sample taken
6. Again using the work experience of the four executives shown in Table 7.6.1., the σ of the population (using sample estimate formula)
   a. 4.3493
   b. 3.7663
   c. 2.38
   d. Cannot tell because it depends on the sample taken
7. Again using Table 7.6.1., the $\sigma_{\bar{X}}$ for samples of size 2 without replacement (treating the samples as the entire population and using finite population correction) is
   a. 2.666
   b. 2.17
   c. 2.38
   d. 3.06
   e. Cannot tell because it depends on the sample taken
8. Again using Table 7.6.1., the $\sigma_{\bar{X}}$ for samples of size 2 with replacement (treating the samples as the entire population) is
   a. 2.666
   b. 2.17
   c. 2.38
   d. 3.06
   e. Cannot tell because it depends on the sample taken

For the remaining MC questions, use this information:
Kroger Corp. is interested in estimating the average number of cola drinks purchased per shopper. Assuming that the relevant population is the population of shoppers, it surveyed a random sample of 49 shoppers and found that they were planning to purchase on an average 24 cans. The standard deviation of purchases from the population of shoppers from an earlier study was known to be 7 cans.

9. The estimated mean number of cans purchased by this population?
   a. 24
   b. 49
   c. 7
   d. Cannot tell
10. The 99% confidence interval for the number of cans purchased by this population (μ)
    a. (20, 27)
    b. (21.42, 26.58)
    c. (24, 49)
    d. Cannot tell
11. The 95% confidence interval for the number of cans purchased by this population (μ)
    a. (22.04, 25.96)
    b. (21.42, 26.58)
    c. (24, 49)
    d. Cannot tell
12. If the Kroger Sales Manager wants to know the true mean of the population with an accuracy of ±2 cans, with a 99% confidence level, how many customers should be surveyed?
    9. 60
    10. 82
    11. 48
    12. 200
13. If the Kroger Sales Manager wants to know the true mean of the population with an accuracy of ±2 cans, with a 95% confidence level, how many customers should be surveyed?
    a. 60
    b. 82
    c. 48
    d. 200

7.7 Glossary

Central Limit Theorem
A result that states that for large samples, the distribution of the sample mean, 0, is approximately normal regardless of the shape of the sampled population.

cluster sample
A sample obtained by randomly selecting groups (clusters) of elements from the population.

confidence interval
An interval believed to contain the corresponding population parameter with a specified level of confidence.

confidence level
The confidence associated with the ability of a confidence interval to contain the true value of the corresponding parameter.

degrees of freedom
A value that specifies which t curve (distribution) is being used from the family of t curves. When constructing a confidence interval for a population mean using the t distribution, the degrees of freedom is $n - 1$, where n is the sample size.

finite population correction (fpc)
An adjustment to the standard error of the sample mean when sampling from a finite population; it is equal to the square root of $(N - n)/(N - 1)$ for the actual standard error and is equal to the square root of $(N - n)/N$ when calculating the estimated standard error.

inference
The process of drawing conclusions about a population based on the results of a statistical sample.

margin of error (E)
The amount that is added to and subtracted from the sample mean when constructing a confidence interval for the population mean.

parameter
A value that describes the population, such as the population mean (:).

point estimate
A single value of a sample statistic used as an estimate of a population parameter.

population
The set of all possible measurements of interest.

sampling distribution
The probability distribution of a sample statistic.

sample unit
A collection of elements (cluster) or an individual element selected from the population to be included in a sample.

sampling design
A plan that specifies the manner in which the sampling units are to be selected for the sample, such as simple random sampling, systematic sampling, stratified sampling or cluster sampling.

sampling frame
A list of population elements from which the sample is to be selected. Ideally, this should be identical to the population.

simple random sample
A sample of size n for which every sample of size n has the same chance of being selected.

standard error
The standard deviation of the sample mean.

statistic
A value that describes the sample, such as the sample mean . A sample statistic can be used to estimate a population parameter.

stratified sample
A sample obtained by first partitioning the population into non-overlapping strata and then selecting random samples within each stratum. The strata should be more homogeneous (contain less variation) than the population as a whole.

systematic sample
A sample for which every *k*th value is selected, for some $k > 0$, after determining a random starting point.

t distribution
A distribution used to construct confidence intervals for the population mean when the population standard deviation is unknown; the sample standard deviation (s) is used in the construction of this interval. Use of this distribution assumes that the sampled population has a normal or nearly normal distribution.

7.8 Solution to Self-test Problems

Solution to Self-test Problem 7.6.1

a. The answer is obtained by finding the probability of randomly picking a number greater than 11,500 in a normal distribution with mean 10,000 and standard deviation 2000. That is, the area to the right of 11,500 in such a normal distribution. That is, the same as the area to the right of the corresponding *Z*-value in the *Z*-distribution. $Z = (11500\text{-}10000)/2000 = 0.75$. The area from 0 to 0.75 in the *Z* distribution is found by looking up the table in the *Z*-distribution, and it is equal to 0.2734. The area to the right of the *Z*-value = 0.5000-0.2734 = 0.2266. Probability for any salesperson to get this award = 0.2266

b. The average for a group of 9 salespersons follows a normal distribution with mean = 11,500 and standard deviation = 2000/sqrt(9) = 666.66. The probability of getting the Group High Sales Achievement Award is given by the area to the right of 11,500 in a normal distribution with mean = 10000 and standard deviation = 666.66. That is the same as the area to the right of the corresponding *Z*-value. $Z = (11500\text{-}10000)/666.66 = 2.25$. From the *Z*-table, the area from 0 to 2.25 = 0.4878. The area to the right of *Z* value of 2.25 is 0.5000-0.4878 = 0.0122. Probability that Cunningham's group will get the Group high sales achievement award = 0.0122

c. Has it become more or less difficult to get Monthly High Sales Achievement Award: There has been no change in the level of difficulty, because the distribution for each salesperson remains the same.
Has it become more or less difficult to get Monthly Group High Sales Achievement Award: Since the group size is increased, it is synonymous to increasing sample size (n), which reduces $\sigma_{\overline{X}} = \dfrac{\sigma}{\sqrt{n}}$, and hence achieving average sales of $11,500 or more would have become more difficult, meaning probability would go down.

Solution to Self-test Problem 7.6.2.

The *Z*-value corresponding 92% is obtained by finding the *Z* which makes the area from 0 to *Z* equal to 0.92/2 = 0.46. *Z*-value of 1.75 corresponds to 0.4599 and a *Z*-value of 1.76 corresponds to 0.4608. You can pick *Z*-value of 1.75, being the closest to 0.46. The 92 % confidence interval is obtained by substituting the appropriate values in the confidence interval expression.

$$\left[198,000-1.75\left[\frac{15,000}{\sqrt{64}}\right]\right] \text{to} \left[198,000+1.75\left[\frac{15,000}{\sqrt{64}}\right]\right]$$

and simplifies to [194,718.75, 201,281.25].

Solution to Self-test Problem 7.6.3.

a. *Z*-value for 95% confidence interval is 1.96. Population standard deviation is sqrt((0.2(1-0.2))/50). Hence, the interval is: 0.2 ± 1.96 sqrt(0.2(0.8))/50) or [0.15, 0.25].
b. *Z*-value for 90% interval is 1.65. (The value of *Z* that makes the right tail equal to (1-0.9)/2 = 0.05) and hence the confidence interval is: 0.8 ± 1.65 sqrt((0.8(0.2)/50) = [0.727, 0.872]

Answers to Multiple-Choice Questions

Question #	Answer	Question #	Answer	Question #	Answer
1	c	5	b	9	a
2	d	6	a	10	b
3	b	7	b	11	a
4	b	8	a	12	b
				13	c

CHAPTER 8 HYPOTHESIS TESTING FOR THE MEAN AND VARIANCE OF A POPULATION

Chapter Overview and Learning Objectives

Anytime a sample is taken to check the value of a population parameter, sampling error will be present. In other words, it is not reasonable to expect $\overline{X}$ to exactly equal the true mean, although it should be close. But how close is "close enough"? This chapter presents statistical methods for determining how close is close enough, along with the consequences of that determination. By the end of the chapter, the student should be able to:

1. Discuss what is meant by the terms "statistically significant difference" and "hypothesis test".
2. Carry out a hypothesis test on the mean and variance of a population.
3. Discuss the implication of a given decision resulting from a hypothesis test.

Chapter Outline

8.1 Hypothesis Testing on the Mean of a Population: Large Sample
8.2 One-Tailed Test for the Mean of a Population: Large Sample
8.3 Reporting Testing Results Using a *p*-value
8.4 Hypothesis Testing on the Mean of a Normal Population: Small Sample
8.5 Inference for the Variance and Standard Deviation of a Normal Population
8.6 Self-Test Problems
8.7 Glossary
8.8 Solution to Self-Test Problems

8.1 Hypothesis testing on the mean of a population: Large sample

Review Problem 8.1

a. Academic Vice President Jim Jones of The University of Jamesville believes that the summer income of their students was Normal with mean of \$6000 and a standard deviation of \$300. Mr. Jones ordered a survey to verify his belief. A random sample of 60 students had a mean income of \$5700. Is there sufficient evidence to support the belief of the Vice-President? Use 0.05 significance level.
b. What is the range of values of the sample mean with the same sample size that will lead to the decision to reject H_0?
c. What is the power of the test in part (a), if the population mean is \$6100 and population standard deviation is \$300 (same as the population when H_0.is true.)?
d. Construct a 95% confidence interval for the population mean of the summer income of students at the University of Jamesville.

Solution

All hypothesis tests use the 5-step procedure given in the text. The first task is to determine the appropriate test. In this problem: sample size is large; population standard deviation is known; key words from the problem: "believes that the summer income of their students was Normal with mean of \$6000" and "Is there sufficient evidence to support the belief" suggests a two-tailed Z-test.

Step 1. Type of hypothesis? Look for a "clue" or key word in the problem: Here, "Support the belief" Since no direction is specified, it must be a two-sided test:
H_0: $\mu = 6000$
H_a : $\mu \neq 6000$ (H_a is always the compliment of H_0).

Step 2. Test Statistic for this problem

$$(1) \quad Z = \frac{\overline{X} - \mu}{\sigma / \sqrt{n}}$$

or if the population standard deviation is unknown, the sample standard deviation may be used.

$$(2) \quad Z = \frac{\overline{X} - \mu}{s / \sqrt{n}}$$

Follows Z distribution.

Step 3. For significance level of 0.05, the rejection region will have a total area of 0.05. Since it is a two tailed test the two tails together must add up to 0.05. Because of symmetry, each tail will be .025. In a Z-distribution, the area to the right of the mean will be 0.5. To find the critical value we look for Z value corresponding to 0.5-0.025 = 0.475. In the Z-table, look inside the table for the number nearest to .475,

Z	0.06
1.9	0.475

The corresponding Z- value is 1.96. Because it is a two-tailed test, the reject H_0 region is all values > 1.96 and all values < -1.96. (1.96 is the critical value on the right tail) and -1.96 (is the critical value on the left tail) Fail to reject H_0 region is all values between -1.96 and +1.96 as shown in the following Figure.

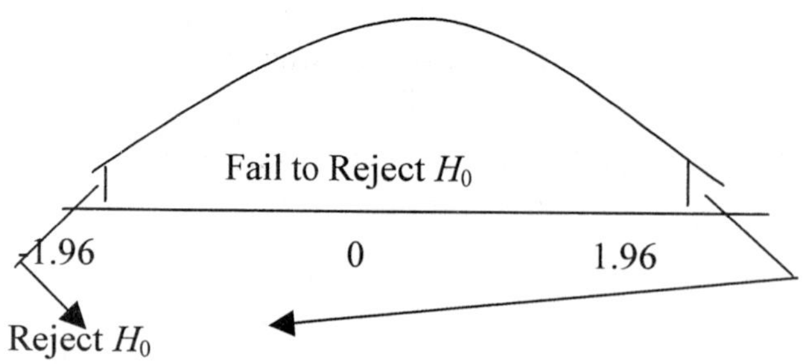

Step 4. Calculate the value of the test statistic:

$$Z = \frac{5700 - 6000}{300/\sqrt{60}}$$
$$= -7.7459$$

Since the test statistic falls in the reject H_0 region, reject H_0.

Step 5. Conclusion: The Vice-President's belief is not supported by statistical evidence.

a. What is the range of values of sample mean with the same sample size that will lead to the decision to reject H_0? First we will find the Fail to Reject H_0 region. As shown in Step 3 of (a) above, Fail to reject H_0 region is all values of Z between -1.96 and +1.96. Using this information and the test statistic equation given in (1), we can write the following equations.

$$-1.96 \leq \frac{\overline{X} - \mu}{\sigma/\sqrt{n}} \text{ and } \frac{\overline{X} - \mu}{\sigma/\sqrt{n}} \leq 1.96$$

These may be rearranged to find the range of values of sample mean ($\overline{X}$) that will lead to a decision to Fail to Reject H_0.

$$\mu - 1.96\left|\frac{\sigma}{\sqrt{n}}\right| \leq \overline{X} \text{ and } \overline{X} \leq \mu + 1.96\left|\frac{\sigma}{\sqrt{n}}\right|$$

Substituting $\mu = 6000$, $\sigma = 300$ and $n = 60$, the above expression may be re-written in terms of

Range of $\overline{X}$: $6000 - 1.96\left|\frac{300}{\sqrt{60}}\right|$ and $6000 + 1.96\left|\frac{300}{\sqrt{60}}\right|$

Shortened format [5924.09, 6075.91]. If the sample mean $\overline{X}$ falls in this range, we fail to reject H_0. Otherwise, we will reject H_0.

b. Power of the test in Part (a) when the population mean $\mu = 6100$ and population standard deviation is 300 (same as the population when H_0.is true.) Power of a test is the probability of rejecting H_0 when H_0 is false. H_0 is false whenever μ is not equal to 6000 which is the hypothesized value of μ when H_0 is true. There is one value of power of the test corresponding to each possible value for μ. Here we are asked to find the power of the test when $\mu = 6100$. That is, if we take random sample of size 60 from such a population of students, what is the probability that H_0 will be rejected? That is, what is the probability that sample mean $\overline{X}$ will fall outside the range found in part (b) , namely [5924.09, 6075.91]. Next we find the corresponding Z values, denoted as z_1 and z_2 where

$$z_1 = \frac{6075.91 - 6100}{300/\sqrt{60}}. \quad \text{and} \quad z_2 = \frac{5924.09 - 6100}{300/\sqrt{60}}.$$

z_1 = -0.622 and z_2 =. -4.54

The power of the test is the area to the right of z_1 (plus) the area to the left of z_2 . $P(Z > z_1)$ = .2324 + .5 = 0.7324. Note that the area to the right of -.622, is the area from -.622 to 0 plus the area from 0 to infinity. The first part as looked up from the Z-table is equal to .2324 (approximating .622 as .62) and the second part is 0.5. $P(Z < z_2)$ = almost 0 (as seen from the Z-table).

c. Confidence interval is for the population mean. Here 95% confidence interval means that on an average, if we take 200 samples and construct 200 of these 95% confidence intervals for the population mean, approximately 190 (that is 95% of 200 or 0.95(200) = 190) of these intervals will contain the population mean. In other words, we can have 95% confidence that any one interval will contain the population mean. The 95% is called the confidence level for the interval. The greater the confidence level, wider will be the interval. In order to find any confidence interval , we need the confidence level required, the standard error of the distribution of the test statistic, sample mean and the correct formula to be used. For a test statistic following *Z*-distribution, C.I is given by:

$$\left[\overline{X} - k\left[\frac{\sigma}{\sqrt{n}}\right]\right] to \left[\overline{X} + k\left[\frac{\sigma}{\sqrt{n}}\right]\right]$$

k is to be found using the *Z*-table, because the underlying test statistic follows *Z*-distribution. For 95% confidence interval, you want to find that pair of values of *Z* that contains the central 95% of the *Z*-distribution. So the tails together must contain 5% of the area. Each tail must have 2.5% of the area. Since *Z*-distribution is symmetric with mean 0, the area to the right of 0 is always 50%. If the tail is 2.5%, the k value is the *Z*-value that corresponds to 47.5% or 0.475. Look inside the *Z*-table for 0.475 or number/s close to it (and are on both sides of 0.475). As shown in Part (a), *Z* value is equal to 1.96, which makes the k for this problem 1.96.

The 95% confidence interval is:

$$\left[5700 - 1.96\left[\frac{300}{\sqrt{60}}\right]\right] to \left[5700 + 1.96\left[\frac{300}{\sqrt{60}}\right]\right]$$

Shortened format, [5624.09, 5775.91].

8.2: One-Tailed Test For The Mean Of A Population: Large Sample

Review Problem 8.2

a. Kathy Smith, Vice-President (Student Affairs) of The University of Jamesville believes that the student population receives on an average $7000 per year of financial support from all outside sources. Ms. Jane Romer, the newly elected student Government President asserted that the figure is lot lower. In order to settle the issue, Kathy and Jane agree to conduct a sample study of 64 students. The sample revealed a mean of $6900 and a sample standard deviation of \$800.Is there sufficient evidence to support Jane's assertion? Use 0.05 significance level.

b. What is the range of values of the sample mean with the same sample size that will lead to the decision to reject H_0?

c. What is the power of the test in part (a), if the population mean is \$6950 and population standard deviation is \$800 (same as the population when H_0.is true.)?

Solution

a. In this problem: sample size: Large; Population Standard deviation: unknown; key words from the problem: "asserted that the figure is a lot lower; suggests a one-sided *t*-test. Let us use the Five-Step hypothesis testing procedure.

Step 1. Type of hypothesis? Key words in the problem: Here, "figure is lot lower." Since direction is specified, it must be a one-sided test. Since lot lower implies that the sample mean is lower than the "believed" population mean. The test is to differentiate between cases, where the sample is so low that the H_0 will be rejected or is it just a little low which may be attributed to chance causes.

H_0: $\mu \geq 7000$

H_a : $\mu < 7000$ (H_a is always the compliment of H_0).

Step 2. Test Statistic for this problem (if σ is known and for large sample size)

$$(3) \qquad Z = \frac{\overline{X} - \mu}{\sigma/\sqrt{n}}$$

or if population standard deviation is unknown, as in this case, sample standard deviation may be used.

$$(4) \qquad Z = \frac{\overline{X} - \mu}{s/\sqrt{n}}$$

Follows *Z*-distribution.

Step 3. The key question here is: Is the sample mean of 6900 sufficiently smaller than the population mean according to H_0, which is 7000? The Reject H_0 region is in the left tail of the *Z*-distribution. For a significance level of 0.05, the rejection region will have a total area of 0.05. Since it is a one-tailed test, the area from the midpoint (0) of the *Z*-distribution to the critical value should be 0.5-.05 = 0.45. Look inside the *Z*-table for 0.45 or number/s close to it (and are on both sides of 0.45) as shown below. Look for the value of *Z* corresponding to those number/s. Here, one of the values 0.4495 corresponding to a *Z*-value of 1.6 + 0.04 = 1.64 and the other value 0.4505 corresponding to a *Z*-value of 1.6 + 0.05 = 1.65. The correct *Z* value is between the two *Z*-values and is estimated to be 1.645. (Because of the non-linear nature of the *Z*-distribution, it is difficult to find the exact *Z* value. In most applications, it is enough if you approximate as shown below.

Z	0.04	0.05
1.6	0.4495	0.4505

Because the reject H_0 region is in the left tail, the critical value will be -1.645. Reject H_0 if the calculated test statistic value is less than -1.645. If it is more than 1.645, you Fail to reject H_0.

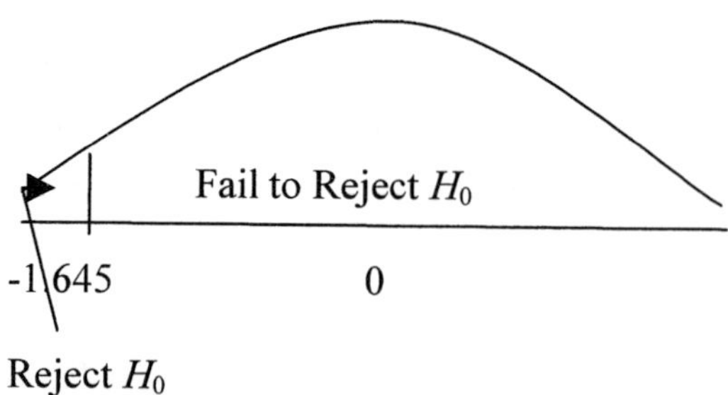

Step 4. Calculate the value of the test statistic:

$$Z = \frac{6900 - 7000}{800/\sqrt{64}}$$
$$= -1.0$$

Since the test statistic falls in the Fail to Reject H_0 region, you fail to Reject H_0.

Step 5. Conclusion: Jane's assertion is not supported by statistical calculations.

b. What is the range of values of sample mean with the same sample size that will lead to the decision to reject H_0? First we will find the Fail to Reject H_0 region. As shown in Step 3 of (a) above, Fail to reject H_0 region is all values of Z between -1.645 to infinity. Using this information and the test statistic equation given in (4), we can write the following equations.

$$-1.645 \leq \frac{\overline{X} - \mu}{s/\sqrt{n}}$$

These may be rearranged to find the range of values of sample mean ($\overline{X}$) that will lead to a decision to Fail to Reject H_0.

$$\mu - 1.645\left|\frac{s}{\sqrt{n}}\right| \leq \overline{X}$$

Substituting $\mu = 7000$, $\sigma = 800$ and n = 64, the above expression may be re-written in terms of

Range of $\overline{X}$: $7000 - 1.645\left|\frac{800}{\sqrt{64}}\right|$ to ∞, or in shortened version [6835.5 , ∞].

If the sample mean $\overline{X}$ falls in this range, we fail to reject H_0. Otherwise, we will reject H_0.

c. What is the power of the test in part (a), if the population mean is $6950 and population standard deviation is $800 (same as the population when H_0.is true)? In this case H_0 is false.

Power of the test is the probability of rejecting H_0 when it is false. That is what is the probability that a random sample from a population with mean $6950 will fall in the range [- ∞, 6835.5]. First, find a value z_1, where

$$z_1 = \frac{6835.5 - 6950}{800/\sqrt{64}} = -1.145$$

Corresponding to the critical value of 6835.5. Area from -∞ to z_1 in a *Z*-distribution is obtained from the *Z*-table.

Z	0.04	0.05
1.1	0.3729	0.3749

Area from -∞ to -1.145 is the same as area from 1.145 to ∞ (because of symmetry). The area from 0 to 1.145 is given by the average of the two values in the table = (0.3729 + 0.3749) /2, = 0.3739. and the area from 1.145 to ∞ is equal to 0.5 - 0.3739 = .1261, which is the power of the test.

8.3 Reporting Testing Results using a *P*-Value

A *p*-value is the probability of obtaining the test statistic value or a more extreme value from a random sample given that H_0 is true.

- For a two-tailed test, it is the area from the test statistic value till ∞ in the underlying distribution of the test statistic, multiplied by 2.
- For a left-tailed test, it is the area from - ∞ till the test statistic value in the underlying distribution of the test statistic.
- For a right-tailed test, it is the area from test statistic value to ∞ in the underlying distribution of the test statistic.

Review Problem 8.3

Academic Vice-President Jim Jones of The University of Jamesville believes that the summer income of their students was Normal with mean of $6000 and a standard deviation of $300. Mr. Jones ordered a survey to verify his belief. A random sample of 60 students had a mean income of $5700. Is there sufficient evidence to support the belief of the Vice-President? What is the *p*-value?

This hypothesis-testing problem was solved in Review Problem 8.1. For finding the *p*-value, we first calculate the value of the test statistic.

$$Z = \frac{5700 - 6000}{300/\sqrt{60}}$$

$$= -7.7459$$

***p*-value calculations:** First find the area of the *Z*-distribution from -7.7459 to -∞. By symmetry, this is the same as area from 7.7459 to ∞ in *Z*-distribution. For this, let us find the area from 0 to 7.7459. From the *Z*-table, this area is almost 0.4999999. Hence area from 7.7459 to ∞ is 0.5-0.4999999 = .0000001. The *p*-value is 2(0.0000001). In effect, the answer is *p*-value = almost 0.

Another Use of p-value: Most computer programs will just give you the p-value for a given sample value and the sample size. We can use the following to rules to reject H_0 or fail to reject H_0.

- reject H_0 if p-value $< \alpha$
- fail to reject H_0 if p-value $\geq \alpha$

8.4 Hypothesis Testing On The Mean Of A Normal Population: Small Sample

t-distribution: In this section, a hypothesis test that follows the t-distribution is introduced. T-distribution is similar to the Z-distribution in some ways, (both are symmetric, with mean 0). The t-distribution is a family of distributions. The particular member of the family used in a particular test is given by the degrees of freedom, which is (n-1) for a single sample test, where n is the sample size.

Review Problem 8.4

Professor Nada Zero, a very strict Statistics Professor claimed in the first class that students unfairly accuse him of giving very low grade. He hypothesized that the average grade given by him was 2.9. The class, with his permission, sent an anonymous survey to his former students and found that the average grade point of the random survey respondents turned out to be 2.8 with a standard deviation of 0.2, with 16 returned surveys.

a. Do the students have a basis for accusing Professor Zero of giving grades whose population mean is lower than 2.9, the value claimed by Professor Zero? Use 0.10 significance level.
b. Find the p-value.

Solution

a. The first task is to determine the appropriate test. Answers to the questions are given in Table 8.4.1. In this problem: sample size is Small, Population Standard deviation is unknown, key words from the problem are "population mean is lower," which suggest a one-tailed t - test.

1	Sample size?	Large		Small	
2	Population's Standard deviation?	Known		Unknown	
3	Type of test?	One-sided		Two-sided	
4	Distribution of the test statistic?	Z	t	Chi-square	F

Table 8.4.1. Important Questions To Decide Upon The Correct Test To Be Used For Hypothesis Testing

Step 1. H_0: $\mu \geq 2.9$

H_a: $\mu < 2.9$ (H_a is always the compliment of H_0).

Step 2. Test statistic:

(5) $$t = \frac{\overline{X} - \mu}{s/\sqrt{n}}$$

where degrees of freedom is n-1 = 16-1 = 15.

Step 3. Using a significance level of 0.10, from (5) and the fact that it is a one-sided test, it is clear that the Reject H_0 region is on the left tail. Refer to the *t*-distribution table given below.

t-distribution

df	$t_{.10}$	$t_{.05}$	$t_{.025}$
15	1.341	1.753	2.131

For *t*-distribution with 15 degrees of freedom, the area to the right of a *t*-value of 1.341 is equal to 0.10. Since our problem involves left tail, the symmetric nature of the *t*-distribution makes the critical value -1.341. Reject H_0 if the value of the test statistic is less than -1.341. Fail to reject H_0 if the test statistic value is more than -1.341.

Step 4. Calculate the value of the test statistic:

$$t = \frac{2.8 - 2.9}{0.2/\sqrt{16}} = -2.0$$

Step 5. Reject H_0. That is, mean grade given by Prof. Zero is indeed lower than 2.9.

b. Finding the *p*-value: For the *t*-test, *p*-values cannot be exactly found. But range of *p*-values may be found by finding where the absolute value of the test statistic falls in the row of values corresponding to the d.f. in the *t*-table, and then reading off the corresponding areas. Since the |test statistic| = 2.0, and it falls between 1.753 and 2.131, and the area corresponding to these two values are .05 and .025 and hence the range of *p*-values are given as follows.

$0.05 \geq p\text{-value} \geq 0.025.$

If the |test statistic| is such that the there is no value that is higher than that in the table, (in this example if test statistic = 4, there will be no value in the table), then the lower limit on the *p*-value will be 0. The maximum limit on the *p*-value for any one-tailed test is 0.5 and for two-tailed tests it is 1.0.

8.5 Inference For The Variance And Standard Deviation Of A Normal Population.

Confidence interval for Variance: The test statistic that helps us find this confidence interval follows Chi-square (χ^2) distribution. It is continuous, non-negative, and skewed to the right. It is a family of distributions corresponding to each degree of freedom.

If we take samples from a population following normal distribution with mean μ and standard deviation = σ, and calculate a series of sample standard deviation s^2 , then the following random variable denoted by the right hand side of the following equation follows chi-square distribution.

$$\chi^2 = \frac{(n-1)s^2}{\sigma^2}$$

Let the degrees of freedom be (n-1) and let the confidence level be α.
The above equation can be rewritten as a confidence interval for σ as follows.

$$\sqrt{\frac{(n-1)s^2}{\chi^2_{\alpha/2,n-1}}} \quad \textit{to} \quad \sqrt{\frac{(n-1)s^2}{\chi^2_{1-\alpha/2,n-1}}}$$

Review Problem 8.5.1

Consumer report magazine was examining consumer complaints against Fly by Night Grocery. They weighed 10 one-pound bags and found the total weight adding up to more than 160 oz. They decided to find a 95% confidence interval for the standard deviation of weights of potato chips bags. The actual weights in ounces are:

16.84	16.16	16.2	17.59	16.88	16.68	16.33	16.89	16.59	17.66

Adding up to more than 160 ounces. The variance of weights of potato Chips bags sold can easily be calculated by using the standard deviation of the data. s = 0.52. The χ^2 value may be looked up from the table below.

df	$\chi^2_{.975}$	$\chi^2_{.950}$	$\chi^2_{..050}$	$\chi^2_{.025}$
9	2.70039	3.32511	16.9190	19.0228
11	3.81575	4.57481	19.6751	21.9200

The confidence interval is found by:

$$\sqrt{\frac{(10-1)(0.52)(0.52)}{2.70039}}$$

Note that the denominators in the first of the two expressions correspond to the right tail value of chi-square and the second expression's denominator corresponds to the left tail. confidence interval for population σ:

[0.357 , 0.949].

Review Problem 8.5.2

A Make It Right First Time auto parts is supplying a crucial brake component whose weight variance should be no more than 0.2. This implies that the standard deviation must be no more than sqrt(0.2) = 0.4472. A random sample of 12 brake parts from a lot of brake parts was found to have a variance of 0.25. Test whether this lot meets the specification at a significance level of 0.05.

Two-tailed tests:
Step 1. H_0: $\sigma \leq 0.4472$
H_a: $\sigma > 0.4472$
Step 2. Test statistic followed chi-square distribution with d.f. of 14.
Step 3. With a significance level of 0.05, the critical value found from the table is 19.6751. If calculated chi-square value is less than or equal to 19.6751, Fail to reject H_0. If the calculated chi-square is more than 19.6751, reject H_0.

Step 4. Calculate the value of the test statistic: (Note that H_0 is in terms of σ though the test statistic is in terms of variance.)

$$\chi^2 = \frac{(12-1)(0.25)}{(0.4472)(0.4472)}$$

$$= 13.75$$

Step 5. Since the test statistic value (13.75) is less than 19.6751, we Fail to reject H_0. The standard deviation is not significantly more than 0.2

8.6 Self-Test Problems

Self-Test Problem 8.6.1.

a. The Vice President of Student affairs of The University of Jamesville believes that the average score in the final exam of students is 68.0 inches and the population standard deviation is 3.0 inches. He ordered a new employee to take a random sample of 49 students to verify his belief. The new employee found the average score of his sample to be 69.0 inches. Is there sufficient evidence to support the belief of the Vice-President? Use 0.05 significance level. (Use the 5-step hypothesis testing procedure.)
b. What is the range of values of sample mean with the same sample size that will lead to the decision to reject H_0?
c. What is the power of the test in part (a), if the population mean $\mu = 68.5$ inches and population standard deviation is 3.0 (same as the population when H_0.is true.)?
d. Construct a 95% confidence interval for the population mean of the height of students at the University of Jamesville.

Self-Test Problem 8.6.2.

Lightning-Speed Pizza outlet on the campus of The University of Jamesville claims that it can deliver Pizza in 10 minutes or less to any dorm room. Some sophomores want to check the claim after experiencing delays several times. They took a random sample of 81 recent customers and found that the average delivery time was 12 minutes with a standard deviation of 2.0 minutes.

a. They were wondering whether there was sufficient evidence to disprove the claim of Lightning-Speed Pizza outlet? Use a significance level of 0.01.
b. What is the range of values of the sample mean with the same sample size that will lead to the decision to reject H_0?
c. What is the power of the test in part (a), if the population mean is 12.0 minutes and population standard deviation is approximated by 2.0 minutes?

Self-test Problem 8.6.3.

The Vice President of Student Affairs at The University of Jamesville believes that the average final exam score of students is 68.0 inches and the population standard deviation is 3.0 inches. He ordered a new employee to take a random sample of 49 students to verify his belief. The new employee found the average score of his sample to be 69.0 inches. Is there sufficient evidence to support the belief of the Vice-President? What is the *p*-value?

Self-test Problem 8.6.4.

Professor Soft Touch, a Statistics Professor who is very easy on grades announced in the first class that on an average his students get a grade point of 3.5 in his course. He wanted to convey a message that he was not really giving away A's to everybody, as alleged by his colleagues. He encouraged his class to help him refurbish his image with his colleagues. The class, with his permission, sent an anonymous survey to his former students and found that the average grade point of the random survey respondents turned out to be 3.57 with a standard deviation of 0.15, with 25 returned surveys.

a. Do his colleagues have a basis for accusing Prof. Touch of giving grades, which are much higher than his claim? Use 0.025 significance level.
b. Find the *p*-value.

Self-test 8.6.5.

Find the 90% confidence interval for the variance of weights of a population of potato chips bags. A sample of 20 bags had a variance of 0.5.

Self-test 8.6.6.
Test whether a population of critical bolts supplied to NASA, meets the specification that the variance in their length should be no more than 0.4. The actual lengths of 15 bolts are:

15.44	17.33	16.03	16.89	16.72	17.91	16.22	16.2
16.51	16.09	17.95	17.17	17.27	17.51	16.17	

Test the hypothesis at a 0.05 significance level.

Self-test Multiple Choice:

1. A *p*-value is a probability value and hence is always >= 0.
   a. True.
   b. False

2. Test statistic for testing population mean using large sample size when population standard deviation is unknown is given by
   a. (X-bar - μ) / ($\sigma/\sqrt{n}$)
   b. (X-bar - μ) / (σ/ n)
   c. (X-bar - μ) / (s/ n)
   d. (X-bar - $\mu/\sqrt{n}$) / ($\sigma/\sqrt{n}$)
   e. None of the above
3. A lab is testing radial tires, whose manufacturer says that the tire will last for 40,000 miles. Assume that the population standard deviation is 3600 miles. The lab took a sample of 64 tires and found that the sample on an average lasted 39000 miles. Is the lab's experience any different from the population? To check this, what is the correct alternate hypothesis?
   a. $\mu \neq 40000$
   b. $\mu = 40000$
   c. $\mu = 39000$
   d. $\mu \neq 39000$
   e. None of the above
4. A lab is testing radial tires, whose manufacturer says that the tire will last for 40,000 miles. Assume that the population standard deviation is 3600 miles. The lab took a sample of 64 tires and found that the sample on an average lasted 39000 miles. Is the lab's experience any different from the population? To check this, using the correct test statistic, the value of the test statistic (close to at least one decimal accuracy) will be:
   a. 1.67
   b. –1.67
   c. 10
   d. –10
   e. None of the above
5. A lab is testing radial tires, whose manufacturer says that the tire will last for 40,000 miles. Assume that the population standard deviation is 3600 miles. The lab took a sample of 64 tires and found that the sample on an average lasted 39,000 miles. Is the lab's experience any different from the population? To check this, using the correct test statistic value, and significance level of 0.05, you would:
   a. Fail to reject H_0
   b. Reject H_0
   c. Cannot conclude
   d. Fail to reject H_0 and H_1
   e. None of the above
6. In general, significance level is the probability of
   a. Failing to Reject H_0
   b. Failing to Reject H_1
   c. Rejecting H_0 when it is true
   d. Usually 95%
   e. None of the above
7. In a two-tailed hypothesis test using a test statistic following normal distribution with mean = 0 and standard deviation = 1, if 2% level of significance is used and the computed value of z is +1.65, what is right decision?
   a. Fail to reject H_0
   b. Reject H_0
   c. Reject H_1
   d. None of the above

8. Test statistic for testing population mean using large sample size when population standard deviation is known is given by
   a. (X-bar - μ) /($\sigma/\sqrt{n}$)
   b. (X-bar - μ)/(σ/n)
   c. (X-bar - μ)/(s/$\sqrt{n}$)
   d. (X-bar - $\mu/\sqrt{n}$)/($\sigma/\sqrt{n}$)
   e. None of the above
9. A lab is testing radial tires, whose manufacturer says that the tire will last for 40,000 miles. The lab took a sample of 64 tires and found that the sample on an average lasted 41000 miles. Sample standard deviation was found to be 1800 miles. Are these tires really lasting for more miles than the manufacturer's claim? To check this, what is the correct null hypothesis?
   a. $\mu \leq 40000$
   b. $\mu \geq 40000$
   c. $\mu \leq 39000$
   d. $\mu \geq 39000$
   e. None of the above
10. A lab is testing radial tires, whose manufacturer says that the tire will last for 40,000 miles. The lab took a sample of 64 tires and found that the sample on an average lasted 41000 miles. Sample standard deviation was found to be 1800 miles. Are these tires really lasting for more miles than the manufacturer's claim? Based on the correct null hypothesis and significance level of 0.05, your conclusion will be:
    a. Reject H_0
    b. Fail to Reject H_0
11. When you find *p*-value, using *Z*-table, you can generally find the answers as a number rather than as a range.
    a. True
    b. False
12. When you find *p*-value, using *t*-table with appropriate degrees of freedom, you can generally find the answers as a number rather than as a range.
    a. True
    b. False
13. If the null and alternative hypotheses are Null hypothesis: $\mu \leq 1000$ and Alternate hypothesis: $\mu > 1000$, the reject the null hypothesis area is on the:
    a. Left-tail
    b. Right-tail
    c. Both tails
    d. None of the above
14. A lab is testing an automatic garage door motor, because of report from a consumer group that doors will only last for 30000 operations. The manufacturer claims that it will last for more than 30000. Using a sample of size 25, the lab found that the mean number of operations for its sample was 30100 and the sample standard deviation was found to be 1000. Test whether based on the lab's experience one can certify the manufacturer's claim that the doors actually last for more than 30000 operations. The correct pair of hypotheses is:
    a. H_0: $\mu = 30000$; H_1: $\mu \neq 30000$
    b. H_1: $\mu = 30000$; H_0: $\mu \neq 30000$
    c. H_0: $\mu = 30100$; H_1: $\mu \neq 30100$
    d. H_0: $\mu \leq 30000$; $H_{1:}$ $\mu > 30000$
    e. H_0: $\mu \geq 30000$; H_1: $\mu < 30000$

15. A lab is testing an automatic garage door motor, because of report from a consumer group that doors will only last for 30000 operations. The manufacturer claims that it will last for more than 30000. Using a sample of size 25, the lab found that the mean number of operations for its sample was 30100 and the sample standard deviation was found to be 1000. Test whether based on the lab's experience one can certify the manufacturer's claim that the doors actually last for more than 30000 operations. If 5% level of significance is used, what will be the critical value/s for the test?
    a. 1.711
    b. –1.711
    c. –2.064 to +2.064
    d. 2.064
    e. None of the above
16. A lab is testing an automatic garage door motor, because of report from a consumer group that doors will only last for 30000 operations. The manufacturer claims that it will last for more than 30000. Using a sample of size 25, the lab found that the mean number of operations for its sample was 30100 and the sample standard deviation was found to be 1000. Test whether based on the lab's experience one can certify the manufacturer's claim that the doors actually last for more than 30000 operations. What is your conclusion?
    a. Reject H_0
    b. Fail to reject H_0
    c. Insufficient information.
    d. None of the above
17. Type I error is the probability of
    a. Rejecting H_0 when H_0 is false
    b. Rejecting H_0 when H_0 is true
    c. Failing to reject H_0 when H_0 is false
    d. Failing to reject H_0 when H_0 is true.
18. Type II error is the probability of
    a. Rejecting H_0 when H_0 is false
    b. Rejecting H_0 when H_0 is true
    c. Failing to reject H_0 when H_0 is false
    d. Failing to reject H_0 when H_0 is true.
19. Correct decision has been made if one
    a. Rejects H_0 when H_0 is false
    b. Rejects H_0 when H_0 is true
    c. Fails to reject H_0 when H_0 is false
    d. Fails to reject H_0 when H_0 is true.
    e. (a) and (d)
20. Critical value is a value
    a. From a statistical table
    b. Depends on the significance level
    c. Calculated using the sample data
    d. Helps find the reject H_0 region
    e. (a), (b) and (d)

8.7 Glossary

alternative hypothesis
A statement in contradiction to the null hypothesis; the researcher is attempting to determine whether this statement can be supported.

critical value
A value selected from an appropriate table in order to define the rejection region for a statistical test of hypothesis. This value depends on the significance level of the test.

null hypothesis
A statement (equality or inequality) concerning a population parameter; the researcher wishes to discredit this statement.

one-tailed test
A test of hypothesis in which the null hypothesis is rejected if the value of the test statistic lies in a particular tail of the corresponding distribution.

***p*-value**
The value of alpha at which the hypothesis test procedure changes conclusions for a given set of data.

power
For a specified value of the population parameter, the probability of rejecting the null hypothesis.

rejection region
Values of the test statistic for which the null hypothesis is rejected.

significance level
The probability of making a Type I error. This value is selected prior to obtaining the sample.

test statistic
A function of the sample observations that provides the value that is used in determining whether to reject or fail to reject the null hypothesis.

two-tailed test
A test of hypothesis in which the null hypothesis is rejected if the value of the test statistic lies in either tail of the corresponding distribution.

Type I error
The error that you make by rejecting the null hypothesis (H_0) when, in fact, it is true
The probability of this error occurring is the predetermined significance level, ∀.

Type II error
The error that you make by failing to reject the null hypothesis (H_0) when, in fact, it is false. The probability of this error occurring for a specified value of the population parameter is ß.

8.8 Solutions for Self-Test Problems

Solution to Self-Test Problem 8.6.1.

a.

Step1. Type of hypothesis? Look for a "clue" or key word in the problem: Here, key words from the problem: "believes that the average score of students is 68.0" and "Is there sufficient evidence to support the belief?" Since no direction is specified, it must be a two-sided test:

H_0: μ = 68.0
H_a : μ ≠ 68.0 (H_a is always the compliment of H_0).

Step 2. Test Statistic for this problem, since σ is known,

$$Z = \frac{\overline{X} - \mu}{\sigma / \sqrt{n}}$$

Follows Z distribution.

Step 3. For significance level of 0.05, two-sided test, Z value from the table is ± 1.96. Because it is a two-sided test, the reject H_0 region is all values > 1.96 and < -1.96. 1.96 is the critical value on the right tail) and -1.96 is the critical value on the left tail. Fail to reject H_0 region is all values between -1.96 and +1.96.

Step 4. Calculate the value of the test statistic:

$$Z = \frac{69 - 68}{3/\sqrt{49}}$$
$$= 2.33$$

Since the test statistic falls in the reject H_0 region, reject H_0.

Step 5. Conclusion: The Vice-President's belief is not supported by statistical evidence.

b. What is the range of values of sample mean with the same sample size that will lead to the decision to reject H_0? First we find the Fail to Reject H_0 region. As shown in Step 3 of (a) above, Fail to reject H_0 region is all values of Z between -1.96 and +1.96. The range of values of a sample mean ($\overline{X}$) that will lead to a decision to Fail to Reject H_0.

$$\overline{X} \geq \mu - 1.96\left|\frac{\sigma}{\sqrt{n}}\right| \quad \text{and} \quad \overline{X} \leq \mu + 1.96\left|\frac{\sigma}{\sqrt{n}}\right|$$

Substituting μ = 68.0, σ = 3, and n = 49, the above expression may be re-written in terms of

Range of $\overline{X}$: $68.0 - 1.96\left|\frac{3}{\sqrt{49}}\right|$ and $68.0 + 1.96\left|\frac{3}{\sqrt{49}}\right|$ or [67.16, 68.84].

If the sample mean $\overline{X}$ falls in this range, we fail to reject H_0. Otherwise, we will reject H_0.

c. Power of the test in Part (a) when the population mean μ = 68.5 and population standard deviation is 3 (same as the population when H_0.is true.) Power of a test is the probability of rejecting H_0 when H_0 is false. H_0 is false whenever μ is not equal to 68. Here we are asked to find the power of the test when μ = 68.5. That is, if we take random sample of size 49 from such a population of students, what is the probability that H_0 will be rejected? That is, what is the probability that sample mean $\overline{X}$ will fall outside the range found in part (b) , namely [67.16, 68.84]. Next we find the corresponding Z values, denoted as z_1 and z_2 where

$$z_1 = \frac{68.84 - 68.5}{3/\sqrt{49}} \quad \text{and} \quad z_2 = \frac{67.16 - 68.5}{3/\sqrt{49}} \quad \text{or}$$

$z_1 = 0.79$ and $z_2 = -3.13$.

The power of the test is the area to the right of z_1 (plus) the area to the left of z_2.
$P(Z > z_1) = 0.5 - 0.2852 = 0.2148$.
$P(Z < z_2) = 0.5 - 0.4991 = 0.0009$.

Power of the test (when $\mu = 68.5$) = 0.0009 + 0.2148 = 0.2157

d. Construct a 95% confidence interval for the population mean of the height of students at the University of Jamesville. The appropriate formula is:

$$\left[\overline{X} - k\left[\frac{\sigma}{\sqrt{n}}\right]\right] \text{ to } \left[\overline{X} + k\left[\frac{\sigma}{\sqrt{n}}\right]\right]$$

k is the *Z* value corresponding to 95%, which is ± 1.96. The 95% confidence interval is:

$$\left[69.0 - 1.96\left[\frac{3}{\sqrt{49}}\right]\right] \text{ to } \left[69.0 + 1.96\left[\frac{3}{\sqrt{49}}\right]\right] \text{ or } [68.16, 69.84].$$

Solution to Self-test Problem 8.6.2.

a.

Step 1. Type of hypothesis? Key words in the problem: "disprove the claim of 10 minutes or less."So one of the hypotheses should be to say, the delivery time is indeed higher than 10 minutes, thus disproving the claim. This would be the alternate hypothesis.

H_0: $\mu \leq 10$
H_a : $\mu > 10$ (H_a is always the compliment of H_0).

Step 2. Follows *Z*-distribution. Test Statistic for this problem (if σ is known and for large sample size) is

$$Z = \frac{\overline{X} - \mu}{\sigma / \sqrt{n}}$$

or if population standard deviation is unknown, as in this case, sample standard deviation may be used.

$$Z = \frac{\overline{X} - \mu}{s / \sqrt{n}}$$

Step 3. The key question here is: Is the sample mean of 12 sufficiently larger than the population mean according to H_0 which is 10. The Reject H_0 region is in the right tail of the *Z*-distribution. For a significance level of 0.01, the rejection region will have a total area of 0.01. Since it is a one-tailed test, the area from the mid point (0) of the *Z*- distribution to the critical value should be 0.5-.01 = 0.49. Look inside the *Z*-table for 0.49 or number/s close to it (and are on both sides of 0.49) as shown below. Look for the value of *Z* corresponding to those number/s. Here, one of the values 0.4898 corresponding to a *Z*-value of 2.3 + 0.02 = 2.32 and the other value 0.4901 corresponding to a *Z*-value of 2.3 + 0.03 = 2.33. The correct *Z* value is between the two *Z*-values and is estimated to be 2.327 usually 2.33 is used.

Z	0.02	0.03
2.3	0.4898	0.4901

Because the reject H_0 region is in the right tail, the critical value will be 2.33. Reject H_0 if the calculated test statistic value is more than 2.33. If it is less than 2.33, you Fail to reject H_0.

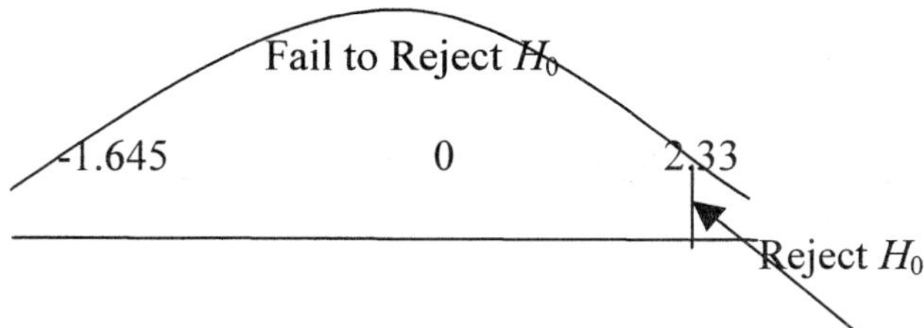

Step 4. Calculate the value of the test statistic:

$$Z = \frac{12 - 10}{2/\sqrt{81}}$$

$$= -9.0$$

Since the test statistic falls in the Reject H_0 region, you Reject H_0.

Step 5. Conclusion: Pizza chain's assertion is not supported. There is statistical evidence to show that indeed, the delivery time is higher.

b. What is the range of values of sample mean with the same sample size that will lead to the decision to reject H_0 ? First we will find the Fail to Reject H_0 region. As shown in Step 3 of (a) above, Fail to reject H_0 region is all values of *Z* between – infinity and 2.33. Using this information and the test statistic equation given in Step 4, we can write the following equations.

$$2.33 \geq \frac{\overline{X} - \mu}{s/\sqrt{n}}$$

These may be rearranged to find the range of values of sample mean ($\overline{X}$) that will lead to a decision to Fail to Reject H_0.

$$\overline{X} \leq \mu + 2.33 \bullet \frac{s}{\sqrt{n}}$$

Substituting $\mu = 10$, $s = 2$ and $n = 81$, the above expression may be re-written in terms of

Range of $\overline{X}$: $-\infty$ to $10 + 2.33 \bullet \frac{2}{\sqrt{81}}$ that is $-\infty$ to 10.5178.

If the sample mean $\overline{X}$ falls in this range, we fail to reject H_0. Otherwise, we will reject H_0.

c. What is the power of the test in part (a), if the population mean is 12 and population standard deviation is 2 (same as the population when H_0.is true.)? In this case H_0 is false. Power of the test is the probability of rejecting H_0 when it is false. That is what is the probability that a random sample from a population with mean 12 will fall in the range [10.5178, ∞]. First, find a value $z_{1,}$ where

$$z_1 = \frac{10.5178 - 12}{2/\sqrt{81}} = -6.6699$$

We need the area in the Z-distribution from –6.6699 to ∞. You may be worried as to what to do since –6.6699 (or for that matter 6.6699) are not in the Z-table. However, it well known (normal rule) that -3 to + 3 in the Z-distribution covers 99.75 of the area. So –6.6699 to + ∞ would almost cover the entire area, close to 1.0.

Solution to Self-test Problem 8.6.3.

The hypothesis testing was already done in self-test Problem 8.1. *p*-value: first of all, find the area from 2.33 (the calculated value of the test statistic, as found in self-test 8.1) to ∞. From the Z-table, area from 0 to 2.33 is 0.4901. Hence the area from 2.33 to ∞ is equal to 0.5-0.4901 = .0099. The *p*-value (because, the underlying hypothesis test is two-tailed) is equal to 2(0.0099) = .0198.

Solution to Self-test Problem 8.6.4.

a. In this problem: sample size is Small; population standard deviation: unknown; key words from the problem: "population mean is lower"; suggests a one-tailed *t*-test.
Step 1. H_0: $\mu \leq 3.5$
H_a: $\mu > 3.5$ (H_a is always the compliment of H_0).
Step 2. Test statistic:

$$t = \frac{\overline{X} - \mu}{s/\sqrt{n}}$$

where degrees of freedom is n-1 = 25-1 = 24.
Step 3. Using a significance level of 0.02, from (5) and the fact that it is a one-sided test, it is clear that the Reject H_0 region is on the right tail. Refer to the *t*-distribution table given below; the critical value is: 2.064. Reject H_0 if the value of the test statistic is greater than 2.064. Fail to reject H_0 if the test statistic value is less than 2.064.

t-distribution

df	$t_{.05}$	$t_{.025}$	$t_{.01}$
24	1.711	2.064	2.492

Step 4. Calculate the value of the test statistic:

$$t = \frac{3.57 - 3.5}{0.15/\sqrt{25}} = -2.333$$

Step 5. Reject H_0. That is, mean grade given by Prof. Touch is indeed higher than 3.5.

b. p-value: Since the absolute value of the test statistic = 2.333, and it falls between 2.064 and 2.492, and the area corresponding to these two values are .025 and .01 and hence the range of p-values are given as follows.

$0.025 \geq p\text{-value} \geq 0.01.$

Solution to Self-test Problem 8.6.5

df	$\chi^2_{.975}$	$\chi^2_{.950}$	$\chi^2_{..050}$	$\chi^2_{.025}$
19	8.9065	10.1170	30.1435	32.85234

The confidence interval by population standard deviation (σ):

$$\sqrt{\frac{(20-1)(0.5)}{30.1435}} \quad \text{to} \quad \sqrt{\frac{(20-1)(0.5)}{10.1170}} \quad \text{or, in shortened form [0.513, 0.969]}$$

Solution to Self-test Problem 8.6.6.

First of all find the sample standard deviation of the lengths using the data. It comes to:
$s^2 = 0.558$; $s = 0.747$

Two-tailed tests:
Step 1. H_0: $\sigma \leq 0.632$ (SQRT(0.4) specified in the problem)
$H_{a:}$ $\sigma > 0.632$

Step 2. Test statistic followed chi-square distribution with degrees of freedom of 14.

df	$\chi^2_{.975}$	$\chi^2_{.950}$	$\chi^2_{..050}$	$\chi^2_{.025}$
14			23.6848	

Step 3. With a significance level of 0.05, the critical value found from the table is 23.6848. If calculated chi-square value is less than or equal to 23.6848, Fail to reject H_0.
If the calculated chi-square is more than 23.6848, reject H_0.

Step 4. Calculate the value of the test statistic:

$$\chi^2 = \frac{(15-1)(0.558)}{0.4}$$

$$= 19.53$$

Step 5. Since the test statistic value (19.53) is less than 23.6848, we Fail to reject H_0.
The variance is not significantly more than 0.4.

Answers To Multiple-Choice Questions:

Question #	Answer	Question #	Answer	Question #	Answer
1	a	8	a	15	a
2	c	9	a	16	b
3	a	10	a	17	b
4	e	11	a	18	c
5	b	12	b	19	e
6	c	13	b	20	e
7	a	14	d		

CHAPTER 9
INFERENCE PROCEDURES FOR TWO POPULATIONS

Chapter Overview and Learning Objectives

Previous chapters have discussed the use of hypothesis testing for the testing of population means and variances. This chapter will extend that treatment to the testing of two means. This chapter will also discuss the situation presented by matched (paired) samples. By the end of the chapter, the student should be able to answer the following questions:

1. What is the difference between dependent (matched) samples and independent samples?
2. How do you test for a significant difference between means collected from independent samples?
3. How do you test for a significant difference between means collected from dependent (matched) samples?
4. How do you test for a difference between the variances of two normal populations?

Chapter Outline

9.1 Independent vs. dependent Samples
9.2 Comparing Two Means Using Two Large Samples, Independent Samples
9.3 Comparing Two Normal Population Means Using Two Small, Independent samples
9.4 Comparing the Variances of Two Normal Populations Using Independent samples (Hypothesis testing for $s_1 = s_2$)
9.5 Comparing the Means of Two Normal Populations Using Paired Samples
9.6 Self-test Problems
9.7 Glossary
9.8 Solution to Self-Test Problems

9.1 Independent vs. Dependent Sampling

Two populations are said to be related if the there is some underlying relationship between he two. Examples include husbands and wives, siblings, population of workers before undergoing a quality control training programs and the same population after the training, population of consumers before seeing a specific advertisement and the same population of consumers after seeing a specific advertisement. While studying two related populations, it often more powerful if we sample the population in such a way that the relationship is preserved. For example, if we want to test the effectiveness of a quality control program on reducing defects in a production process, we may want to sample a set of workers before the training, collect data on the defects produced, send them for training and then sample the same workers for defects produced after the training and maintain the data on defects produced by each worker before and after the training as one paired sample for statistical analysis. Other examples could be salary of male and female employees with identical qualification and experience to be kept as a pair in a study of salaries of male and female workers.

If there is a definite reason for pairing, then it is a dependent sample. If two samples are obtained independently and no reason for pairing, then it is an independent sample.

Dependent sample may allow us to improve accuracy for a given sample size.

9.2 Comparing Means of Two populations (Using Large samples):

Review Problem 9.2.1

Vice-President of student affairs Kathy Norton (a former professor of Statistics) of the University of Jamesville is interested in constructing a confidence interval for the difference in the population means of summer earnings of male students (μ_1) and female students (μ_2) She instituted a study, which collected data from a random sample of 40 male and 50 female students and reported the following results.

	Sample 1 (male students)	Sample 2 (female students)
Sample size	$n_1 = 40$	$n_2 = 50$
Sample average	$\overline{X}_1 = 5150$	$\overline{X}_2 = 5100$
Sample standard deviation	$s_1 = 300$	$s_2 = 400$

Table 9.2.1. Data for Review Problem 9.2.1.

What is the 95% confidence interval for the difference in means of the population ($\mu_1 - \mu_2$)?

Discussion: Since both samples are greater than 30, we can use the fact that the statistic

(9.1)
$$Z = \frac{(\overline{X}_1 - \overline{X}_2) - (\mu_1 - \mu_2)}{\sqrt{\frac{\sigma_1^2}{n_1} + \frac{\sigma_2^2}{n_2}}}.$$

follows a normal distribution with mean 0 and standard deviation 1.0. The answer is the same as the answer to the question: What are the *Z*-values that contain 95% of the area (equal area on both sides of the mean) around the mean?

Solution

Look up the *Z*-value corresponding to ((0.95/2) = 0.475)? From the *Z*-table, we get 1.96. By symmetry, the answer is -1.96 to + 1.96. Using these *Z* values and rearranging Formula 9.1, we get the 95% confidence interval for ($\mu_1 - \mu_2$) as given below.

(9.2)
$$(\overline{X}_1 - \overline{X}_2) - 1.96\sqrt{\frac{\sigma_1^2}{n_1} + \frac{\sigma_2^2}{n_2}} \text{ to } (\overline{X}_1 - \overline{X}_2) + 1.96\sqrt{\frac{\sigma_1^2}{n_1} + \frac{\sigma_2^2}{n_2}}$$

Population standard deviations, σ_1 and σ_2 are unknown. So we cannot directly use this formula. However, sample standard deviations s_1 and s2 are given. Since both sample sizes are greater than 30, we can substitute the sample standard deviation for the population standard deviation to get the following (9.3).

(9.3)
$$(\overline{X}_1 - \overline{X}_2) - 1.96\sqrt{\frac{s_1^2}{n_1} + \frac{s_2^2}{n_2}} \text{ to } (\overline{X}_1 - \overline{X}_2) + 1.96\sqrt{\frac{s_1^2}{n_1} + \frac{s_2^2}{n_2}}$$

Substituting the appropriate values from the problem in (9.2) we get the following:

$$(5150-5100)\text{-}1.96\sqrt{\frac{300^2}{40}+\frac{400^2}{50}} \text{ to } (5150-5100)\ +1.96\sqrt{\frac{300^2}{40}+\frac{400^2}{50}}$$

which simplifies to: [-94.69 to 194.69]

Note for other confidence intervals: The appropriate value of *Z* must be substituted in (9.2) and (9.3) See table for *Z*-values.

Confidence level or (1-α) where α is the level of significance	For confidence intervals and two sided tests	One-sided left tailed tests (reject H_O area is on the left)	One-sided right tailed tests (reject H_O area is on the right)
80% or α = 0.20	± 1.28	-0.84	+0.84
90% or α = 0.10	± 1.645	-1.28	+1.28
95% or α = 0.05	± 1.96	-1.96	+1.96
99% or α = 0.01	± 2.575	-2.33	+2.33

Table 9.2.2 Typical values of *Z* for various tests

Margin of error: It is the estimate of the amount error in your point estimate for the population estimate of the population mean. If you want to know $(\mu_1-\mu_2)$ of two populations, the $(\overline{X_1}-\overline{X_2})$ is the point estimate for it and the error in that point estimate is given by one half of the length of the confidence interval. In Problem 9.2, it is ((194.69 - (-94.69))/2) = 144.69. If you want to reduce this error, one method would be to take a larger sample from both populations. Let n be the common sample size for both samples. This just makes the calculation of n easier. Suppose also that in Problem 9.2, we want to reduce the error for 95% confidence interval to 100. The sample size required can be obtained by

$1.96\sqrt{\frac{s_1^2}{n_1}+\frac{s_2^2}{n_2}}$ = 100, since we assumed that $n_1 = n_2 = n$, we can substitute n in place of both n_1 and n_2 and rearrange the terms to find a numerical value for n.

Use $1.96\sqrt{\frac{s_1^2}{n}+\frac{s_2^2}{n}} = 100$. Square both sides to get $1.96^2\,(\frac{400^2}{n}+\frac{300^2}{n}) = 100^2$.

Simplifying this expression, we get n = 96. The general formula for sample size, assuming common sample size (n) for both is

$$n=\frac{Z_{\alpha/2}^2 s_1^2 s_2^2}{E^2}$$

Hypothesis Testing for Difference in Population means (Large samples):

Review Problem 9.2.2

Vice-President of Student Affairs Kathy Norton (a former professor of Statistics) of the University of Jamesville in interested in checking the claim that summer earnings of male students *differ* from that of female students on their campus. Let μ_1 be the population mean of summer income of male students and μ_2 be the population mean of summer income of female students. She instituted a study, which collected data from a random sample of 40 male and 50 female students and reported the following results. Conduct a hypothesis test to help the Vice President make the correct decision. Use a significance level of 0.05.

	Sample 1 (male students)	Sample 2 (female students)
Sample size	$n_1 = 40$	$n_2 = 50$
Sample average	$\overline{X}_1 = 5150$	$\overline{X}_2 = 5100$
Sample standard deviation	$s_1 = 300$	$s_2 = 400$

Table 9.2.3. Data for Review Problem 9.2.2.

Step 1. Hypothesis:(Key words do not indicate a direction. Since null hypothesis will always contain the " = " sign, we get)

$$H_O: \mu_1 = \mu_2$$
$$H_a: \mu_1 \neq \mu_2$$

Step 2: Test Statistic to be used: From previous discussion (rewriting Formula 9.1 using the null hypothesis: $\mu_1 = \mu_2$ or the fact that $\mu_1 - \mu_2 = 0$) the following test statistic will be appropriate:

$$Z = \frac{\overline{X_1} - \overline{X_2}}{\sqrt{\frac{s_1^2}{n_1} + \frac{s_2^2}{n_2}}}$$

(If population sigma were known we could have used it in place of the sample standard deviations.)

Step 3: Rejection region: Since it is a two-sided test, the rejection region is both tails of the distribution of the test statistic; that is, both sides of the Z distribution. Using a significance level of 0.05, (see Table 9.2.2) we get $Z > 1.96$ and $Z \leq 1.96$ as the rejection region.

Step 4: Find the value of the test statistic:

$$Z = \frac{\overline{X_1} - \overline{X_2}}{\sqrt{\frac{S_1^2}{n_1} + \frac{S_2^2}{n_2}}} \quad \textit{Substituting, we get;} \quad Z = \frac{5150 - 5100}{\sqrt{\frac{300^2}{40} + \frac{400^2}{50}}}$$

$= 0.6777$

Step 5: Conclusion: Since 0.677 (calculated value of the test statistic) is in the Fail to reject H_O area, we conclude that there is no difference in males and female summer incomes. How will the problem be worded, if we want to test whether the higher male summer income of 5150 is significantly higher that female summer income of 5100? This takes us to Problem 9.2.3

Review Problem 9.2.3

Vice President of Student Affairs Kathy Norton (a former professor of Statistics) of the University of Jamesville in interested in checking the claim that summer earnings of male students are *higher* than that of and female students on their campus. Let μ_1 be the population mean of male students and μ_2 be the population mean of female students. She instituted a study, which collected data from a random sample of 40 male and 50 female students and reported the following results. Conduct a hypothesis test to help the Vice President make the correct decision. Use a significance level of 0.05.

	Sample 1 (male students)	Sample 2 (female students)
Sample size	n_1 = 40	n_2 = 50
Sample average	$\overline{X}_1 = 5150$	$\overline{X}_2 = 5100$
Sample standard deviation	s_1 = 300	s_2 = 400

Table 9.2.4. Data for Review Problem 9.2.3.

Step 1. Hypothesis: (Key word *higher* indicates a direction.). In order to conclude that males indeed do earn more than females, we must find the corresponding Z value obtained by setting population 1 to be male and population 2 to be female, and finding the test statistic Z's value with numerator equal to $\overline{X}_1 - \overline{X}_2$.

Notice that if the question of testing male income higher than female income arises only because $\overline{X}_1 > \overline{X}_2$. If $\overline{X}_1 \leq \overline{X}_2$, no further testing will be needed. We can conclude that such a sample will *never* lead to a conclusion that population mean of male (population 1) income is higher than the population mean of female (population 2) income.

Now back to the problem. One of the conclusions we would like to make in this problem is: $\mu_1 < \mu_2$. Hence one of the hypotheses should be "$\mu_1 > \mu_2$." Since > is used in the hypothesis, this can only be an Alternate hypothesis. The null hypothesis for any problem is the compliment of the alternate hypothesis, which leads to the following set of hypotheses.

$H_O: \mu_1 \leq \mu_2$
$H_a: \mu_1 > \mu_2$

Step 2: Test Statistic to be used: From previous discussion, the following test statistic will be appropriate:

$$Z = \frac{\overline{X}_1 - \overline{X}_2}{\sqrt{\frac{s_1^2}{n_1} + \frac{s_2^2}{n_2}}}$$

(If population sigma were known we could have used it in place of the sample standard deviations.)

Step 3: Rejection region. Since it is a one-sided test, and since the alternate hypothesis is of the type: $\mu_1 > \mu_2$; the rejection region is in both tails of the distribution of the test statistic, that is both sides of the Z distribution. Using a significance level of 0.05, the rejection region (see Table 9.2.2) we get $Z > 1.96$ and $Z < -1.96$ as the rejection region.

Step 4: Find the value of the test statistic:

$$Z = \frac{\overline{X_1} - \overline{X_2}}{\sqrt{\frac{S_1^2}{n_1} + \frac{S_2^2}{n_2}}} \qquad \textit{Substituting, we get;} \qquad Z = \frac{5150 - 5100}{\sqrt{\frac{300^2}{40} + \frac{400^2}{50}}}$$

$$= 0.6777$$

Step 5: Conclusion. Since 0.677 (calculated value of the test statistic) is in the Fail to Reject H_O area, we conclude that there is no difference in males and female summer incomes.

9.3 Comparing Two Normal Population Means Using Two Small, Independent samples

Discussion: This section applies for small samples ($n_1 < 30$, $n_2 < 30$) and populations that are normal. As before, going from large to small samples, test statistics are derived by using the sample standard deviations (Here it is not assumed that the two populations are having the same variance). Since the samples are small, the resulting test statistic follows approximate *t*-distribution with a messy expression for the degrees of freedom. We can find confidence interval and also test hypothesis.

The first order of business in determining the confidence interval is to find the appropriate test statistic. It is known that

$$t' = \frac{\overline{X_1} - \overline{X_2}}{\sqrt{\frac{s_1^2}{n_1} + \frac{s_2^2}{n_2}}}$$

follows the t distribution with degrees of freedom

$$\text{degrees of freedom for } t' = \frac{\left[\frac{s_1^2}{n_1} + \frac{s_2^2}{n_2}\right]^2}{\frac{\left(\frac{s_1^2}{n_1}\right)^2}{n_1 - 1} + \frac{\left(\frac{s_2^2}{n_2}\right)^2}{n_2 - 1}}$$

(1-α)(100%) confidence interval is

$$(\overline{X_1}-\overline{X_2}) - t_{\alpha/2,df}\sqrt{\frac{s_1^2}{n_1}+\frac{s_2^2}{n_2}} \quad \text{to} \quad (\overline{X_1}-\overline{X_2}) + t_{\alpha/2,df}\sqrt{\frac{s_1^2}{n_1}+\frac{s_2^2}{n_2}}$$

Review Problem 9.3.1

Two major competing models of SUV are advertising that their brand costs less to maintain in the first year. The following data was collected from a random sample of buyers of the SUV brands on the first anniversary of their purchase.

a. Find the 90% confidence interval for $\mu_1 - \mu_2$

b. Test using appropriate hypothesis testing procedure whether the means are equal at a significance level of 0.10.

Parameter	Value	Parameter	Value
$\overline{X_1}$	250	$\overline{X_2}$	300
s_1	30	s_2	20
n_1	10	n_2	8

Table 9.3.1 Data for Review Problem 9.3.1

Solution

a. For the confidence interval formula:

$$\text{degrees of freedom for } t' = \frac{\left[\frac{30^2}{10}+\frac{20^2}{8}\right]^2}{\frac{\left(\frac{30^2}{10}\right)^2}{10-1}+\frac{\left(\frac{20^2}{8}\right)^2}{8-1}} = 15.59$$

Degrees of freedom rounded up is 16.0, and t value = 1.746.

$$(250-300) - 1.746\sqrt{\frac{900}{10}+\frac{400}{8}} \quad \text{to} \quad (250-300) + 1.746\sqrt{\frac{900}{10}+\frac{400}{8}}$$

simplifies to: [-70.66,-29.34]

b. Step 1. Hypothesis. (Key words: whether "means are equal" but does not indicate a direction. Since Null hypothesis will always contain " = " sign, we get)

H_0: $\mu_1 = \mu_2$

H_a: $\mu_1 \neq \mu_2$

Step 2: Test Statistic to be used: follows *t*-distribution.

$$t' = \frac{\overline{X_1}-\overline{X_2}}{\sqrt{\frac{s_1^2}{n_1}+\frac{s_2^2}{n_2}}}$$

Step 3: Rejection region. Since it is a two sided test, the rejection region is on both tails of the distribution of the test statistic, that is both sides of the t distribution. This problem requires complicated degrees of freedom calculation. Fortunately, we have done it already in part (a) and the degrees of freedom Are 16. Using a significance level of 0.10, the rejection region (see Table A.5) we get $t' > 1.746$ and $t' < -1.746$ as the rejection region.

Step 4: Find the value of the test statistic:

$$t' = \frac{250 - 300}{\sqrt{\frac{900}{10} + \frac{400}{8}}} = -4.225$$

Step 5: Conclusion. Since -4.225 (calculated value of the test statistic) is in the reject H_O region, we conclude that there is significant difference in the average first year maintenance cost of SUVs.

Intuitive Reasoning on the *t* -test:

Note that this is similar to all other tests involving difference in means. It is just that the degrees of freedom had to be calculated using a complicated formula.

Note also that the 90% confidence interval calculated in part a. It did not contain 0. That means, the difference is significant. If we conduct two-sided tests, with significance level of (100-90)%, we will reject the Null hypothesis. Conversely, if the interval contained 0, then there is no significant difference, i.e. Fail to reject the null hypothesis of no difference at a significance level of (100-90)%.

Comparing Two Normal Population Means Using Two Small, Independent samples, where the Populations have Equal Variances

Discussion: This section applies for small samples ($n_1 < 30$, $n_2 < 30$) and populations that are normal. As before, going from large to small samples, test statistics are derived by using the sample standard deviations *(Here it is assumed that the two populations are having the same variance, which makes the test statistic follow the t-distribution exactly*) and the degrees of freedom $n_1 + n_2 - 2$. We can find confidence interval and also test hypothesis.

Confidence Interval:

First order of business in finding the confidence interval is to find the appropriate test statistic. Since population variances are equal, we can find a better estimate of the variance of the underlying population by pooling the sample variances using the formula given next.

$$s_p^2 = \frac{(n_1 - 1)s_1^2 +)(n_2 - 1)s_2^2}{n_1 + n_2 - 2}$$

and the test statistic is:

$$t = \frac{\overline{X}_1 - \overline{X}_2}{\sqrt{\frac{s_p^2}{n_1} + \frac{s_p^2}{n_2}}} = \frac{\overline{X}_1 - \overline{X}_2}{s_p\sqrt{\frac{1}{n_1} + \frac{1}{n_2}}}$$

It follows t distribution with degrees of freedom = $n_1 + n_2$ - 2. The (1-α)(100%) confidence interval is

$$(\overline{X_1} - \overline{X_2}) - t_{\alpha/2,df}\sqrt{\frac{s_1^2}{n_1}+\frac{s_2^2}{n_2}} \quad \text{to} \quad (\overline{X_1} - \overline{X_2}) + t_{\alpha/2,df}\sqrt{\frac{s_1^2}{n_1}+\frac{s_2^2}{n_2}}$$

Next, let us re-do the Review Problem 9.3.1. under the assumption of equal population variances, which becomes Review Problem 9.3.2. We will also compare the differences.

Review Problem 9.3.2 .

Two major competing models of SUV are advertising that their brand costs less to maintain in the first year. The following data was collected from a random sample of buyers of the SUV brands on the first anniversary of their purchase. Assume that the population variance of the first year costs for both models are equal.

a. Find the 90% confidence interval for $\mu_1 - \mu_2$

b. Test using appropriate hypothesis testing procedure whether the means are equal at a significance level of 0.10.

Parameter	Value	Parameter	Value
$\overline{X_1}$	250	$\overline{X_2}$	300
s_1	30	s_2	20
n_1	10	n_2	8

Table 9.3.2 Data for Review Problem 9.3.2

$$s_p^2 = \frac{(10-1)900 + (8-1)400}{10+8-2} = 681.55$$

$$s_p = 26.10$$

a. First order of business is to calculate the pooled variance.

Next task is to look up the *t*-value from Appendix A, for the corresponding degrees of freedom (in this case 10 + 8 - 2 = 16) and the 90% confidence level, which translates to finding that *t*-value which has a tail area of (100-90)/2 = 5% or 0.05. From the *t*-table, we get 1.746.

Final task is to substitute the numbers in the confidence interval formula:

$$(250-300) - 1.746\sqrt{\frac{681.55}{10}+\frac{681.55}{8}} \quad \text{to} \quad (250-300) + 1.746\sqrt{\frac{681.55}{10}+\frac{681.55}{8}}$$

which simplifies to: [-71.62, -28.37]

Note that this interval is just slightly smaller. The assumption of equal population variance allowed us to get a little tighter with the interval.

b. Step 1. Hypothesis: (Key words: whether "means are equal". but does not indicate a direction. Since Null hypothesis will always contain " = " sign, we get)

$$H_O : \mu_1 = \mu_2$$
$$H_a : \mu_1 \neq \mu_2$$

Step 2: Test Statistic to be used: follows *t*-distribution.

$$t = \frac{\overline{X_1} - \overline{X_2}}{\sqrt{\frac{s_p^2}{n_1} + \frac{s_p^2}{n_2}}} = \frac{\overline{X_1} - \overline{X_2}}{s_p\sqrt{\frac{1}{n_1} + \frac{1}{n_2}}}$$

Step 3: Rejection region. The degrees of freedom is 16. It is a two-sided test. Using a significance level of 0.10, the rejection region (see Table A.5) we get $t > 1.746$ and $t < -1.746$ as the rejection region.

Step 4: Find the value of the test statistic:

$$t = \frac{250 - 300}{\sqrt{\frac{681.55}{10} + \frac{681.55}{8}}} = -4.03$$

Step 5: Conclusion. Since -4.225 (calculated value of the test statistic) is in the Reject H_O region, we conclude that there is significant difference in the average first year maintenance cost of SUVs.

9.4 Comparing Variances of Two Normal Populations using Independent Samples

Discussion: In the previous section, there was a test, which assumed population variances are equal. There are also other tests that require population variances to be equal. Here is a formal test to check whether they are equal. Other applications include checking whether processes produce equal variance or checking whether a set of assembly line type workers have equal variance in their time to complete their portion of the task, etc.

If we had two normal populations and you take samples of size n_1 and n_2 from each population, and plot a histogram of the ratio of

$$F = \frac{s_1^2}{s_2^2}$$

you will get a specially shaped graph called an **F-distribution.** Table 9.4.1 lists important properties of F-distribution. This is an important distribution from hypothesis testing point of view, because many test statistics to be used in future chapters follow F-distribution.

Properties	Values
Name	F-Distribution
Formula	$F = \frac{s_1^2}{s_2^2}$
Possible values of the random variable	0 to $+\infty$
Skewness	Skewed to the right
Reject H_0 area of the test statistic, One-tailed test	Could be left tail or right tail
Reject H_0 area of the test statistic, Two-tailed test	Both tails of the test
Finding right tail: Values and areas	Look up in the table
Finding left tail: Values and areas	Switch the numerator and denominator degrees of freedom and find the right tail F-value, and then take its reciprocal
A trick to simplify matters for hypothesis tests	Label the sample variances such that the larger sample variance is labeled as numerator, smaller will be labeled as denominator, and the use just right side only. If it is two-sided test with 0.10 as sig. level, use 0.05 as the significance level. For one-sided tests, this transformation will always give you reject H_0 area on the right tail.
Finding confidence interval for the ratio of population variances	No simple trick. You have to find the right- and left- tail value of the F-distribution
Single or Family	Family of distributions
Degrees of freedom	Uses two degrees of freedom: Numerator degrees of freedom and denominator degrees of freedom

Review Problem 9.4.1.

A special manual assembly of a very expensive car involves just two operations. It is important to have equal processing time and equal processing time variance in the assembly time to smooth out the assembly operation. In this problem, based on the sample data:

a. Test whether the variances are equal at 0.10 significance level..

b. Obtain a 90 % confidence level for the ratio of

$$\frac{\sigma_1^2}{\sigma_2^2}$$

Data is given in Table 9.4.1.

Property	Value of sample 1	Value of sample 2
Sample size	8	10
standard deviation	5.25	4.25

Table 9.4.1. Data for Review Problem 9.4.1.

Solution

a. Step 1: We are interested in checking whether the population variances are equal.

$$H_0: \sigma_1^2 = \sigma_2^2$$
$$H_1: \sigma_1^2 \neq \sigma_2^2$$

Step 2: The test statistic

$$F = \frac{s_1^2}{s_2^2}$$

Step 3: We have to find the critical F-value on the right tail and the left tail. Right tail: Look up the 0.05 right tail area corresponding to the degrees of freedom of numerator (8-1) and denominator (10-1), which gives 2.51. Left tail calculations: First find the F-value corresponding to the numerator degrees of freedom of (10-1) (Note that the degrees of freedom of numerator and denominator are reversed.), and the denominator degrees of freedom of (8-1). The value is 2.72. Now we have to take the reciprocal of this, which is 0.368.

Critical values: F-value of more than 2.51 or less than 0.368 will result in reject H_0.

F- value between these two extremes will result in Fail to reject H_0 .

Step 4: Test statistic: F = (5.25)(5.25)/(4.25)(4.25) = 1.5259

Step 5: Since the calculated test statistic value is in the Fail to reject H_0 region, you conclude that there is not much difference in the standard deviations.

b. The 90% confidence interval for the ratio of variances:

Lower limit: (5.25)(5.25)/(4.25)(4.25)(1/2.51) = 0.608. (For the lower limit of the confidence interval, use the right-tail value)

Upper limit: (5.25)(5.25)/(4.25)(4.25)(1/0.368) = 4.14 (For the upper limit of the confidence interval, use the left-tail value)

Limits: [0.608, 4.14]

9.5 Comparing Means of Two Normal Populations Using Paired Samples:

This is the case where samples are dependent, like before training and after training machining times by the same set of individuals, husband-wife pair giving an opinion of spouses, etc.

Review Problem 9.5.1.

A poll of husband wives, asks each of them to estimate overall amount of excess calories consumed by the husband. (One set of data is self-rating by the husband and the other set of data is rating the husband's excess by the wife). A sample of 10 husband-wife pairs were surveyed and the results are given in Table 9,5.1. It is claimed that wives are more critical of their husbands eating than the husbands themselves, and hence the population mean for the wives' values will be higher than that of the husbands.

a. Use paired sampling approach to find the 95% confidence interval for the (wife-husband) calorific value.
b. Test, using a significance value of 0.05, whether wives report significantly higher value than the husbands.

Solution

Wife	Husband	Wife-Husband
100	120	-20
120	95	25
311	250	61
234	200	34
121	120	1
-100	-200	100
50	10	40
-150	-120	-30
200	120	80
300	170	130
	Total	421
	Average	42.1

d-bar = 42.1 (as shown in Table 9.5.1)
Standard deviation of difference: 51.61 (calculations not shown)

Table 9.5.1. Data for Review Problem 9.5.1

a. For 95% confidence interval find the *t*-value for a right tail area of 0.025 and degrees of freedom of 10-1 = 9. The *t*-values are: +2.2.62 and -2.2.62.
μ_d = wife - husband.

90 % confidence interval, Lower limit = 42.1 - 2.262 (51.61/sqrt(10)) = 5.18
90 % confidence interval, Lower limit = 42.1 + 2.262(51.61/sqrt(10)) = 79.01
[5.18,79.01]

b. Step 1: H_0: μ_d (wife - husband) ≤ 0
H_1: μ_d (wife - husband) > 0
Step 2: Test statistic is a *t*-distribution. with (10-1) degrees of freedom
Step 3: At a significance level of 0.05, and the critical value being in the right tail (since wife-husband is expected to be positive and if it is sufficiently high, the corresponding test statistic will be significantly positive and hence reject H_0 must be in the right tail. Critical value is: 1.833 (degrees of freedom 9, and right tail area is 0.05). Reject H_0 if test statistic > 1.833. Otherwise fail to reject H_0.
Step 4: t = (42.1-0)/(51.61/sqrt(10))
= 2.5795
Step5: Since *t*-value is higher than the critical value, reject H_0. Wives report a significantly higher value on their husbands' excess calorific consumption.

9.6. Self-test Problems

Self-Test Problem 9.6.1

Vice-President of Academic Affairs James Hathaway of the University of Jamesville is interested in constructing a confidence interval for the difference in the population means of student GPA's of Engineering (μ_1) and Business (μ_2) students. He instituted a study, which collected data from a random sample of 60 Engineering students and 30 Business students.

	Sample 1 (Engineering students)	Sample 2 (Business students)
Sample size	n_1 = 60	n_2 = 30
Sample average	$\overline{X_1} = 3.11$	$\overline{X_2} = 3.32$
Sample standard deviation	s_1 = 0.24	s_2 = 0.2

Table 9.6.1. Data for Self-test Problem 9.2.1.

What is the 90% confidence interval for the difference in means of the population ($\mu_1 - \mu_2$)? (Hint: The answer needed here is the same as the answer to the question: What are the *Z*-values that contain 90% of the area (equal area on both sides of the mean) around the mean?)

Self-test Problem 9.6.2

Assume that you have pollen allergy and you are planning a vacation in one of the two resort areas: Mt. Saint Helen or Mt. Everest. The pollen count based on a random sample is given as follows. Assume that the two regions' pollen counts are independent and that their variances are equal.

Place	Sample Size	Average Pollen Count	Sample Standard Deviation
Mt. St. Helens	15	76	5
Mt. Everest	12	73	3

Table 9.6.2. Data for Problem 9.6.2.

a. At 0.05 level of significance, is there a difference between the pollen counts of the two areas? Which place would be a good vacation destination for you, considering only the pollen count?
b. What is the p-value or range within which the p-value will be contained?

Self-test Problem 9.6.3

Time for assembling a toy before and after a training program at XYZ Inc. is given in Table 9.6.3.

Employee #	1	2	3	4	5	6	7	8	9
Before training	18	7	26	11	26	22	19	20	28
After training	16	9	21	14	26	27	18	14	30
After-before	-2	2	-5	3	0	5	-1	-6	2

Table 9.6.3. Data for Problem 9.6.3.

Standard deviation of the difference ($\mu_{after} - \mu_{before}$) is 3.667.

a. At the 0.05 level of significance, has there been a decrease in assembly time after instituting the training program?
b. What is the p-value?
c. What will be your decision if you used a 0.01 level of significance?

Multiple Choice Questions

Use the following to answer questions 1-3:
The results of an English placement exam for two campuses at Mercy College are as follows. Use 0.05 level of significance.

Campus	Sample Size	Mean	Standard Deviation
1	200	78	5
2	250	82	7

1. What is the ***null*** hypothesis if we want to test the hypothesis that the population mean of the score in both campuses are equal?
   a. $\mu_1 - \mu_2 \leq 0$
   b. $\mu_1 - \mu_2 \geq 0$
   c. $\mu_1 - \mu_2 = 0$
   d. $\mu_1 - \mu_2 \neq 0$
   e. None of the above
2. What is the computed value of the test statistic?
   a. 9.3
   b. 7.06
   c. 3.4
   d. -7.06
   e. None of the above
3. What will the conclusion?
   a. Fail to Reject H_0
   b. Reject H_0
   c. Cannot conclude
   d. None of the above

Questions 4-6 refer to the following problem.
Independent random samples were drawn from two populations (one in Perrysburg, Ohio and the other in Ottawa Hills, Ohio) in order to study the amount spent on dinner by single women. In a random sample of 14 observations from Perrysburg, Ohio, the sample mean was $18 and the sample variance was $10. In a random sample of 18 observations from Ottawa Hills, Ohio, the sample mean was $19 and the sample variance was $8. Test the hypothesis that the population mean for amount spent on dinner by single women in Perrysburg, Ohio is indeed lower than the population mean for amount spent on dinner by single women in Ottawa Hills, Ohio. Use a 0.05 level of significance. Assume that the population variances are equal.

4. The correct set of hypothesis:
   a. H_0: μ_P - $\mu_O \leq 0$; H_1: μ_P - $\mu_O > 0$
   b. H_0: μ_P - $\mu_O \geq 0$; H_1: μ_P - $\mu_O < 0$
   c. H_0: μ_P - $\mu_O = 0$; H_1: μ_P - $\mu_O \neq 0$
   d. None of the above
5. The correct value of the test statistic is:
   a. −1.63
   b. 1.63
   c. −1.07
   d. 1.07
   e. None of the above
6. The correct conclusion is:
   a. Fail to reject H_0
   b. Reject H_0

c. Cannot conclude
d. None of the above

Use the following to answer questions 7-9:
The results of a mathematics placement exam for two campuses at Mercy College for two campuses are as follows:

Campus	Sample Size	Mean	Standard. Deviation
1	330	33	8
2	310	31	7

7 What is the null hypothesis if we want to test the hypothesis that the mean score in Campus1 is higher than in Campus 2?
a. $\mu_1 = 0$
b. $\mu_2 = 0$
c. $\mu_1 > \mu_2$
d. $\mu_1 > \mu_2$
e. None of the above

8 What is the computed value of the test statistic?
a. 9.3
b. 2.6
c. 3.4
d. 1.9
e. None of the above

9. What will the degrees of freedom for the distribution of the appropriate test statistic?
a. 15
b. 14
c. 13
d. 12
e. None of the above.

Questions 10-13 refer to the following problem.
A company has been advertising a new, improved version of its gasoline. A consumer group wanted to find out whether the new gasoline is an improvement over the old gasoline. The consumer group took a random sample of 8 cars, and drove each car over the same route twice, once using the old gasoline and once using the new gasoline. Let d = miles per gallon using the old gasoline - miles per gallon using the new gasoline. Test the following set of hypotheses, using significance level = .01. Difference(d) = old gas - new gas.

H_0: $\mu_d \geq 0$ vs. H_1: $\mu_d < 0$

Test Car	MPG Using Old Gasoline	MPG Using New Gasoline
1	20.1	23.2
2	17.2	16.9
3	33.0	34.2
4	37.8	35.2
5	19.9	22.6
6	36.6	36.5
7	27.4	27.8
8	30.8	32.7

10. What is the decision rule?
    a. Reject H_0 if t < -3.499 or if t > 3.499
    b. Reject H_0 if t < -3.143
    c. Reject H_0 if t < -2.998
    d. Reject H_0 if t > 3.143

11. What is the calculated value of the test statistic?
    a. -1.203
    b. -.6494
    c. -.4252
    d. -.2296
12. Based on the result of the hypothesis test, is the new gasoline an improvement over the old gasoline?
    a. Yes
    b. No
13. Which one of the following assumptions had to be made in order to carry out the hypothesis test?
    a. Assume d has a t distribution with 7 degrees of freedom.
    b. Assume d has a standard normal distribution.
    c. Assume d is normally distributed.
    d. Assume d follows F-distribution
14. Suppose this set of hypotheses is tested: H_0: MU_1 - $MU_2 \geq 0$, and H_1: MU_1 - $MU_2 < 0$
    If the null hypothesis is rejected, what is the conclusion?
    a. The mean of population 2 is greater than the mean of population 1.
    b. The mean of population 2 is <u>not</u> greater than the mean of population 1.

9.7 Glossary

dependent samples
Samples in which observation 1 of sample 1 is matched up (paired) with observation 1 in sample 2; observation 2 in sample 1 with observation 2 in sample 2, and so on.

F-distribution
A skewed distribution used (in this chapter) to construct confidence intervals for the ratio of two population variances (or standard deviations) and to perform tests of hypothesis on this ratio.

independent samples
Samples from two or more populations where the observations in each sample are selected independently of the observations in the other sample(s).

mean of the population differences
The parameter of interest for dependent (paired) samples. The population consists of the differences between all values of variable 1 and the paired values of variable 2.

pooled sample variance
An estimate of the common variance of two (or more) populations when it is assumed that the populations have equal variances. It is a weighted average of the two sample variances, giving more weight to the sample variance from the larger sample.

9.8 Answers to Self-Test Problems

Solution to Self-Test Problem 9.6.1.

Look up the Z-value corresponding to $((0.90/2) = 0.45)$? From the Z-table, we get 1.645. By symmetry, the answer is -1.645 to + 1.645.
Using the standard expression for the confidence interval, we get the 90% confidence interval for $(\mu_1 - \mu_2)$ as given below.

$$(3.11\text{-}3.32) - 1.645\sqrt{\frac{0.24^2}{60}+\frac{0.20^2}{30}} \text{ to } (3.11\text{-}3.32) + 1.65\sqrt{\frac{0.24^2}{60}+\frac{0.20^2}{30}}$$

which simplifies to: [-0.28877 to 0.07066]

Solution to Self-test Problem 9.6.2.

a. It is not a dependent set of data. It is not very large sample size. If the two population variances can be assumed to equal and the populations are assumed to be independent and normal, we can use pooled variance. Here these assumptions hold. Hence, use pooled variance. The sample says, Everest has less than St. Helens. So let us test it to see whether it is "True" statistically speaking? That is, we want to a one-sided test to see whether Everest actually has less pollen count.

Step 1: H_0: mu(Everest) $\geq$ mu(St. Helens)
H_1: mu(Everest) $<$ mu(St. Helens)

Step 2: Significance level is 0.05. Test statistic is a t-distribution, with (15+12-2) = 25 degrees of freedom.

Step 3: Decision Rule: From table, (one-tailed, 0.05) t = -1.708. Note that if the test statistic is mildly negative, we cannot conclude that Everest has less pollen. It has to be substantially negative to reach such a conclusion. The fact that 73 is less than 76 tells you that the test statistic will be negative. We want to check : Is it substantially negative, so that we reject H_0? Hence, the critical value is –1.708

Step 4: Calculate the test statistic value:
Pooled variance: Note that we will treat Everest as sample 1 and St. Helens as sample 2.

$$s_p^2 = \frac{(12-1)9+(15-1)25}{12+15-2} = 17.96$$

Test Statistic:

$$t = \frac{73-76}{\sqrt{\frac{17.96}{12}+\frac{17.96}{15}}} = -1.827$$

Step 5: Since it is in the Reject H_0, we conclude that Everest has less pollen count than St. Helens. So I would go to Everest.

b. .05 > p-value > 0.025 From the table and looking up where 1.827 falls in the row corresponding to degrees of freedom of 25 and reading up the one-tailed test values.

Solution to Self-test Problem 9.6.3.

a. Step 1: H_0: $\mu_{after} \geq \mu_{before}$
H_1: $\mu_{after} < \mu_{before}$

Step 2: Test statistic is a *t*-distribution with (n-1) = (9-1) degrees of freedom

Step 3: Significance level: 0.05. Critical values : Using (n-1) = (9-1) degrees of freedom and *t*-table, one-tailed, we get -1.86. Decision rule: If the test statistic is less than –1.86, Reject H_0. Otherwise, fail to reject H_0.

Step 4: Test Statistic: d-bar = sum of (after-before)/9 = -.222
Test statistic = -.222/(3.667/sqrt(9)) = -.1818

Step 5: Decision: Since test statistic is greater than the critical value, we fail to reject H_0. There is no significant difference. Interpretation: The time has not been reduced after training.

b. P-value: Since .1818 is less than the value of 1.397 corresponding to 0.1 for one-tailed test, the 0.5 > p-value > 0.1
For 0.01, critical value will be –2.896, since -.1818 is still in the Accept H_0 region, the conclusion will be the same.

Answers for Multiple-Choice questions

Question #	Answer	Question #	Answer
1	c	8	c
2	d	9	e
3	b	10	c: From *t*-table, degrees of freedom = 7, one-sided, we find: -2.998
4	b	11	a: X(diff)-Bar/(standard deviation(diff)/sqrt(n) = (-0.7575)/(1.8519/sqrt(8)) = -1.203
5	e: correct answer is -0.9424	12	b: We fail to reject H_0 since -1.203 (test statistic value) is in the Fail to reject H_0 region. So no improvement.
6	a: value is -1.697	13	a
7	e	14	a

CHAPTER 10 ESTIMATION AND TESTING FOR POPULATION PROPORTIONS

Chapter Overview and Learning Objectives

The last several chapters have discussed the topic of hypothesis testing with respect to situations involving a continuous, typically normal, distribution. This chapter applies those same techniques to situations involving proportions (percentages). By the end of the chapter, the student should be able to:

1. Construct confidence intervals for a population proportion or for the difference between two population proportions.
2. Perform tests of hypothesis using samples involving proportions.
3. Calculate the required sample size(s) for situations involving proportions.

Chapter Outline

10.1 Estimation and Confidence Intervals for a Population Proportion
10.2 Hypothesis Testing for a Population Proportion
10.3 Comparing Two Population Proportions (Large and Independent Samples)
10.4 Self-Test Problems
10.5 Glossary
10.6 Solution to Self-Test Problems

10.1 Estimation and Confidence Intervals for a Population Proportion

Discussion: Consider:

- A business, which is interested in knowing "How many people saw its million dollar Super Bowl advertisement."
- American Lacrosse Association's desire to know how many Americans are involved in Lacrosse in some shape or form.
- A politician's desire to know how many voters support his position

All of these questions can be answered with the materials in this chapter. As usual, we will also find confidence intervals and present procedures for hypothesis testing of claims.

For a single population proportion, one can find confidence intervals, do hypothesis tests and determine appropriate sample sizes. Specific notations used in this chapter:

$\hat{p}$ is sample proportion

p is the population proportion

p_0 is the population proportion when H_0 is true.

p_1 is the population proportion of population 1

$\bar{p}$ is the pooled proportion

First we summarize the important differences between confidence intervals and hypothesis testing in the contest of proportions in Table 10.1.1. In most other tests, they have almost identical formulas, which are rearranged for each application. In the context of proportions, there are some subtle differences. If we list them up front, there is a good chance, you can look for them and learn the differences well. It is also an easy reference.

Test For Proportions	Points To Be Noted
One population, confidence interval: Small sample	Refer to Table A.8, giving lower and upper bounds (based on binomial distribution) using the **sample proportion found** in the survey.
One population, hypothesis testing: Small sample	Refer to Table A.8, giving lower and upper bounds (based on binomial distribution) using the proportion as per the **sample proportion found.**
One population, confidence interval: Large sample	Find the confidence interval using sample proportion found in the problem and (n - 1) in the denominator.
One population, hypothesis testing: Large sample	Use the **population proportion as per the Null hypothesis** and n in the denominator
Two populations, confidence interval	Use **sample proportions**, and $(n_1 - 1)$ and $(n_2 - 1)$ in the denominator.
Two populations, hypothesis testing of equality of proportions.	Use **pooled sample proportion** in the denominator, and n_1 and n_2 in the denominators.

Table 10.1.1. Important details about confidence intervals and hypothesis testing in the contest of proportions.

Review Problem 10.1.1

Democrat Jennifer Granholm in the party primary. On a recent random survey of 300 democratic voters, 120 preferred Granholm. Construct a 90% confidence interval on Ms. Granholm's preference by democratic voters.

The test statistic follows Z distribution. The $100(1 - \alpha)\%$ confidence interval value is 1.645 and the confidence interval is given by the formula:

$$\hat{p} - Z_{\alpha/2}\left(\sqrt{\frac{\hat{p}(1-\hat{p})}{n-1}}\right) \text{ to } \hat{p} + Z_{\alpha/2}\left(\sqrt{\frac{\hat{p}(1-\hat{p})}{n-1}}\right)$$

$$0.4 - 1.645\left(\sqrt{\frac{0.4(1-0.4)}{300-1}}\right) \text{ to } 0.4 + 1.645\left(\sqrt{\frac{0.4(1-0.4)}{300-1}}\right)$$

In brief form: [0.353, 0.446]

Note: We use (n - 1) in the denominator to make it a better estimate of the confidence interval.

Review Problem 10.1.2.

Democrat Jennifer Granholm in the party primary. On a recent random survey of 300 democratic voters, 120 preferred Granholm. Suppose that Ms. Granholm wants to find the range of voter preference in her favor within a margin of error of 0.03, significance level 0.05. What should be the sample size? Note that It is always + or - 0.03.

The formula for sample size is:

$$n = \frac{Z^2_{\alpha/2}(\hat{p})(1-\hat{p})}{E^2} + 1$$

n = ((1.645)(1.645)(0.4)(1 - 0.4)/(.03)(0.03)) + 1
= 722.6 or 723

10.2 Hypothesis Testing for Population Proportion (Small sample $5 < n < 30$):

For small samples, the process of finding the confidence interval is quite straightforward. You simply look it up in Table A.8. The principle behind that is simply the fact that this process is like conducting a binomial experiment with n trials. Let p_0 be the proportion that a specific property of a population is hypothesized to be. Using small samples, we can find the confidence interval as well as find answers to the hypothesis test. Examples will clarify matters.

Review Problem 10.2.1

A small mobile ice cream vendor believed that at least 3 out of 4 children love his ice cream. He wanted to test the popularity of his business and asked a random sample of 12 children about how they liked his ice cream. 8 out of the 12 loved his ice cream.

a. Construct a 95% confidence interval for the proportion of kids that love his ice cream.
b. Test the hypothesis that at least 75% (3 out of 4) kids love his ice cream.

Solution to Review Problem 10.2.1

a. Since it is a one sided test, and since $\alpha = .05$, we have to double it to 0.1 and look up $n = 12$ and X = 8 in Table A.8. [0.391, 0.877].

b. H_0: $p \geq 0.75$
H_1: $p < 0.75$.
Since 0.75 is in the interval [0.391,0.877] found in part a, we fail to reject the H_0 . The only way we will reject H_0 will be if the sample proportion is too small. Here it is not "too small". Even though the sample is a little smaller, it is not significantly smaller than the population proportion hypothesized in H_0. Note that we do not use the 0.75 under the null hypothesis to find the intervals in this case. It may result in fractional values like 0.75 of 15, which is 11.25, cannot be listed in the binomial based table of small samples interval (Table A.8).

Hypothesis testing using large samples is similar to the material in the next section. The test statistic is:

$$Z = \frac{p - p_0}{\sqrt{\frac{p_0(1-p_0)}{n}}}$$

and follows a normal distribution. The usual five-step procedure for any hypothesis testing applies.

Review Problem 10.2.3.

A regional dealer for a national cosmetics maker claims that he controls at least 0.6 (60%) of the market share in his territory. A random sample of 200 consumers in his region revealed that 115 of them are the dealer's clients. Is there sufficient evidence to show that the dealer has 0.6 market share. Use a significance level of 0.1

Step 1. H_0: $p \geq 0.60$
H_1: $p < 0.60$
Step 2. Test statistic is Z. Left tailed with a significance level of 0.1, is that Z which makes the left tail equal to 0.1. Z = -1.28.
Step 3. If the test statistic is less than -1.28, reject H_0. Otherwise fail to reject H_0.
Step 4.

$$Z = \frac{\hat{p} - p_0}{\sqrt{\frac{p_0(1-p_0)}{n}}} = \frac{\frac{115}{200} - 0.6}{\sqrt{\frac{0.6(1-0.6)}{200}}} = 0.72$$

Step 5: Since the test statistic fall in the fail to reject H_0 region, you conclude that there is no evidence to show that the dealer has less than 60% market share.

10.3 Comparing Two Population Proportions (Large and Independent Samples)

Review Problem 10.3.1

Democrat Jennifer Granholm and Republican Richard Posthumus are running for Governor of Michigan in their respective party primaries. On a random survey of 300 democratic voters, 120 preferred Granholm. On a survey of 400 republicans, 250 preferred Posthumus.

a. What is the 95% confidence interval for the difference in preference for Granholm and Posthumus (G - P)?
b. Since the interval is entirely in negative territory, does it mean, Posthumus will certainly win?

Solution

a. The test statistic follows Z distribution. Value for the (1 - α)100% confidence interval is 1.645 and the confidence interval is given by the formula:

$$\left(\hat{p}_1 - \hat{p}_2\right) - Z_{\alpha/2}\sqrt{\frac{\hat{p}_1\left(1-\hat{p}_1\right)}{n_1 - 1} + \frac{\hat{p}_2\left(1-\hat{p}_2\right)}{n_2 - 1}} \text{ to}$$

$$\left(\hat{p}_1 - \hat{p}_2\right) + Z_{\alpha/2}\sqrt{\frac{\hat{p}_1\left(1-\hat{p}_1\right)}{n_1 - 1} + \frac{\hat{p}_2\left(1-\hat{p}_2\right)}{n_2 - 1}}$$

$\hat{p}_1 = \frac{x_1}{n_1}$ and $\hat{p}_2 = \frac{x_2}{n_2}$

Applying the formula, we get: $\hat{p}_1 = \frac{120}{300} = 0.40$ and $\hat{p}_2 = \frac{250}{400} = 0.625$,

$$(0.40 - 0.625) - 1.96\sqrt{\frac{0.40(1-0.40)}{300-1} + \frac{0.625(1-0.625)}{400-1}} \text{ to}$$

$$(0.40 - 0.625) + 1.96\sqrt{\frac{0.40(1-0.40)}{300-1} + \frac{0.625(1-0.625)}{400-1}}$$ and simplifies to [-0.28055, -0.1695]

b. No. It depends on uncommitted voters and the relative strength of the two parties, non-party/third party voters and all that may happen between now and Election Day.

Review Problem 10.3.2.

For a court case filed by residents of an economically poor area against an auto-insurer, the following data were collected. Assume that nobody had more than one accident. Clearly, many did not have accidents.

Area	Sample Size	Number of accidents
Economically Rich	400	130
Economically Poor	300	95

Table 10.3.2. Data for Review Problem 10.3.2.

As a court statistician, report on whether there is a significant difference in the proportion of people who had accident between the two areas at a significance level of 0.05. Test a suitable hypothesis and report on the p-value.

Solution

Discussion: The sample sizes are large and we are interested in the difference. So a test statistic that follows Z distribution should be available.

Step 1. H_0: $p_1 = p_2$
H_1: $p_1 \neq p_2$

Step 2. The test statistic is

Discussion: All tests are done assuming the null hypothesis is true. In this case, if the two proportions are equal, then a better estimate of the underlying standard deviation can be found by pooling the proportions in the two samples to get a common value.

$\bar{p} = \frac{x_1 + x_2}{n_1 + n_2}$ where x_1 and x_2 are number of successes, and n_1 and n_2 are sample sizes.

$$Z = \frac{\hat{p}_1 - \hat{p}_2}{\sqrt{\frac{\bar{p}(1-\bar{p})}{n_1} + \frac{\bar{p}(1-\bar{p})}{n_2}}}$$

Step 3: Z value corresponding to a significance level of 0.05, and two tailed will be ±1.96. Fail to reject H_0 if the calculated Z value is > -1.96 and < 1.96. Otherwise reject H_0 .

Step 4: Calculate the test statistic:

$$Z = \frac{\frac{130}{400} - \frac{95}{300}}{\sqrt{\frac{\frac{130+95}{400+300}(1-\frac{130+95}{400+300})}{400} + \frac{\frac{130+95}{400+300}(1-\frac{130+95}{400+300})}{300}}} = 0.2336$$

Step 5: Since the test statistic falls in the Fail to reject H_0 region, you conclude that there is not significant difference between the two regions in terms of accidents.

10.4 Self test Problems

Self-test Problem 10.4.1

Great Motors Inc. has been losing its small car market share for the last few years. It has launched a new small car sales campaign for the last 1 year. On a survey of opinions of "Small car buyers of the year 2003", 120 of the 300 surveyed had said that they plan to buy Great Motors's small car in the year 2003.

a. Find the 95% confidence interval for the proportion planning to buy Great Motors' small car in the year 2003.

b. If they plan to achieve 45% small car market share, is there enough evidence to show that they will achieve it, assuming that survey is a reflection of reality and significance level of 95%.

Self-test Problem 10.4.2

Family Motors Inc., a large family-operated auto company sells two identical cars with different nameplates: Work-Horse and Race-Horse. It is a long held belief that Work-Horse owners are less satisfied than Race-Horse owners. A survey of 250 Work-Horse owners revealed 150 were satisfied, whereas a survey of 400 Race-Horse owners revealed that 260 were satisfied.

a. Construct a 90% confidence interval for the difference in satisfaction proportions of the underlying populations.
b. Test whether the satisfaction level among Work-Horse owners is really less than that of Race-Horse owners, at a significance level of 0.10.

Multiple Choice Questions:

Questions 1-5 are based on this problem:
A soft drink manufacturer wants to check the claim of its regional distributor that it controls 50% of the market in that region. The management feels that the distributor's actual market is lot less. The management took a random sample of 1000 consumers and found that 475 of them were using their brand. The management wants to test whether there is enough evidence to "prove" that the distributor actually controls less than 50% of the market. Use a significance level of 0.05.

1. The **Null hypothesis** to be used for testing the claim is:
   a. $p \leq 0.5$
   b. $p = 0.5$
   c. $p \leq 0.475$
   d. $p \geq 0.475$
   e. $p \geq 0.50$
2. What will be the distribution of the appropriate test statistic to be used in this problem:
   a. Normal
   b. *t*-distribution with degrees of freedom = 999
   c. *t*-distribution with degrees of freedom = 10
   d. *F*-distribution
   e. None of the above
3. What is the alternate hypothesis?
   a. $p \leq 0.5$
   b. $p < 0.5$
   c. $p \leq 0.475$
   d. $p > 0.475$
   e. $p > 0.50$
4. The value of the test statistic is:
   a. -1.58
   b. 1.58
   c. 1.28
   d. -1.28
   e. None of the above
5. The null hypothesis will be rejected.
   a. True b. False

Questions 6-10 are based on the following problem:
In a recent study investor confidence in old economy vs. new economy stocks, a random set of 300 were questioned on new economy stocks and 102 people expressed confidence in them. In another survey of 400 on old economy stocks 116 people expressed confidence in them.

6. The lower limit of the 90% confidence interval for the difference in the (new-old) is:
   a. 0.05
   b. -0.05
   c. -0.0085
   d. 0.008
   e. 0.1085
7. The upper limit of the 90% confidence interval for the difference in the (new-old) is:
   a. 0.05
   b. -0.05
   c. -0.0085
   d. 0.008
   e. 0.1085
8. For conducting a hypothesis test to check whether the two proportions are same or different, the pooled proportion will be::
   a. 0.29
   b. 0.311
   c. 0.34
   d. 0.05
9. For conducting a hypothesis test, with a significance level of 0.05, to check whether the two proportions are same or different, the test statistic will be:
   a. -1.414
   b. 1.414
   c. -1.96
   d. 1.96
10. For conducting a hypothesis test, with a significance level of 0.05, to check whether the two proportions are same or different, the conclusion will be to reject H_0.
   a. True   b. False

10.5 Glossary

proportion (p)
A parameter equal to the proportion of population elements having a specified attribute.

standard error of $\hat{p}$

The estimated standard deviation of the statistic $\hat{p}$ equal to $s_{\hat{p}} = \sqrt{\dfrac{\hat{p}(1-\hat{p})}{n-1}}$

unbiased
A desirable property of a sample statistic implying that if samples were obtained indefinitely, the average value of the statistic is equal to the parameter it is estimating.
Examples of unbiased estimators:

$\hat{p}$ is an unbiased estimator of p,

$\overline{X}$ is an unbiased estimator of the population mean, and
s^2 is an unbiased estimator of the population variance.

10.5 Solution to Self-Test Problems

Solution to Self-test Problem 10.4.1.

a. *p*-hat = 120/300 = 0.4
Z = 1.96 (that Z which makes the area to its right tail equal to ((100 - 95)/2)% or 025.)
0.4 - 1.96(sqrt((0.4(1 - .4)/(300 - 1)) to 0.4 +1.96(sqrt((0.4(1 - .4)/(300 - 1))
Shortened form, [0.344, 0.455].

b. To answer this, let us do the following hypothesis test:
Step 1. H_0: $p \geq 0.45$
H_1 : $p < 0.45$
Step 2. Test stat is Z. On a one-sided test, Z value that makes the left tail equal to 0.05 is -1.645.
Step 3. If Z is less than -1.645 reject H_0. Otherwise, Fail to reject H_0.
Step 4. Test statistic = (0.40 - 0.45)/sqrt((0.45(1 - .45)/(300)) = -1.741
Step 5. Reject H_0 . The market share controlled by the dealer is significantly less.

Solution to Self-Test Problem 10.4.2.

a. $\hat{p}_1 = \frac{150}{250} = 0.60 \ \ and \ \ \hat{p}_2 = \frac{260}{400} = 0.65$

Confidence interval: (.6 - .65) - 0.0644, (.6 - .65) + .0644,
and shortened form: [0.1144, 0.0144]

b. Step 1. H_0: $p_1 \geq p_2$
H_1: $p_1 < p_2$
Step 2. Test statistics is Z.
Step 3. For 0.1 significance level, and left-tailed, the Z value is -1.28. If test statistic is less than -1.28, reject H_0. Otherwise fail to reject H_0.
Step 4. Calculate the test statistic:
P-bar = (150 + 260)/(250 + 400) = 0.6307
Standard deviation of test statistic: sqrt(((0.6307)(1 - .6307)/250) + ((0.6307)(1 - 0.6307)/400))
Z = -1.2850
Step 5: Reject H_0. There is evidence that the Work-Horse owners are less satisfied than Race-Horse owners.

Answers to Multiple choice questions

Question #	Answer	Question #	Answer	Question #	Answer
1	e	5	b	9	b
2	b	6	c	10	b
3	a	7	e		
4	a	8	b		

CHAPTER 11 ANALYSIS OF VARIANCE

Chapter Overview and Learning Objectives

This chapter introduces the ANOVA procedure, which can be used to test for the equality of two or more group means. The completely randomized design (one-factor ANOVA), the randomized block design, and the two-way factorial design are discussed. Procedures for constructing confidence intervals for mean differences using these designs are described along with a test for equal variances using the completely randomized design. Multiple comparison procedures are also introduced. Upon completion of this chapter, the student should be able to:

1. Construct an ANOVA table to test for equal group means.
2. Discuss the assumptions behind the use of an experimental design.
3. Use Hartley's test for investigating the assumption of equal variances.
4. Construct confidence intervals for mean differences.
5. Understand the concept of blocking and be aware of when blocked designs are appropriate.
6. Perform a multiple comparisons procedure when using the completely randomized, randomized block, or two-way factorial designs.

Chapter Outline

11.1 Comparing Two Means: Another Look
11.2 One-Factor ANOVA Comparing More Than Two Means
11.3 Designing an Experiment
11.4 Randomized Block Design
11.5 The Two Way Factorial Block Design
11.6 Self-Test Problems
11.7 Glossary
11.8 Solution to Self-Test Problems

11. 1 Comparing Two Means: Another Look

Consider a factor called fertilizer applied at different levels, called Fertilizer 1, Fertilizer 2. Suppose that we are interested in studying crop yields by using each brand of fertilizer, a natural question is: Are the population mean yield of the two brands are equal or not. To check this we can take samples of size n_1 and n_2 from the fields using the two brands and conduct hypothesis tests of equality of means. If we assume that the standard deviation of the populations are equal, we can refine the test further by using a pooled estimate of the variance in order to calculate the standard deviation of the test statistic, which follows t-distribution with n_1-n_2-2 degrees of freedom All of these were illustrated in Chapter 9. *H*owever, what if we had 4 brands of fertilizers? We still want to test for equality of means. We further assume that standard deviation of the underlying populations are the same. Another way to ask the same question: Is the factor called Fertilizer has significant impact on yield?

11.2 One-Factor ANOVA Comparing More Than Two Means

Here a test for 3 or more populations is presented.

Property	Assumption
Samples	Independent
Each Sample	Comes from a Normal distribution
Variance	All normal populations have common equal variance
If all samples are of equal size,	Then violations of equal variance may be tolerated

Table 11.2.1. Assumptions of One-Factor ANOVA

Between-Sample Variation: How much is each sample average differing from other sample averages? More they differ, greater will be the underlying population variance. There is a formula to estimate underlying size σ^2 using the sample means and the grand mean of the entire population. If H_0 is true, these two estimates of the underlying σ^2 will be the same.

Within-sample variation: The sample variances of each sample are a function of the underlying common variance. A simple formula will help us estimate the underlying common variance of the population. (Even if population means are not the same, this procedure will give a good estimate of underlying σ^2.)

Between-Sample Variation (Mean square factor (MS Factor) = Sum of squares of factor /degrees of freedom of factor

Within-sample variation (Mean square error (MSError)) = Sum of squares of Error/degrees of freedom of error

Our next job is to find these values and get an intuitive feeling for them. For example consider a problem with 4 levels in the a factor:

Sum of squares of factor (SSfactor) =

$$n_1\left(\overline{x_1}-\overline{\overline{x}}\right)^2+n_2\left(\overline{x_2}-\overline{\overline{x}}\right)^2+n_3\left(\overline{x_3}-\overline{\overline{x}}\right)^2+n_4\left(\overline{x_4}-\overline{\overline{x}}\right)^2$$

Degrees of freedom for the factors is k-1, where k is the number of factors, in this case k = 4. Let the sample sizes for each of the four factors be n_1, n_2, n_3 and n_4 respectively. Then

Sum of squares of error (SS Error) =

$$\sum_{i=1}^{i=n_1}\left(x_{1i}-\overline{x_1}\right)^2+\sum_{i=1}^{i=n_2}\left(x_{2i}-\overline{x_2}\right)^2+\sum_{i=1}^{i=n_3}\left(x_{3i}-\overline{x_3}\right)^2+\sum_{i=1}^{i=n_4}\left(x_{4i}-\overline{x_4}\right)^2$$

which is similar to the numerator of any standard deviation calculation.

Degrees of freedom for this is $n_1 + n_2 + n_3 + n_4 - 4$.

The test statistic for this test is: F = MS(Factor)/MS(Error)

This follows an F-distribution with numerator degrees of freedom (k-1) and denominator degrees of freedom ($n_1 + n_2 + n_3 + n_4 - 4$) for this example with 4 factors. For more levels, the formula is suitably extended.

Discussion: There are many simplified formulas to calculate the F value. We use first principles to illustrate the formula and the application.

Review Problem 11.2.1.

In a study of low tar cigarettes, three brands A, B and C were tested and the data in micrograms is given below.

Brand A	Brand B	Brand C
12	9	11
14	6	10
13	11	12
11	13	11
15	12	17
	9	16
		14

Table 11.2.1. Data for Problem 11.2.1.

Samples	Properties
Sample sizes	$n_1 = 5$; $n_2 = 6$; $n_3 = 7$
Averages	$\overline{x_1} = 13; \overline{x_2} = 10; \overline{x_3} = 13;$
Grand Average (average of all samples)	$\overline{x} = 12;$
Total sample size (n)	18

Table 11.2.2. Parameters of the data set of Problem 11.2.1.

Test the hypothesis that all means are equal using ANOVA. For a significance level of 0.10,

Step 1: H_0: $\mu_1 = \mu_2 = \mu_3$
H_1: Not all means are equal.
Step 2: Test statistic is F, with (3-1) numerator degrees of freedom and (18-3) = 15 denominator degrees of freedom
Step 3: Reject H_0 if $F > 2.70$. (If degrees of freedom is not listed, choose the nearest.)
Fail to reject H_0 if F is less than 2.70.
Step 4: Calculate the value of the test statistic:

$$\text{SSFactor} = 5\,(13-12)^2 + 6(10-12)^2 + 7(13-12)^2 = 36$$

$$\begin{aligned}\text{SSE} &= (12-13)^2 + (14-13)^2 + (13-13)^2 + (11-13)^2 + (15-13)^2 + (9-10)^2 \\ &\quad + (6-10)^2 + (11-10)^2 + (13-10)^2 + (12-10)^2 + (9-10)^2 + (11-13)^2 \\ &\quad + (10-13)^2 + (12-13)^2 + (11-13)^2 + (17-13)^2 + (16-13)^2 + (14-13)^2 \\ &= 86\end{aligned}$$

$F = 3.14$ as shown below in Table 11.2.3.

Source	SS	DF	MS	F
Treatment	36	2	18	3.14
Error	86	15	5.7333	

Table 11.2.3. ANOVA Calculation Table

Step 5: Since F value falls in the Reject H_0 region, at least one set of means are not equal.

Test for Equality of Variances:
In ANOVA, it was assumed that variances are equal. There is a test statistic called Hartley's H-Statistic, tabulated in Appendix A.14 for a significance level of 0.05, which can be used to test for equality of variances. It assumes equal sample sizes.

Review Problem 11.2.2.

Professor Jim Jones teaches 3 sections of Statistics. On some sections, he had made some mistake in the multiple-choice questions, resulting in everyone getting it right on those questions. However, Professor Jones believes that the variances of the population of scores are equal. Test whether variances in the class scores are equal using the randomly selected sample data collected on the spot in class.

Section 1	Section 2	Section 3
46	88	67
67	46	78
94	78	80
76	56	98
54	45	76

Table 11.2.4

Sample Variance 1	354.8
Sample Variance 2	377.8
Sample Variance 3	128.2

Table 11.2.5 Variances

Step 1: $H_0: \sigma_1^2 = \sigma_2^2 = \sigma_3^2$

H_1: At least one pair of variances are different

Step 2: Test statistic is Hartley's H. The critical values are tabulated in Appendix A.14.

Step 3: H = Test statistic. From Appendix A.14, critical value is 15.5. If the value of test statistic falls below the critical value, fail to reject H_0. Otherwise, reject H_0.

Step 4: H = Largest sample variance/smallest sample variance = 377.8/128.2 = 2.93. Fail to reject H_0.

Step 5: There is not enough evidence to reject H_0.

Discussion: In all cases (whether null hypothesis is rejected or fail to rejected) of ANOVA problem, we can construct 100%(1-α) confidence interval for the difference in means of two populations. We use the pooled variance, which is in fact equal to the MS(Error) for the problem. The underlying tests statistic follows t-distribution, just like the t-test for 2 populations.

Review Problem 11.2.3. Find the 90% confidence interval for the difference in tar content of (Brand A-Brand B) using the data in Table 11.3.1.

(1-0.10)(100 %) confidence interval:

$$\left(\overline{x_A}-\overline{x_B}\right)-t_{\alpha/2,(n-k)}S_P\sqrt{\frac{1}{n_A}+\frac{1}{n_B}} \text{ to } \left(\overline{x_A}-\overline{x_B}\right)+t_{\alpha/2,(n-k)}S_P\sqrt{\frac{1}{n_A}+\frac{1}{n_B}}$$

In this: $\overline{x_A}= 13$ and $\overline{x_B} = 10$; $n_A = 5$; $n_B = 6$; S_P = sqrt(5.7333) = 2.394; $t_{\alpha/2,(n-k)} = 1.753$

With $\alpha/2$ = 0/05 at the right tail and $(n - k) = 15$, substituting the values, we get

$$(13-10)-1.753(2.394)\left(\sqrt{\frac{1}{13}+\frac{1}{10}}\right) \text{ to } (13-10)+1.753(2.394)\left(\sqrt{\frac{1}{13}+\frac{1}{10}}\right)$$

In shortened form, [1.234, 4.765].

11.3 Designing an Experiment

First, highlights of the design of experiments summarized in Table 11.3.1.

Property	Completely Randomized Design	The Randomized Block Design	The Two-Way Factorial Design
Selection of sample items	All elements have the same chance of being selected from each treatment (factor)	Each sample in a given level is related to corresponding samples at other levels. e.g. heights of father, son and grandson. This is one block. The whole data will contain several blocks of data	There are two factors potentially affecting the dependent variable of interest. e.g. Let grade be the dependent variable, and Factor A: 4 categories of number of classes attended (< 50%, 50 - 70%, 70 -85% and Factor B: 85-100%) and 3 categories CGPA (≤ 2.0, 2.0 to 3.0 and >3.0).
Hypotheses to be tested	$\mu_1 = \mu_2 = \mu_3$	$\mu_F = \mu_S = \mu_{GS}$	a. Factor A is not significant. b. Factor B is not significant. c. There is no interaction between factors A and B.
Assumptions		a. Population for each factor level combination is normal b. These have common variance σ^2	

11.4 Randomized Block Design

Discussion: The elementary formulas get a little messier and less intuitive, when it involves blocks. It is best to understand it systematically as shown in the following example.

Review Problem 11.4.1.

It is surmised that prices of milk tend to be closer to each other if the stores are in the same neighborhood. It is also known that some grocery chains sell it for a higher price than others. This is a good example for checking the effect of blocks on ANOVA. Table 11.4.1. gives the details of the prices of milk (in cents per gallon) taken on the same 24 hour interval in 10 different neighborhoods in Ohio and Michigan. Using ANOVA, analyze and report the effects of blocks and factors on milk prices. Use significance level of 0.10 for all tests.

Neighborhood	Meijer	Kroger	Food Town	Totals	Block_Total_Squared
1	181	187	186	554	306916
2	233	247	246	726	527076
3	199	201	199	599	358801
4	267	277	279	823	677329
5	282	287	302	871	758641
6	177	182	206	565	319225
7	169	186	179	534	285156
8	228	235	253	716	512656
9	295	307	308	910	828100
10	250	279	258	787	619369
Totals	2281	2388	2416	7085	50197225
Averages	228.1	238.8	241.6		
Column Total Squared	5202961	5702544	5837056		

Table 11.4.1. Milk Price Data and Related Calculations

SS(Factor) $= (1/10)[2281^2 + 2388^2 + 2416^2] - (7085^2/30) = 1015.267$

SS(blocks) $= (1/3)[554^2 + 726^2 + 599^2 + 823^2 + 871^2 + 565^2 + 534^2 + 716^2 + 910^2 + 787^2]$
$- (7085^2/30) = 57848.83$

SS(total) $= [181^2 + 187^2 + 186^2 + 233^2 + \ldots + 258^2)-(7085^2/30) = 59806.17$

SS(Error) $=$ SS(total) - SS(factor) – SS(blocks) $= 59806.17 - 1015.267 - 57848.83$
$= 942.0667$

All of these are given in Table 11.4.2. in a standard format.

Source	DF	SS	MS	*F*
Factor	2	1015.267	507.6333	$F_1 = 9.699314$
Blocks	9	57848.83	6427.648	$F_2 = 122.8126$
Error	18	942.0667	52.33704	
Total	29	59806.17		

Table 11.4.2. ANOVA Results

ANOVA (Factor effect):

Step 1: H_0: $\mu_1 = \mu_2 = \mu_3$
H_1: Not all means are equal.
Step 2: Test statistic is F, with 2 numerator degrees of freedom and 18 denominator degrees of freedom
Step 3: Reject H_0 if $F > 2.62$. Fail to reject H_0 if F is less than 2.62.
Step 4: Calculate the value of the test statistic: From Table 11.4.2., $F_1 = 9.699$, thus rejecting H_0.
Step 5: Since the F value falls in the Reject H_0 region, at least one set of means are not equal.

ANOVA (Block effect):

Step 1: H_0: There is no block effect.
H_1: There is block effect.
Step 2: Test statistic is F, with 9 numerator degrees of freedom and 18 denominator degrees of freedom
Step 3: Reject H_0 if $F > 2.0$. Fail to reject H_0 if F is less than 2.0.
Step 4: Calculate the value of the test statistic: From Table 11.4.2., $F_2 = 122.81$, thus rejecting H_0.
Step 5: Since F value falls in the Reject H_0 region, there is a block effect.

What if we did not know or recognize the presence of block?

We would have simply done regular one factor ANOVA and the results are shown in Table 11.4.3.

Source	SS	DF	MS	F
Treatment	1015.267	2	507.60	0.233
Error	58790.703	27	2177.44	
Total	59806.170			

Table 11.4.3. ANOVA Calculation Table

It is clear that using the 5-step procedure, we would have failed to Reject H_0, thus concluding there is no difference in the factors, leading to wrong conclusion.

11.5 The Two-Way Factorial Design

*H*ere there are two factors of interest. the main competitor's market share in the market (Factor A) and Amount spent in advertising in the market (Factor B). Let the dependent variable be the per capita daily sales (oz) of soft drinks in a market.

Review Problem 11.5.1.

Suppose that we want to model the per capita daily sales of soft drinks in various markets. It is believed that this depends on the two factors listed above. Let us say we have 3 (in general r) replicates of data for each market. Let a be the number of levels of factor A and b be the number of levels of factor B. Table 11.5.1. presents the raw data for the problem.

Market Share % of Competitors: Factor A	Factor B								
	Advt. level 1			Advt. Level 2			Advt. Level 3		
30	98	68	13	45	72	83	94	96	92
40	83	40	27	21	71	28	63	99	61
50	150	31	15	132	137	47	110	101	33
60	15	43	54	72	10	92	84	34	60

Table 11.5.1. Raw Data

	Advt. Level 1	Advt. Level 2	Advt. Level 3	
Competitor's Market Share (%)	Total of all replicates	Total of all replicates	Total of all replicates	Totals
30	179	200	282	661
40	150	120	223	493
50	196	316	244	756
60	112	174	178	464
Totals	637	810	927	2374

Table 11.5.2. Totals of All replicates (in this case 3 replicates)

Source	DF	DF (Numerical values)	SS	MS	*F*
Factor A	a-1	3	6425.889	2141.963	1.518883
Factor B	b-1	2	3547.722	1773.861	1.257859
Interaction	(a-1)(b-1)	6	3642.944	607.1574	0.43054
Error	ab(r-1)	24	33845.33	1410.222	
Total	abr-1	35	47461.89		

Table 11.5.3. ANOVA Table

In this problem Factor A represents the competitor's market share (4 different % of market share) Factor B represents the advertisement levels (3 of them), and 3 replicates of the dependent variable sales per capita. Finally, Table 11.5.3. gives the ANOVA table. The details of the formula for the SS are left to the reader; refer to the book since they are very cumbersome.

a. Test the significance of factor A at 0.10 level of significance.
b. Test the significance of factor B at 0.10 level of significance.
c. Test the significance of interaction of Factors A and B at 0.10 level of significance.

Solution:

a. The test statistic is *F* with 2 (a-1) for the numerator degrees of freedom and 24 ab(r-1) for the denominator. Reject H_0 (factor A is not significant), H_1 (factor A is significant), gives a critical value of 2.54. Since the corresponding *F* is 1.51, we fail to reject H_0.

b. The test statistic is *F* with 3 (b-1) for the numerator degrees of freedom and 24 ab(r-1) for the denominator. Reject H_0 (factor B is not significant), H_1 (factor B is significant), gives a critical value of 2.33. Since the corresponding F is 1.257, we fail to reject H_0.

c. The test statistic is F with 6 (a-1)(b-1) for the numerator degrees of freedom and 24 ab(r-1) for the denominator. Reject H_0 (interaction of factors AB is not significant), H_1 (interaction of factors AB is significant), gives a critical value of 2.04. Since the corresponding F is 0.430, we fail to reject H_0.

Self-test Problems

Self-test Problem 11.6.1.

There are four models of SUV that are made respectively by Toyota, *H*onda, Ford and Subaru. Random samples for almost identically equipped SUV's price quotes are given in the Table 11.6.1. Test whether the population means of prices are equal at 0.10 level of significance using ANOVA test.

*H*onda-CRV	Ford-Escape	Toyota-Rav4	Subaru-Forrester
22760	24500	25500	22000
21800	23400	24750	24100
22460	24500	23900	25100
22200	22900	26100	23600
24100	23500	27000	
	21000		

Table 11.6.1. Data for Problem 11.6.1.

Groups	Count	Sum	Average
*H*onda-CRV	5	113320	22664
Ford-Escape	6	139800	23300
Toyota-Rav4	5	127250	25450
Subaru-Forrester	4	94800	23700

Table 11.6.2. Averages for the data set.

Self-test Problem 11.6.2

Find the 95% confidence interval for the difference in the population mean prices of (*H*onda-CRV- Toyota-Rav4), using the data in Tables 11.6.1. and 11.6.2.

Self-Test Problem 11.6.3.

In a study of cost of oversees computer software development, data was collected on per hour development cost in three countries: India, China and Philippines. In order to be thorough, 10 different types of software projects, such as online, web-based, new software development, applications on existing packages, and so on were studied. The data for 10 types of projects in the three countries are tabulated in Table 11.6.3. Using significance level of 0.10 for all tests, test

a. Whether their means are same?
b. Whether there is a block effect?

Neighborhood	India	China	Philippines	Totals	
1	55.31	64.99	63.15	183.45	33653.9
2	64.46	80.64	126.06	271.16	73527.75
3	59.61	59.94	99.92	219.47	48167.08
4	69.72	83.31	98.2	251.23	63116.51
5	79.3	88.12	108.18	275.6	75955.36
6	68.43	83.1	89.46	240.99	58076.18
7	70.13	72.09	121.8	264.02	69706.56
8	61.35	75.46	120.41	257.22	66162.13
9	61.32	79.29	72.77	213.38	45531.02
10	58.45	65.47	105.28	229.2	52532.64
Totals	648.08	752.41	1005.23	2405.72	5787489
Averages	64.81	75.24	100.52		
	420007.7	566120.8	1010487		

Table 11.6.3. Software Development Cost per *H*our and Related Calculations

Multiple Choice Questions:

Questions 1-5 are based on the data below. In a study of low sales plans, the total sales (shown as 000s of $) in a district following the plan based on random samples is given below. Test the equality of population means using 0.05 significance level:

Plan A	Plan B	Plan C	Plan D
30	40	50	20
30	45	15	25
45	60	30	25
25	55	45	35
20			50
25			
35			
30			

Table 11.6.4

Groups	Count	Sum	Average	Variance
Plan A	8	240	30	57.14286
Plan B	4	200	50	83.33333
Plan C	4	140	35	250
Plan D	5	155	31	142.5

Table 11.6.5

ANOVA						
Source of Variation	SS	DF	MS	*F*	*P*-value	*F* crit
Treatment	1180	3	393.3333	3.394247	0.042069	3.196774
Error	1970	17	115.8824			
Total	3150	20				

Table 11.6.6.

1. MSE for the problem is:
   a. 3.39
   b. 393.3
   c. 115.9
   d. 1970
   e. None of the above
2. The total sample size n for the problem is:
   a. 17
   b. 20
   c. 21
   d. 3
   e. None of the above
3. Base on the data the critical value will be
   a. 3.2
   b. 5.18
   c. .04
   d. None of the above
4. 90% Confidence interval for the population mean for μ_C is:
   a. $35 \pm (1.771) \times \sqrt{393.33} \times \sqrt{(1/4)}$
   b. $140 \pm (1.740) \times \sqrt{115.9} \times \sqrt{(1/4)}$
   c. $35 \pm (1.740) \times \sqrt{115.9} \times \sqrt{(1/4)}$
   d. $140 \pm (1.771) \times \sqrt{393.33} \times \sqrt{(1/4)}$
   e. None of the above
5. 95% Confidence interval for the population mean of $\mu_A - \mu_C$ is:
   a. $(30-35) \pm (2.11) \times \sqrt{393.33} \times \sqrt{((1/8)+(1/4))}$
   b. $(30-35) \pm (2.11) \times \sqrt{115.9} \times \sqrt{((1/8)+(1/4))}$
   c. $(240-140) \pm (1.74) \times \sqrt{115.9} \times \sqrt{((1/8)+(1/4))}$
   d. $(240-140) \pm (1.74) \times \sqrt{393.33} \times \sqrt{((1/8)+(1/4))}$
   e. None of the above
6. Other things remaining the same, confidence interval will get wider as the degree of freedom associated with MSE increases.
   a. True
   b. False
7. Correlation coefficient for any set of pairs of data will ____________ be between 0 and -1 both inclusive.
   a. sometimes
   b. always
   c. never
   d. None of the above

Data for Questions 8-10.

	X	Y	X^2	Y^2	XY
	42	73	1764	5329	3066
	41	53	1681	2809	2173
	34	63	1156	3969	2142
	28	73	784	5329	2044
	30	52	900	2704	1560
	32	72	1024	5184	2304
	23	75	529	5625	1725
	46	78	2116	6084	3588
Totals	276	539	9954	37033	18602

8. Based on the above data, the SCP_{XY} will be
   a. 37033
   b. 9954
   c. 18606
   d. 6.5
   e. None of the above
9. Based on the above data, the SS_X will be
   a. 276
   b. 9954
   c. 432
   d. -432
   e. None of the above
10. Correlation coefficient for X and Y will be
   a. -.9884
   b. 0.0116
   c. .9884
   d. -0.0116
   e. None of the above

Questions 11-14 are based on the data below: a study of low tar cigarettes. Three brands A, B and C were tested and the data in micrograms is given below.

Brand A	Brand B	Brand C
9	8	6
6	9	6
3	12	9
10	11	4
		5
		5
		7
		6

$$SSE = (9 - ?)^2 + (6 - ?)^2 + (3 - ?)^2 + (10 - ?)^2 + (8 - 10)^2 + (9 - 10)^2 + (12 - 10)^2 + (? - 10)^2 + (6 - 6)^2 + (6 - 6)^2 + (9 - 6)^2 + (4 - 6)^2 + (5 - 6)^2 + (5 - 6)^2 + (7 - 6)^2 + (6 - 6)^2$$

11. Missing numbers in the above expression for SSE in the order in which they are presented:
   a. 9, 6, 3, 10, and 11
   b. 6, 6, 10, 10, and 13
   c. 10, 10, 10, 10 and 6
   d. 6, 6, 6, 6, and 11
   e. 7, 7, 7, 7 and 11
12. The missing numbers (in the order in which they are missing) in the following expression for SSTreatment are:
   SSTreatment = $?(7 - 7.25)^2 + ?(10 - 7.25)^2 + ?(6 - 7.25)^2$
   a. 8, 4, 4
   b. 4, 8, 4
   c. 4, 4, 4
   d. 4, 12, 16
   e. None of the above
13. Complete the table below:

Source	SS	DF	MS	*F*
Treatment	43	2	?	?
Error	56	13	?	

   MSTreatement is:
   a. 43
   b. 56
   c. 21.5
   d. 4.30
   e. None of the above
14. Using 0.05 significance level, suppose that the critical value from the appropriate table is 3.81. The conclusion is:
   a. Fail to reject *Ho*
   b. Reject *Ho*
   c. Cannot get enough information
   d. *P*-value is 0.4 and, hence accept *Ho*
   e. None of the above

Questions 15 and 16 refer to the following problem. Independent random samples were drawn from four populations. Assume that each of the populations is normally distributed and that the population variances are equal. Use the following ANOVA table to determine whether the population means are equal, using a .05 level of significance.

ANALYSIS OF VARIANCE				
SOURCE	DF	SS	MS	*F*
FACTOR	3	90	30	1.339
ERROR		30	672	22.4
TOTAL		33	762	

15. What is the hypothesis structure?
   a. H_0: $\mu_1 = \mu_2 = \mu_3$ vs. H_1: Not all means are same.
   b. H_0: $\mu_1 = \mu_2 = \mu_3 = \mu_4$ vs. H_1: Not all means are same.
   c. H_0: $\mu_1 = \mu_2 = \mu_3 = 0$ vs. H_1: Not all means are same.
   d. H_0: $\mu_1 = \mu_2 = \mu_3 = \mu_4 = 0$ vs. H_1: Not all means are same.
   e. None of the above

16. What is the conclusion?
    a. Fail to reject H_0
    b. Reject H_0
    c. Fail to reject H_0 and H_1
    d. Reject H_0 and Reject H_1
    e. None of the above
17. Sum of squares of Error is ___________equal to (sum of squares of treatment + sum of squares of total) in any ANOVA problem.
    a. Always
    b. Sometimes
    c. Never
    d. Always for some problem structures and never for other problem structures.
18. You use ANOVA – Randomized block design if each set of data corresponding to a level of the factor
    a. Comes from the same person
    b. Is coming from samples related in some way
    c. Independent samples
    d. a and b
    e. None
19. If you ignore the blocking effect when the blocks are present you might come to wrong conclusion.
    a. True
    b. False
20. In two way factorial designs, there are two factors and a set of blocks corresponding to the two factors.
    a. True
    b. False

11.7 Glossary

analysis of variance (ANOVA)
A statistical procedure for testing whether the means of two or more populations (groups) are equal.

between sample variation
The variation of the sample means when using one-factor ANOVA, measured by MS(factor).

block
In the randomized block design, a group of experimental observations that are grouped together because they belong to the same city, person, point in time, or other variable creating dependent samples.

completely randomized design
The experimental design used for one-factor ANOVA; it contains one factor of interest and uses independent samples.

dependent variable
In an experimental design, the measured variable of interest that is being compared across two or more groups.

factor
The nominal variable (such as gender) that defines the groups to be compared in a completely randomized or randomized block design. For a two-way factorial design, there are two such variables (such as gender and marital status).

interaction
In a two-way factorial design, the situation in which the relationship between one of the factors and the dependent variable depends on the level of the other factor.

level
A value of the nominal variable used to define the groups (populations) to be compared For example, the factor GENDER has two levels, male and female.

main effect
A term used in two-way factorial designs to denote the effect of one of the factors on the dependent variable.

mean square (MS)
A measure of variation equal to a sum of squares (SS) divided by its corresponding degrees of freedom.

multiple comparisons
A follow-up procedure to determine which population (group) means are in fact different. This procedure is used only in the event that the null hypothesis (H_0: all means are equal) is rejected during the analysis procedure.

randomized block design
The experimental design containing one factor of interest and using dependent samples.

replicate
A sample value obtained using the same treatment under nearly equal conditions.

sum of squares (SS)
A measure of variation for a main effect, block effect, or interaction effect.

treatment
For the completely randomized and randomized block designs, a level of the factor of interest. For the two-way factorial design, a combination of a level of the first factor with a level of the second factor.

two-way factorial design
An experimental design that considers all levels of one factor with all levels of another factor. This design has two factors of interest and allows testing for main effects and for interaction between the two factors.

within sample variation
The variation of the sample values within the individual samples in one-factor ANOVA, measured by MS(error).

11.8. Solution to Self-Test Problems

Solution to Self-test Problem 10.6.1.

We would use the five step process to test the hypothesis.
Step 1: H_0: $\mu_1 = \mu_2 = \mu_3 = \mu_4$
H_1: Not all means are equal.
Step 2: Test statistic is F, with numerator degrees of freedom equal to 3 and denominator degrees of freedom 16.
Step 3: Reject H_0 if $F > 2.46$. Fail to reject H_0 if F is less than 2.46. Otherwise, reject H_0 .

Step 4: Calculate the value of the test statistic:

$$\text{SSFactor} = 5\,(22264 - 23758.5)^2 + 6(23300 - 23758.5)^2 + 5(25450 - 23758.5)^2 + 4(23700\text{-}23758.5)^2 = 21570535$$

$$\begin{aligned}\text{SSE} = &(22760 - 22664)^2 + (21800 - 22664)^2 + (22460 - 22264)^2 \\ &+ (22200 - 22264)^2 + (24100 - 22264)^2 + (24500 - 23300)^2 \\ &+ (23400 - 23300)^2 + (24500 - 23300)^2 + (22900 - 23300)^2 \\ &+ (23500 - 23300)^2 + (21000 - 23300)^2 + (25500 - 25450)^2 \\ &+ (24750 - 25450)^2 + (23900 - 25450)^2 + (26100 - 25450)^2 + (27000\text{-}25450)^2 \\ &+ (22000 - 23700)^2 + (24100 - 23700)^2 + (25100 - 23700)^2 + (23600 - 23700)^2 \\ &= 22194720\end{aligned}$$

$F = 5.18$ as shown below in Table 11.8.1.

ANOVA				
Source of Variation	SS	DF	MS	F
Between Groups	21570535	3	7190178	5.183343
Within Groups	22194720	16	1387170	
Total	43765255	19		

Table 11.8.1. ANOVA Calculation Table

Step 5: Since F value falls in the Reject H_0 region, at least one set of means are not equal.

Solution to Self-test Problem 11.6.2

Let A be *H*onda-CRV and B be Totyota-Rav4, with (1-0.05)100 % confidence interval:

$$\left(\overline{x_A} - \overline{x_B}\right) - t_{\alpha/2,(n-k)} S_P \sqrt{\frac{1}{n_A} + \frac{1}{n_B}} \; to \left(\overline{x_A} - \overline{x_B}\right) + t_{\alpha/2,(n-k)} S_P \sqrt{\frac{1}{n_A} + \frac{1}{n_B}}$$

In this: $\overline{x_A} = 22664$ $\overline{x_B} = 25450$; $n_A = 5$; $n_B = 4$; S_P= sqrt(1387170) (from Table 11.6.3.) = 1177.78;

$t_{\alpha/2,(n-k)}$ = 2.120 (α/2 = 0.05/2 = 0.025 at the right tail and (n-k) = 15).

Substituting the values, we get

$$(22264-25450)-2.12*1177.78*\sqrt{\frac{1}{5}+\frac{1}{5}} \text{ to } (22264-25450)+2.12*1177.78*\sqrt{\frac{1}{5}+\frac{1}{5}}$$

Shortened format, [-4765, -1606.83]

Solution to Self-test Problem 11.6.3

SS(Factor) = (1/10) [$648.08^2 + 752.41^2 + 1005.23^2$] – ($2405.72^2$/30) = 6745.294
SS(blocks) = (1/3)[$183.45^2 + 271.16^2 + 219.47^2 + 251.23^2 + 275.6^2 + 240.99^2 + 264.02^2$
$+ 257.22^2 + 213.38^2 + 229.2^2$] - ($2405.72^2$/30) = 2560.086
SS(total) = [$55.31^2 + 64.99^2 + 63.15^2 + 64.46^2 + \ldots + 105.28^2$) - ($2405.72^2$/30) = 11862.42
SS(Error) = SS(total) - SS(factor) – SS(blocks)
= 11862.42 - 6745.294 - 2560.086 = 2557.09

All of these values are given in Table 11.8.2. in a standard format.

Source	DF	SS	MS	F
Factor	2	6745.294	3372.647	$F_1 = 23.74139$
Blocks	9	2560.086	284.454	$F_2 = 2.002383$
Error	18	2557.039	142.0577	
Total	29	11862.42		

Table 11.8.2. ANOVA Results

ANOVA (Factor effect):

Step 1: H_0: $\mu_1 = \mu_2 = \mu_3$
H_1: Not all means are equal.
Step 2: Test statistic is F, with 2 numerator degrees of freedom and 18 denominator degrees of freedom
Step 3: Reject H_0 if $F > 2.62$. Fail to reject H_0 if $F < 2.62$.
Step 4: Calculate the value of the test statistic: From Table 11.4.2, $F_1 = 23.74139$, thus rejecting H_0.
Step 5: Since F value falls in the Reject H_0 region, at least one set of means are not equal.

ANOVA (Block effect):

Step 1: H_0: There is no block effect.
H_1: There is block effect.
Step 2: Test statistic is F, with 9 numerator degrees of freedom and 18 denominator degrees of freedom
Step 3: Reject H_0 if $F > 2.0$. Fail to reject H_0 if $F < 2.0$.
Step 4: Calculate the value of the test statistic: From Table 11.4.2. $F_2 = 2.002383$, thus rejecting H_0.
Step 5: Since F value falls in the Reject H_0 region, there is a block effect.

Answers to Multiple Choice Questions

Question #	Answer	Question #	Answer	Question #	Answer
1	c	8	d	15	b
2	c	9	e	16	a
3	a	10	b	17	c
4	c	11	e	18	d
5	b	12	e	19	a
6	b	13	c	20	b
7	a	14	b		

CHAPTER 12 QUALITY IMPROVEMENT

Chapter Summary and Learning objectives:

This chapter introduces the philosophy and many of the techniques related to quality improvement and quality assurance. The basic principles of total quality management (TQM) are discussed. The philosophy and criteria of the Malcolm Baldrige National Quality Award (MBNQA) are outlined. Additional quality improvement tools are explained. The idea behind the use of control charts is developed, as well as the procedures used for constructing such charts for variables sampling and attribute sampling. The capability of a process is explained and ratios for measuring process capability are defined. Upon completion of this chapter, the student should be able to:

1. Explain the basic concepts of total quality management
2. Explain the history, intent, and criteria associated with the Malcolm Baldrige National Quality Award
3. Understand the reason for, and the construction of, flowcharts and cause-and-effect diagrams
4. Construct $\overline{X}$ and *R* charts
5. Detect nonrandom patterns in $\overline{X}$ charts
6. Construct p and c charts
7. Determine capability ratios Cp, Cpk, and Cpm

Chapter Outline

12.1 Quality Improvement
12.2 The Malcolm Baldrige National Quality Award and ISO9000 Registration
12.3 Quality Improvement Tools
12.4 Statistical Process Control, Process Variation and Control Charts
12.5 Control Charts for Variables Data: The *X*-bar and *R*-Charts
12.6 Control Charts for Attribute Data: The *p* and *c* charts
12.7 Process capability
12.8 Self-test Problems
12.9 Glossary
12.10 Solution to Self-Test Problems

12.1 Quality Improvement

Total Quality Management (TQM) is a philosophy to meet or exceed customer expectations. Components are: continuous improvement, team work and attention to voice of the customer. TQM involves everybody in the organization. TQM is not a quick fix.

Some historical figures in quality:

Edward Deming: Some important points in his 14 point set: create constancy of purpose for the product/service, constant improvement, eliminate slogans, quotas, barriers , annual merit rating, vigorous encouragement of self-improvement. He has achieved results in Japan earlier and had a great impact on the American industries in the 70s and 80s. Heavy proponent of statistical quality control (SQC).

Joseph Juron: Quality planning, control and improvement. Identify the customer, develop products to meet their needs, and get the whole organization to buy into it. Relied on statistical quality control (SQC).

Philip Crosby: Zero defects and quality is free, two slogans eschewed by Deming. Non-technical approach.

12.2 The Malcolm Baldrige National Quality Award and ISO9000 Registration

Malcolm Baldrige National Quality Award: Instituted by US congress in 1987, to be given to the organization (service, manufacturing and small business: at most one each) for achieving dramatic quality improvement. It is based on outcome or results; it is based on elaborate criteria.

ISO9000: It is procedure and documentation based registration, which helps doing business in Europe. High level of details about the procedures and proof of compliance required to get registration.

12.3 Quality Improvement Tools

Pareto Chart: The important few and the unimportant many; and how to handle each.

Flow chart Draw a picture/diagram of the process and understand how it works

Cause-and-effect diagram: Relate causes and effects.
Learn more about these from your textbook.

12.4 Statistical Process Control, Process Variation and Control Charts

Statistical Process control (SPC) is a way to measure and analyze variations in the process. Deming's funnel experiment involves a funnel on a stand, and a paper with a bull's eye at the bottom of the funnel. The idea is to drop marbles through the funnel, so that the marble stops at the bull's eye. It illustrates the causes and effects of corrective action in a simple process with variation.

Strategy 1: Do not react to each marble drop, recognize that there will be variation. (Contains least variation.)

Strategy 2: Measure the distance of the marble's resting place from the bull's eye and move the funnel this distance in the opposite direction. (Contains more variation than Strategy 1, but stable.)

Strategy 3: Measure the distance of the marble's resting place from the bull's eye. Move the funnel from the bull's eye in the opposite direction starting with from the bull's eye. (Eventually becomes unstable.)

Management must help educate workers to understand and apply the right strategy.

12.5 Control Charts for Variables Data: The *X*-bar and *R*-Charts

Discussion: Imagine a potato chips bagging plant. It wants to fill in 16-ounce bags. The process may put in a little more or a little less than 16 ounces. How do we tell whether an on-going process is performing as "Usual" or whether something has gone out of whack, and hence it must be brought back under control by looking for causes and removing he causes. Control charts help us achieve this.

We first identify how much variation the process will naturally create, estimate its variability and if acceptable, then use these values to figure out when a process is under control and when it has gone out of control.

Intuitive Explanation: All quality control procedures flow from the central limit theorem. "Distribution of sample averages from a population with mean μ and standard deviation σ is approximately normal with mean and standard deviation given by the following:

$\mu_{\overline{X}} = \mu$ and $\sigma_{\overline{X}} = \dfrac{\sigma}{\sqrt{n}}$ where *n* is sample size.

The 99.7% confidence interval for the population mean is given by:

$$\overline{\overline{X}} \pm 3\frac{\sigma}{\sqrt{n}} = \overline{\overline{X}} \pm 3\frac{\hat{\sigma}}{\sqrt{n}} = \overline{\overline{X}} \pm 3\frac{\left(\overline{R}/d_2\right)}{\sqrt{n}}$$

In the above equation, since population standard deviation may not be known, we first substitute it with an estimate, and then we substitute the estimate with values, which can be calculated. The upper limit of this confidence interval is known in quality control as Upper control limit (UCL) and the lower limit of this confidence interval is know as Lower Control Limit (LCL). Formulas are:

$$\text{UCL} = \overline{\overline{X}} + 3\frac{\left(\overline{R}/d_2\right)}{\sqrt{n}} \quad \text{and LCL} = \overline{\overline{X}} - 3\frac{\left(\overline{R}/d_2\right)}{\sqrt{n}}$$

where $\overline{R}$ and $\overline{\overline{X}}$ are calculated as follows. We will illustrate the problem with setting a statistical process control chart for a potato chips bagging plant. You are asked to set up the system.

Steps to set up *X*-bar chart:

1. Take random samples of potato chips bags (say sample size $n = 4$) once an hour on the hour and weigh the bags and note down the weights.
2. Take these readings for say 10 hours, which will result in 10 samples, each of which is of size 4.
3. Calculate $\overline{\overline{X}}$ which is the average weight of all 40 bags.
4. Calculate R = (Highest weight - Lowest weight) of each set of 4 samples. You will get 10 such R values corresponding to the 10 hours you have sampled.
5. Average all the 10 R values to get $\overline{R}$.

6. Look up in Table 12.3 of your text to find the d_2 value corresponding to sample size 4, which will be 2.059.
7. Use the formulas above for UCL and LCL to determines the X-bar chart.

Developing an R-chart, which is the chart to control the range of values, follows the same principles as the X-bar charts, which in turn flows from the central limit theorem. The UCL and LCL for the R-Chart is given below.

$\text{UCL} = \overline{R} + 3 * s_{\overline{R}}$ and $\text{LCL} = \overline{R} - 3 * s_{\overline{R}}$ where

$s_{\overline{R}} = \overline{R}\left(\frac{d_3}{d_2}\right)$ where d_2 and d_3 are from Table 12.3 in the textbook.

If we substitute $s_{\overline{R}}$ into the UCL and LCL of the R-chart, the equations can be re-written into a commonly used version of the UCL and LCL as follows.

$\text{UCL} = D_4\overline{R}$ and $\text{LCL} = D_3\overline{R}$

Steps to set up *R*-Chart:

1. Take random samples of potato chips bags (say sample size n = 4) once an hour on the hour and weigh the bags and note down the weights.
2. Take these readings for say 10 hours, which will result in 10 samples, each of which is of size 4.
3. Calculate R = (Highest weight - Lowest weight) of each set of 4 samples. You will get 10 such R values corresponding to the 10 hours you have sampled.
4. Average all the 10 R values to get $\overline{R}$.
5. Look up in Table 12.3 of your text to find the D_4 and D_3 values corresponding to sample size 4, which will be 2.282 and 0 respectively.
6. Use the formulas above to determine the UCL and LCL for the R-Chart.

Review Problem 12.5.1.

Data on weights of potato chips bags taken on the hour every hour for 10 hours is given in Table 12.5.1. Construct an (a) X-bar chart and (b) R-Chart

Hour sample taken	Weight of potato chips bag (oz)			
1	15.9	16.3	16.1	15.8
2	16.1	15.3	16.1	16.3
3	15.5	15.5	15.5	16.8
4	15.8	16.7	16.2	15.5
5	15.9	16.1	15.3	16.1
6	16.4	15.6	16.1	15.7
7	16.6	16.2	16.1	15.4
8	16.3	16.1	16.3	16.9
9	16.4	16.6	15.4	16.3
10	16.7	16.9	16.3	16.1

Table 12.5.1. Weights Of Potato Chips Bags Taken On The Hour Every Hour.

Solution

a. We need some calculations to use the procedure outlined earlier for constructing the chart.These are shown in Table 12.5.2.

Hour sample taken	Weight of potato chips bag (oz)				*X*-bar	*R*
1	15.9	16.3	16.1	15.8	16.025	0.5
2	16.1	15.3	16.1	16.3	15.95	1
3	15.5	15.5	15.5	16.8	15.825	1.3
4	15.8	16.7	16.2	15.5	16.05	1.2
5	15.9	16.1	15.3	16.1	15.85	0.8
6	16.4	15.6	16.1	15.7	15.95	0.8
7	16.6	16.2	16.1	15.4	16.075	1.2
8	16.3	16.1	16.3	16.9	16.4	0.8
9	16.4	16.6	15.4	16.3	16.175	1.2
10	16.7	16.9	16.3	16.1	16.5	0.8
				X-double bar	16.08	9.6
					R-bar	0.96

Table 12.5.2. Calculations for *X*-bar and *R*-chart Construction.

$$\text{UCL} = \overline{\overline{X}} + 3 * \frac{\left(\overline{R}/d_2\right)}{\sqrt{n}} = 16.08 + 3 * \frac{(0.96/2.059)}{\sqrt{4}} = 16.78$$

$$\text{LCL} = \overline{\overline{X}} - 3 * \frac{\left(\overline{R}/d_2\right)}{\sqrt{n}} = 16.08 - 3 * \frac{(0.96/2.059)}{\sqrt{4}} = 15.38$$

Centerline: 16.08

b. *R*-Chart calculations

$$\text{UCL} = D_4\overline{R} = 2.282 * 0.96 = 2.191$$

$$\text{LCL} = D_3\overline{R} = 0 * 0.96 = 0.$$

Centerline = 0.96

Review Problem 12.5.2

Jim Smith, a new intern set up the control chart for Potato chips bagging facility in Mr. Chips Potatoes Inc. He then collected 8 more hourly data as presented in Table 12.5.3.

a. Using the new data, and control limits from Review Problem 12.5.1. plot *X*-bar chart
b. Using the new data, and control limits from Review Problem 12.5.1. plot *R*-Chart
c. Is the process under control? Comment.

Hour #	Weight of Potato Chips bags (oz)			
1	15.2	16.8	16.1	16.9
2	15.8	15.9	14.8	16.4
3	15.8	16.8	16.2	17.2
4	16.8	15.2	15.5	16.4
5	16.6	15	16	16.5
6	15.7	16.9	16	15.8
7	15.7	16.4	16.1	16.9
8	16.4	16.2	16.7	16.8

Table 12.5.3. Data collected for 8 additional hours.

a. Plot of *X*-bar chart. Calculations

Hour #	Weight of Potato Chips bags (oz)				*X*-bar	R
1	15.2	16.8	16.1	16.9	16.25	1.7
2	15.8	15.9	14.8	16.4	15.725	1.6
3	15.8	16.8	16.2	17.2	16.5	1.4
4	16.8	15.2	15.5	16.4	15.975	1.6
5	16.6	15	16	16.5	16.025	1.6
6	15.7	16.9	16	15.8	16.1	1.2
7	15.7	16.4	16.1	16.9	16.275	1.2
8	16.4	16.2	16.7	16.8	16.525	0.6

Table 12.5.4. Calculations for plot of *X*-bar and *R*-chart.

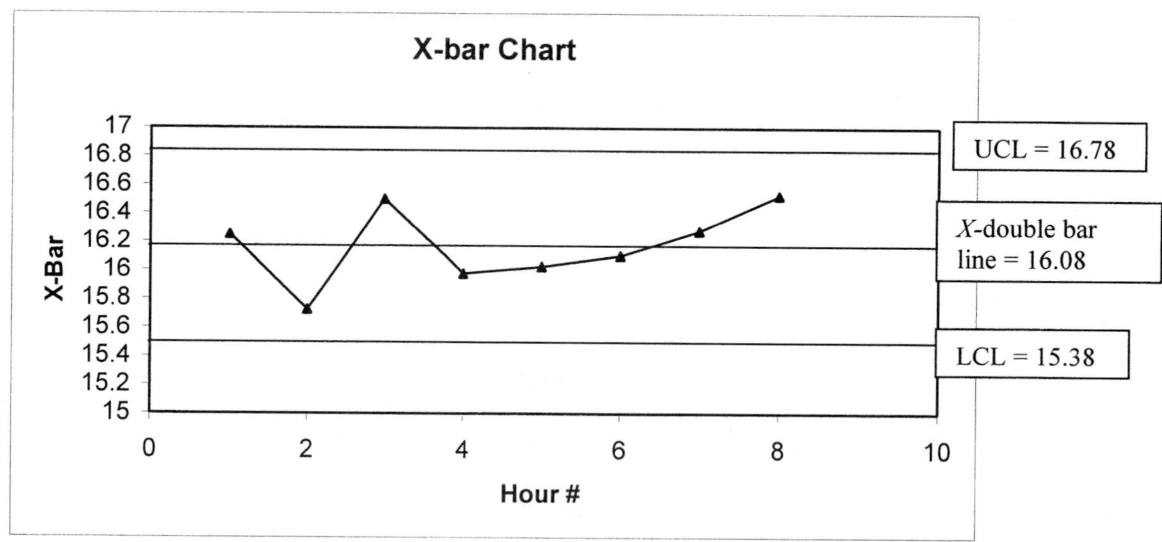

Figure 12.5.1. *X*-bar Chart

b. *R*-Chart

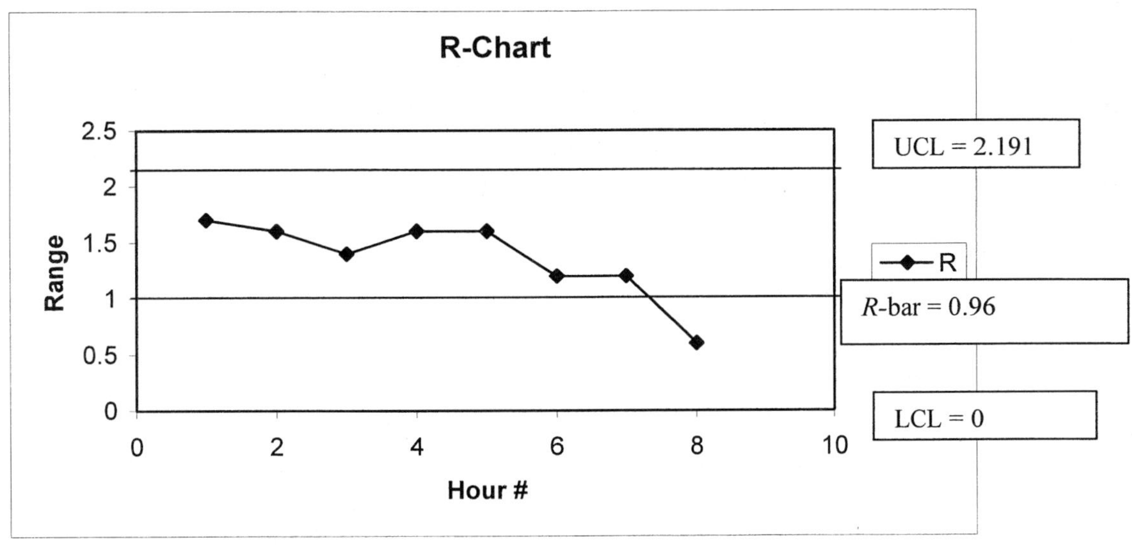

c. All the points are within the lower and upper control limits in both charts and hence the process must be in control.

12.6 Control Charts for Attribute Data: The *p* and *c* charts

***p*-charts:**
Uses: When you control proportion of defectives in a process, proportion of impurities in a process, proportion of non-conforming parts, etc.

Let us examine the proportion of potato chips bags that do not "look right" (may be because of the bagging materials, the way it bulges or whatever). If too many of these show up the process is out of control. Again it is most important to have a procedure for finding the UCL and LCL. Then it is just a matter of taking samples, plotting the samples and then looking for assignable causes, if any of the many conditions such as: one point outside the limit, 9 points in a row all one side of the center line, etc. For complete details refer to Figure 12.12. in the text.

Setting up *p*-chart:
p-chart is based on binomial distribution and sampling from a binomial population. Take n samples at random at one time and take samples m times (e.g. 10 hours on the hour). Suppose n = 20 and m = 10, in all you will have 200 samples. Find the number of non-conforming defects) in the 200 items and define *p*-bar = (# non-conforming/200). The control limits for the *p*-chart are:

$$\text{UCL} = \bar{p} + 3\sqrt{\frac{\bar{p}(1-\bar{p})}{n}} \text{ and LCL} = \bar{p} - 3\sqrt{\frac{\bar{p}(1-\bar{p})}{n}} \text{ and centerline} = \bar{p}.$$

Lower limit is set to 0, if it turns out to be negative.

***c*-Chart:**
This is useful for tracking number of defects in one item (e.g. number of paint blemishes in a new car, number of loose bolts in an assembled item). Again center line, UCL and LCL have to

be found first. Then future points are plotted and out of control scenarios are watched using guidelines in Figure 12.12. in your text.

Setting up *c*-Chart:
Sample m items (say m cars or m assemblies), count the number of blemishes in each of the item 9car or assembly), denoted as c_i for I = 1,2,...,m. Add up all the blemishes and get the following:

$$\bar{c} = \frac{\sum_{i=1}^{m} c_i}{m}.$$

$$\text{UCL} = \bar{c} + 3.\sqrt{\bar{c}} \quad \textit{and} \quad \text{LCL} = \bar{c} - 3.\sqrt{\bar{c}}$$

LCL is set to 0, if the calculations turn out to make the LCL negative.

12.7 Process capability

A process may be under control, meaning it is within the natural variations of the process, but may not be acceptable, because of the requirements of the user (specifications). Lower specification limit (LSL) and Upper specification limit (USL) are the limits given by the consumer.
Process spread = 6(estimate of the process standard deviation).
Process standard deviation is to be estimated using sample runs etc.

If the process spread > (USL - LSL), then there is no way to meet the requirements with the given process.

If the process spread < (USL - LSL), then it will be possible to meet the specifications. However, one may have to adjust the center of the process to coincide with the middle of the specification ((LSL+USL)/2), also called process target T, as much as possible in order to produce to specifications.

Process Capability (C_p) assumes that

- Process output is centered within specifications
- Process is normally distributed
- Process is stable

$$C_p = \frac{\text{USL - LSL}}{6\hat{\sigma}}$$

$$C_p = \frac{\text{USL} - \overline{X}}{3\hat{\sigma}} \text{ when only USL counts: missing rivets}$$

$$C_p = \frac{\overline{X} - \text{LSL}}{3\hat{\sigma}} \text{ when only LSL counts: burst strength}$$

$C_P \geq 1.33$, good
$1 \leq C_P < 1.33$ adequate
$C_P < 1$ Inadequate.

How does process location affect things?

Process Capability (C_{pk}) assumes that

- Process output is centered within specifications
- Process is normally distributed
- Process is stable
- Control charts are used to monitor the process over time.

$$C_{pk} = \text{Min}\left(R_L = \frac{\overline{X} - \text{LSL}}{3\hat{\sigma}}; R_U = \frac{\text{USL} - \overline{X}}{3\hat{\sigma}} \right)$$

$C_{pk} = 1.0$ is considered adequate. By definition, it is clear that
$C_{pk} \leq C_p$.
If $C_{pk} < 1.0$, you have to use vigorous quality improvements to see whether you can raise it above 1.0

Review Problem 12.7.3.

Table 12.7.1. presents the specifications, process mean and process standard deviations.

a. Which measure of process capability C_{pk} or C_p seems more appropriate?
b. Compute the appropriate measure for each process.
c. Estimate the number of non-conforming units per million for each process, using Table 12.4 of your text.

Process	Specifications	Mean	Sample standard deviation
A	120 ± 5	121	2.05
B	50 ± 1	47	0.05
C	70 ± 2	69.7	0.5

Solution to Review Problem 12.7.3.

Parts a and b

Process A: One of the assumptions of *Cp* is the process is centered within specifications. It is almost satisfied.

$$C_p = \frac{125 - 115}{6(2.05)} = 0.813$$

Since C_p is less than 1.0, the process capability is not adequate.
C_{pk} = Min (((121 - 115)/3.(2.05)),((125 - 121)/3.(2.05))
= Min (0.97,0.65)
= 0.65

Process B:
Since middle of the process is 50 and the process mean is 47, it is not coinciding. Let us use C_{pk} to check the capability.

$$C_{pk} = \text{Min}\left(R_L = \frac{47-49}{3.(0.05)}; R_U = \frac{51-47}{3.(0.05)} \right)$$

= Min (-13.33,26.66)
= -13.33

Clearly, this does not make much sense. The reason is, the process is centered at 47, whereas specifications are (49,51). Looking at the sample standard deviation of the process, it seems capable of meeting the specifications, provided we center it to coincide with the middle of the specification limit.

Process C:
The process centered pretty close to the middle of the specification limit. So let us use C_p

C_p = (72 - 68)/6(0.5) = 1.33 which is good for process capability.

C_{pk} = Min (((69.7 - 68)/3.(0.5)),((72 - 69.7)/3.(0.5)))
= Min (1.13,1.533)
= 1.13

c. Process A: From Table 12.4 of your text, the number of non-conforming parts per million corresponding to a C_{pk} of 0.65 is over 24,448 but less than 133,614..

Process B: The process center is outside the specification limits. So nothing makes much sense.

Process C: From Table 12.4 of your text, the number of non-conforming parts per million corresponding to a C_{pk} of 1.13 is over 96 but less than 2700.

12.8 Self-Test Problems

Self-Test Problem 12.8.1.

Data on diameter of an aerospace component taken on the hour every hour for 10 hour is given in Table 12.8.1. Construct

a. *X*-bar chart
b. *R*-Chart

	Diameter in (mm)				
Hour #	1	2	3	4	5
1	20.6	20.4	21.8	21.7	21.1
2	21.7	20.8	21.8	21.7	21.3
3	20.8	20.4	20.9	21.3	20.3
4	21	21.2	21.9	22	20.8
5	21.7	21.3	20.4	21.8	21.4
6	21.3	21.5	21.3	21.3	21.2
7	21.4	21.3	21.5	21.2	21
8	21.4	21.2	21.1	21.4	21.1
9	21.4	21.3	21.5	21.2	21.2
10	21.2	21.3	21.2	21.3	21.4

Table 12.8.1. Diameter of an aerospace component taken on the hour every hour.

Self-Test Problem 12.8.2.

Using the data given in Self-test Problem 12.8.1. test whether the following samples (Table 12.8.2) taken on hour 11 and hour 12 are with in the limits of the

a. *X*-bar, b. *R*-charts.

	Diameter in (mm)				
Hour #	1	2	3	4	5
11	21.9	21.1	20.3	21.6	22.4
12	19.5	22.4	19.7	21.3	21.9

Table 12.8.2. Data

Self-Test Problem 12.8.3

An auto-parts manufacturer manufactures brake components. He is controlling the length of the component on a go-no-go basis. That is, if it fits a particular widget, it is a "go". Otherwise, it is a no-go. He takes samples of size 200 on the hour and finds out the proportion of "go". He did a preliminary test to produce a *p*-chart, which he plans to use for control. Table 12.8.3. gives data from the initial study. Find all the parameters needed for a *p*-chart.

Hour #	Sample size	Number "No-Go"
1	200	2
2	200	6
3	200	10
4	200	6
5	200	7
6	200	2
7	200	1
8	200	8
9	200	2
10	200	7
	2000	51
	p-bar	0.0255

Table 12.8.3. Data for *p*-chart

Self-Test Problem 12.8.4

Two competing processes are offered by two suppliers (Carlos and Vikram) to produce a critical component you need. Carlos can supply at $3.00 per unit whereas Vikram can do it only at $3.20 per unit. The details of the processes are shown in Table 12.8.4.

a. Are both processes capable of meeting your needs?
b. Using process capability analysis, find the "better" of the two processes
c. Which supplier will you choose and why?
d. If you assume that your supplier will be willing to listen to your suggestions and re-center the processes as you so desire, which supplier would you choose? Why?

Process	Your Specification	Mean	Sample standard deviation
Carlos' process	120±2	119	0.3
Vikram's	120±2	120	0.4

Table 12.8.4. Data on two competing processes

Multiple Choice Questions

1. In a process control chart for cement bagging machines, let x-double bar be 51.5 pounds. Let sample size be 5. Let *R*-bar be 1.3 The UCL is:
   a. 52.25
   b. 52.8
   c. 49.75
   d. 52.25
   e. 51.5
2. In a process control chart for cement bagging machines, let x-double bar be 51.5 pounds. Let sample size be 5. Let *R*-bar be 1.3 The LCL is:
   a. 50.75
   b. 55.5
   c. 50.3
   d. 51.25
   e. 50.5
3. In a process control chart for cement bagging machines, let x-double bar be 51.5 pounds. Let sample size be 5. Let *R*-bar be 1.3 If sample at 9.00 a.m. has an *X*-bar of 51.5 and at 10.00 a.m. it is 51.65, there is enough reason to look for assignable causes.
   a. True b. False
4. In a process control chart for cement bagging machines, let sample size be 4. Let *R*-bar be 1.5 UCL for the *R*-chart is:
   a. 1.5
   b. 3.423
   c. 0
   d. 2.282
   e. 2.7495
5. In a process control chart for cement bagging machines let sample size be 4 and *R*-bar be 1.5. If sample at 9.00 a.m. has an R value of 4.5 and at 10.00 a.m. it is 4.3, there is enough reason to look for assignable causes.
   a. True b. False
6. Control chart for process control is based on the theorem that sample average for all possible samples of size n follows normal distribution with mu of x-bar = population mu and sigma of x-bar equals population sigma/sqrt(sample size).
   a. True b. False
7. In a process control chart for cement bagging machines, let x-double bar be 50.5 pounds. Let sample size be 5. Let *R*-bar be 1.8 The UCL is:
   a. 51.8
   b. 55.5
   c. 49.75
   d. 51.25
   e. None of the above
8. In a process control chart for cement bagging machines, let x-double bar be 50.5 pounds. Let sample size be 5. Let *R*-bar be 1.3 The LCL is:
   a. 51.8
   b. 55.5
   c. 49.75
   d. 51.25
   e. 50.5

9. In a process control chart for cement bagging machines, let x-double bar be 50.5 pounds. Let sample size be 5. Let R-bar be 1.2 If sample at 9.00 a.m. has an X-bar of 51.5 and at 10.00 a.m. it is 51.65, there is enough reason to look for assignable causes.
   a. True b. False
10. In a process control chart for cement bagging machines, let sample size be 5. Let R-bar be 1.3 UCL for the R-chart is:
    a. 1.3
    b. 50.5
    c. 0
    d. 2.115
    e. 2.7495
11. In a process control chart for cement bagging machines let sample size be 5. If sample at 9.00 a.m. has an R value of 1.7 and at 10.00 a.m. it is 1.5, there is enough reason to look for assignable causes.
    a. True b. False
12. Even if the process is not centered within specification, we can use C_p to analyze process capability and make a decision.
    a. True b. False
13. A value of less than 1.0 for C_p means the process is fully capable of meeting the specifications.
    a. True b. False
14. Process variation is more important than process center for the purpose of long term quality control.
    a. True b. False
15. If a process is under control, it will ____________ meet the specifications.
    a. Always
    b. Sometimes
    c. Never

12.9 Glossary

assignable cause
A cause of process variation that can be specifically explained and controlled, generally due to improperly adjusted machines, operator error, or defective raw material.

attribute data
Data that consist of the number of nonconformities or the number of nonconforming items.

***c* chart**
A control chart for monitoring the number of nonconformities per item.

chance cause
Variation in a process encountered during the in-control state.

control chart
A statistical chart used to monitor various aspects of a process and to determine if the process is in control (stable) or out of control (unstable).

control limits
Limits for a control chart that when exceeded, signal an out-of-control state.

C_p
A measure of process capability that compares the width of the process specs to the process spread, assuming that the process is centered within the specification limits.

C_{pk}
A measure of process capability equal to the distance from the process center to the nearest spec limit, divided by three standard deviations.

C_{pm}
A measure of process capability that includes the effect of a drift away from the process target.

cause-and-effect (fishbone) diagram
A quality improvement tool that represents the relationships between potential problems within a process and their possible causes.

flowchart
A quality improvement tool which is a diagram of the entire process that allows you to view the process as a system and observe potential problem areas or opportunities for improvement.

Malcolm Baldrige National Quality Award (MBNQA)
An annual award given by the US government that recognizes those companies that have demonstrated a high degree of quality emphasis, both internally and externally.

Pareto chart
A quality improvement tool that is an enhanced bar chart, useful for identifying quality problems having the largest impact.

***P* chart**
A control chart for monitoring the proportion of nonconforming items.

process
Any combination of people, machinery, material and methods that is intended to produce a product or service.

process capability
A measure that specifies the ability of a process to satisfy the process specifications.

process spread
The range of process operation, defined as six standard deviations.

quality characteristic
A feature of a product that describes its fitness for use, such as length, weight, taste, appearance, and reliability.

***R* chart**
A control chart for monitoring process variation.

specification (spec) limits
Limits that are imposed on a process quality characteristic and determine the product's fitness for use.

statistical process control (SPC)
The application of statistical quality control to measuring and analyzing the variation found in processes.

Total Quality Management (TQM)
A customer-focused management strategy that emphasizes a respect for employees and a constant effort at improving product or service quality.

variables data
Data obtained when a record is mad eof an actual measured quality characteristic, such as weight.

$\overline{X}$ **chart**
A control chart for monitoring process location (process average).

12.11 Solution to Self-Test Problems

Solution to Self-test Problem 12.8.1.

a. We need some calculations to use the procedure outlined earlier for constructing the chart. These are shown in Table 12.10.1.

	Diameter in (mm)						
Hour #	1	2	3	4	5	*X*-bar	Range
1	20.6	20.4	21.8	21.7	21.1	21.12	1.4
2	21.7	20.8	21.8	21.7	21.3	21.46	1
3	20.8	20.4	20.9	21.3	20.3	20.74	1
4	21	21.2	21.9	22	20.8	21.38	1.2
5	21.7	21.3	20.4	21.8	21.4	21.32	1.4
6	21.3	21.5	21.3	21.3	21.2	21.32	0.3
7	21.4	21.3	21.5	21.2	21	21.28	0.5
8	21.4	21.2	21.1	21.4	21.1	21.24	0.3
9	21.4	21.3	21.5	21.2	21.2	21.32	0.3
10	21.2	21.3	21.2	21.3	21.4	21.28	0.2
					X-double bar	21.246	7.6
						R-bar	0.76

12.10.1. Calculations for *X*-bar and *R*-chart construction.

$$\text{UCL} = \overline{\overline{X}} + 3\frac{\left(\overline{R}/d_2\right)}{\sqrt{n}} = 21.246 + 3\frac{(0.76/2.326)}{\sqrt{5}} = 21.684$$

$$\text{LCL} = \overline{\overline{X}} - 3\frac{\left(\overline{R}/d_2\right)}{\sqrt{n}} = 21.246 - 3\frac{(0.76/2.326)}{\sqrt{5}} = 20.807$$

$$\text{Centerline}: 21.246$$

b. *R*-Chart calculations.

$$\text{UCL} = D_4\overline{R} = 2.114*(0.76) = 1.60664$$

$$\text{LCL} = D_3\overline{R} = 0*(0.76) = 0.$$

$$\text{Centerline} = 0.76$$

Solution to Self-test Problem 12.8.2

a. First we will calculate the *X*-bar and R of the samples and show it in Table 12.10.2.

	Diameter in (mm)						
Hour #	1	2	3	4	5	*X*-bar	Range
11	21.9	21.1	20.3	21.6	22.4	21.46	2.1
12	19.5	22.4	19.7	21.3	21.9	20.96	2.9

12.10.2. The new *X*-bar and *R* values.

From self-test Problem 12.8.1:
X-bar Chart: UCL = 21.684; LCL = 20.807.
The two points are within the UCL and LCL.

R-Chart: UCL = 1.606; LCL = 0.0.
The samples have 2.1 and 2.9 as their range. They are clearly out of control. You should look for assignable causes.

Solution to Self-test Problem 12.8.3.

$$\text{UCL} = 0.0255 + 3\sqrt{\frac{0.0255.(1-0.0255)}{200}} = 0.05894$$

$$\text{LCL} = 0.0255 - 3\sqrt{\frac{0.0255.(1-0.0255)}{200}} = 0.0 \text{ (Note: LCL if negative, is rounded to 0.}$$

$$\text{Centerline} = 0.0255$$

Solution to Self-test Problem 12.8.4.

Calculations of process capability:

Carlos' Process:
One of the assumptions of C_p is the process is centered within specifications. It is not quite satisfied. Let us still calculate:

$$C_p = \frac{122-118}{6(0.3)} = 2.222$$

Since C_p is more than 1.33, the process capability is good.
C_{pk} = Min(((119 - 118)/3.(0.3)),((122 - 119)/3.(0.3))
= Min (1.11,3.333)
= 1.111

According to this result, it is adequate.

The number of non-conforming parts produced per million (using Table 12.4 of your text) will be between 96 and 2700, closer to 2700.

Vikram's Process:
One of the assumptions of C_p is the process is centered within specifications. This is well centered. So let us look carefully at C_p .

$$C_p = \frac{122 - 118}{6(0.4)} = 1.666$$

Since C_p is more than 1.33, the process capability is good.
C_{pk} = Min(((120 - 118)/3.(0.4)),((122 - 120)/3.(0.4))
= Min (1.666,1.666)
= 1.666
According to this result, it is good.

The number of non-conforming parts produced per million (using Table 12.4 of your text) will be less than 6.8.

a. Both processes can meet your needs, as detailed above.
b. Vikram's process is centered well and it meets the specifications and produces lot less non-conforming parts. Hence, one could argue that it is the better process.
c. Even though Vikram is a costlier supplier, you should go with Vikram, considering the quality.
d. However, if Carlos can center his process at the target (120), his standard deviation being smaller will produce even a better product. He is also cheaper. Hence he should be preferred.

Discussion: The main point is that variability and ability to center the process on target are keys to improving quality.

Answers to Multiple Choice Questions

Question #	Answer	Question #	Answer	Question #	Answer
1	a	6	a	11	b
2	a	7	e	12	b
3	b	8	c	13	b
4	b	9	a	14	a
5	a	10	e	15	b

CHAPTER 13 APPLICATIONS OF THE CHI-SQUARE STATISTIC

Chapter Overview and Learning Objectives

This chapter discusses applications of the chi-square distribution for testing goodness of fit and independence. The goodness of fit test for the multinomial situation as well as the test for determining whether a set of sample data is from a particular distribution is described. The test of independence is extended to cover the test of homogeneity for several populations. At the completion of this chapter, the student should be able to:

1. Carry out a goodness of fit test for the multinomial situation or a particular distributional form (such as binomial, Poisson, or normal).
2. Set up and complete a test of hypothesis for independence or homogeneity.

Chapter Outline

13.1 Chi-Square Goodness of Fit Tests
13.2 Chi-Square Test of Independence
13.3 Self-Test Problems
13.4 Glossary
13.5 Solution to Self-Test Problems

13.1 Chi-Square Goodness of Fit Tests

Discussion: The purpose of these tests is to check whether a given set of data can be reasonably presumed to come from a known distribution.

Binomial distribution

Suppose that Vikram and Jones (your neighbors who are currently in the ninth grade) are quarrelling about whether an old coin they picked up in the park during a Lacrosse game is Fair. That is, will both sides (H and T) show up with equal frequency? You jump is to use your statistics knowledge to settle the dispute. In that process, you will learn about Chi-Square distribution.

Review Problem 13.1.1

Vikram and Jones are quarrelling about whether an old coin they picked up in the park during a Lacrosse game is Fair. That is, if they toss it many times, will both sides (H and T) show up with equal frequency? They tossed it 200 times, by taking turns (to be fair) and found the results shown in Table 13.1.2.

Use appropriate tests to resolve the dispute, using a significance level of 0.05.

Outcome	Observed Frequency
H	110
T	90

Table 13.1.2. Calculations of Chi-Square

Solution

Basically, if the coin were fair, they would have obtained something close to 100 H's and 100 T's. Clearly, they do not have to be exactly 100 in order to deem the coin as fair. How far off can it be and still be considered a "Fair" coin. We use the fact that the test statistic

$$\chi^2 = \sum_{i=1}^{c} \left(\frac{(O_i - E_i)^2}{E_i} \right) \quad \text{where } c \text{ is the number of categories}$$

follows the Chi-Square distribution with c-1 degrees of freedom. Given the significance level and a table of the Chi-Square distribution, we can allocate reject and fail to reject regions and make a conclusion.

Note: All of Chi-Square distribution will be non-negative and all calculated Chi-Square test statistics would be non-negative. Tests are all two-sided, in the sense of data coming from a particular distribution with specific parameters, or not coming from that distribution with those specific parameters. However, the Reject H_0 area is always on the right tail of the distribution.

Step 1: H_0: The coin is Fair; P(H) = 0.5 and P(T) = 0.5
H_1: Coin is not Fair.

Step 2: Test statistic is:

$$\chi^2 = \sum_{i=1}^{c} \left(\frac{(O_i - E_i)^2}{E_i} \right) \quad \text{where } c \text{ is the number of categories}$$

Step 3: If the calculated $\chi^2 > 3.8415$ (look up in Table A.6 with degrees of freedom = 1, and in the column corresponding to right tail value of 0.05, which is the level of significance.) Reject H_0. Otherwise, Fail to Reject H_0.

Step 4:

Outcome	Observed Number of Observations	Expected Number of Observations	(Obs. - Exp.)^2	(Obs.-Exp.)^2/Exp
H	110	100	100	1
T	90	100	100	1
Total				2

Table 13.1.2. Calculations of Chi-Square

Step 5: Since the calculated Chi-Square is in the Fail to Reject H_0 range, there is no evidence to conclude that the coin is not fair.

Multinomial Distribution

Multinomial distributions have several categories, with each category having a certain expected proportion. We can observe the outcome from a supposed multinomial process and use Chi-Square test to reject or fail to reject H_0.

Review Problem 13.1.2.

A marketing consultant to a large grocery chain proposed that he has developed a program by which he could modify the profile of customers shopping at their chain. At the end of the program, the following will be the expected profile.

Type of Shopper	% (Expected)
Women with Children	20
Men with Children	15
Women alone	40
Men alone	20
Couple	5
Total	100

Table 13.1.3. "Guaranteed" Shopper Profile

The chain's management is impressed, since the consultant gave a money back guarantee if the profile after the program did not match the profile in Table 13.1.3. They agreed to test at a significance level of 0.05. The chain instituted the consultant's program for a few months and observed the following based on a random sample of 400 customers. Use Chi-Square test to check whether to approve the consulting fees.

Type of Shopper	Observed number
Women with Children	63
Men with Children	71
Women alone	170
Men alone	65
Couple	31
Total	400

Table 13.1.4. Observed Shopper Profile

Solution

Step 1: H_0: The observed shopper profile comes from the multinomial distribution of Table 13.1.4.

H_1: The observed shopper profile does not come from the multinomial distribution of Table 13.1.4.

Step 2: Test statistic is:

$$\chi^2 = \sum_{i=1}^{5}\left(\frac{(O_i - E_i)^2}{E_i}\right) \text{ where 5 is the number of categories}$$

Step 3: If the calculated χ^2 > 9.4877 (look up in Table A.6 with degrees of freedom = 5-1, and in the column corresponding to right tail value of 0.05, which is the level of significance.) Reject H_0. Otherwise, Fail to Reject H_0.

Step 4: Calculation of Chi-Square values:

Type of Shopper	Observed Number	Expected %	Expected Number	Chi-Square Value
Women with Children	63	20	80	3.613
Men with Children	71	15	60	2.017
Women alone	170	40	160	0.625
Men alone	65	20	80	2.813
Couple	31	5	20	6.05
Total	400	100	400	15.117

Table 13.1.5. Table of Chi-Square Calculations

Step 5: Since calculated Chi-Square value, 15.117, falls in the reject H_0 region, we reject the null hypothesis. We conclude that the consultant has not achieved what he guaranteed in terms of shopper profile. Hence, he should return his fee.

General Note:

- This procedure can be used for any type of distribution, like Normal, Poisson, and so on provided we can make discrete categories from the underlying distribution and thus make it into a multinomial distribution.
- The expected number of observations must be at least 5 for each category. Otherwise, combine the adjacent categories to make the expected values in each category at least 5.
- If we estimate the parameters of the distribution from the data, (e.g. estimating the mean and standard deviation for a normal distribution or estimating the mean rate for Poisson) you would lose one degrees of freedom for each parameter estimated.

13.2 Chi-Square Tests for Independence

Discussion: Businesses collect data constantly for various purposes. Marketing applications is one major destination for collected data. Suppose that you are a Car dealer. You want to strengthen your negotiating position as well as be "Fair" to your customers and be efficient with your time. Using the Chi-Square test for independence, you can answer questions like: Are age and amount reduced independent? Essentially, we will calculate some expected number of frequencies in all these cross tabulation cells under the assumption that "age and amount reduced are independent" and see whether the expected and observed values are "close enough," thus concluding that the two factors are indeed independent.

Review Problem 13.2.1.

Suppose that you are a major car dealer and you have analyzed the profiles and negotiating behavior of recent customers, and presented it in Table 13.2.1. You want to test whether the age and amount offer is reduced are independent. Use 0.10 as the significance level.

Age of the Customer	Amount Customer Reduced from the Dealer's First Offer.			
	0-500	500-1000	100-1500	>1500
< 23	80	60	50	100
23-30	50	60	120	170
30-40	40	90	100	100
40-60	70	80	50	90
> 60	30	40	70	50

Table 13.2.1. Data on Customers

Solution

Step 1: H_0: The age and amount reduced are independent.
H_1: The age and amount reduced are not independent

Step 2: Test statistic is:

$$\chi^2 = \sum \frac{(O-E)^2}{E}$$

with (c-1)(r-1) degrees of freedom where c is the number of columns and r is the number of rows.

Step 3: If the calculated $\chi^2 > 18.54$ (look up in Table A.6 with degrees of freedom = 12, and in the column corresponding to right-tail value of 0.10, which is the level of significance.) Reject H_0. Otherwise, Fail to Reject H_0.

Step 4: Calculation of Chi-Square values: This involves several the following steps.

- Assume H_0 is true (a common assumption for all hypothesis testing, as you may recall)
- Calculate the row and column totals (Table 13.2.2.)

Age of the customer	Amount the customer reduced from the Dealer's first offer.				
	0-500	500-1000	100-1500	>1500	Marginal Totals
<23	80	60	50	100	290
23-30	50	60	120	170	400
30-40	40	90	100	100	330
40-60	70	80	50	90	290
>60	30	40	70	50	190
Marginal Totals	270	330	390	510	1500

Table 13.2.2. Observed values with Column and Row Totals

- Calculate the expected frequencies in the cells using the formula:
  Expected frequency = ((row total)(column total))/(grand total). (Table 13.2.3)

- Calculate the Chi-Square value using the $\chi^2 = \sum \frac{(O-E)^2}{E}$ (Table 13.2.4)

Age of the Customer	Amount the Customer Reduced from the Dealer's First Offer.				
	0-500	500-1000	100-1500	>1500	Marginal Totals
< 23	(290)(270)/1500 = 52.2	63.8	75.4	98.6	290
23-30	72	88	104	136	400
30-40	59.4	72.6	85.8	112.2	330
40-60	52.2	63.8	75.4	98.6	290
> 60	34.2	41.8	49.4	64.6	190
Marginal Totals	270	330	390	510	1500

Table 13.2.3. Expected values

Age of the customer	Amount the Customer Reduced from the Dealer's First Offer			
	0-500	500-1000	100-1500	> 1500
< 23	$((80-52.2)^2/52.2)$ = 14.805	0.226	8.556	0.02
23-30	6.722	8.909	2.462	8.5
30-40	6.336	4.170	2.350	1.327
40-60	6.070	4.113	8.556	0.750
> 60	0.516	0.078	8.590	3.300

Table 13.2.4. Each element of the Chi-Square expression

Chi-Square value (sum of all the numbers in Table 13.2.4.) is 96.404

Step 5. Conclude. Since the calculated Chi-Square value (96.404) falls in the Reject H_0 region, you conclude that there is not enough evidence of independence of age and amount reduced.

Tests of Homogeneity

If instead of having totally random sample, we have a predetermined number of observations to be collected in each column (or for that matter in each row), then we can test whether columns of data are homogeneous. For example, two columns may represent female and male. The test is whether they have homogeneous opinion on something. The Null Hypothesis is: The columns are homogeneous and the Alternate Hypothesis is that the columns are not homogenous. The calculations, degrees of freedom, and all other things are same and hence can easily be calculated like the previous examples.

13.3 Self-Test Problems

Self-Test Problem 13.3.1.

Test whether the following table of frequencies of income is from a population, which follows Normal distribution with mean 30,000 and standard deviation 1000. The data values are given such that each range represents the noted segments of the normal distribution. Test for normality using a 0.05 level of significance.

Range ($)	Observed Frequency
< 27000	2
27000 - 28000	18
28000 - 29000	123
29000 -30000	345
30000 - 31000	352
31000 - 32000	135
32000 - 33000	22
> 33000	3

Table 13.3.1. Data of Incomes

Self-Test Problem 13.3.2.

Test whether the following set of random numbers are truly random? Use five uniform intervals and the following set of 100 one-digit random numbers for testing. Use a significance level of 0.05.

Random numbers:

4 2 7 1 1 0 8 1 8 2 7 5 9 9 7 7 9 8 6 6 5 8 0 9 5
8 3 3 1 9 8 0 2 9 5 7 9 7 4 1 7 4 1 7 4 5 9 9 8 4
3 7 9 9 4 8 7 3 9 0 9 3 5 3 1 6 8 4 6 3 9 5 2 0 9
8 6 5 1 4 4 9 1 9 9 5 1 8 9 3 3 9 4 3 4 6 9 1 1 4

Self-Test Problem 13.3.3.

200 men were selected at random from various levels of management and interviewed about their concern about economic issues. The response of each person was tallied as follows. Using 0.01 for the level of significance, test whether the concern level and management level are independent.

	No concern	Some concern	Great concern
Top Mgmt.	15	13	12
Middle Mgmt.	20	19	21
Supervisor	7	7	6
Group Leader	28	21	31

Table 13.3.6. Cross Tabulation of Management Level and Concern

Multiple Choice Questions

The first 3 Questions refer to the following problem.

The safety director of SAFETOWN believes that the distribution of accidents is uniform over time of the day. To test this, he took samples at random from the file of minor accidents and classified them according to the time the accident took place. Use a 0.5 level of significance, and answer the following questions.

Time of the Day	Number of Accidents (Observed)	Expected Frequency: (You have to calculate)
8:00 – 9:00	6	
9:00 - 10:00	8	
10:00 – 11:00	12	
11:00 - 12:00	16	
12:00 – 1:00	10	
1:00 - 2:00	7	
2:00 – 4:00	21	
4:00 – 6:00	20	
Total frequency	100	

Table 1: Data On Accident Frequencies

1. Assuming uniform accidents over time, what will the expected frequencies in the respective intervals:
   a. 2.5 in each of the intervals
   b. 10 in each interval
   c. 20 in each interval
   d. 10, 10, 10, 10, 10, 10, 20, 20
   e. None of the above
2. A correct statement of the decision rule for this problem is
   a. Reject *Ho* if χ^2 is greater than 6.846
   b. Reject *Ho* if χ^2 is less than 9.488
   c. Accept *Ho* if χ^2 is less than –2.706
   d. Reject *Ho* if χ^2 is greater than 9.488
   e. None of the above
3. The computed value of the test statistic is
   a. t_2 is equal to 6.95
   b. χ^2 is equal to –6.95
   c. χ^2 is equal to 48.2
   d. χ^2 is equal to 6.95
   e. None of the above
4. If the observed frequencies exactly match the expected frequencies in a chi-square test, the value of the chi-square statistic would be:
   a. Zero
   b. A large positive value
   c. A large negative value
   d. A small positive value
   e. Cannot tell

5. If you want to tilt the test statistic of a chi-square test, so as to ensure that the Null hypothesis is rejected, you should try to
   a. Make the observed as close to the expected as possible
   b. Make the observed much higher than the expected
   c. observed much smaller than the expected
   d. either (b) or (c) or some values higher some values lower
6. In a chi-square test, if the null hypothesis is rejected at a significance level of 0.10, then for the same data, at a 0.05 significance level, the null hypothesis will ______ be rejected.
   a. Sometimes
   b. Always
   c. Never
7. In testing whether a data comes from a normal distribution with mean 300 and standard deviation 20, I have divided the distribution into 6 intervals. ($-\infty$ to 300-2(20), 260 to 280, 280 to 300, 300 to 320, 320 to 340, and more than 340.) If the total sample size is 1500, what will be the expected frequency for the interval 260 to 280?
   a. 250
   b. 204
   c. 512
   d. 408
   e. 34

Answer questions 8-12 based on the following problem.

The safety director of SAFETOWN believes that the distribution of accidents is uniform over time of the day. To test this, he took samples at random from the file of minor accidents and classified them according to the time the accident took place. Use 0.5 level of significance.

Time of Day	Number of Accidents
8:00 – 10:00	12
10:00 – 12:00	28
12:00 – 2:00	15
2:00 – 4:00	25
4:00 – 6:00	20

8. The null and alternate hypothesis are:
   a. *Ho*: The distribution of accidents is uniform, i.e., the number of accidents in each period is the same.
      H_1: The distribution is not uniform.
   b. *Ho*: The number of accidents increases from 8:00 a.m. onwards.
      H_1: The number of accidents remains the same in all periods.
   c. *Ho*: $\mu_1 = \mu_2$
      H_1: $\mu_1 \neq \mu_2$
   d. *Ho*: Time of day and number of accidents are related.
      H_1: Time of day is negatively correlated with number of accidents.
   e. None of the above.
9. The appropriate test to use for this problem is
   a. Chi-squared test for independence of attributes
   b. Kruskal-Wallis Test
   c. Chi-squared test of goodness of fit
   d. None of the above

10. A correct statement of the decision rule for this problem is

a. Reject *Ho* if χ^2 is greater than 6.846
b. Reject *Ho* if χ^2 is less than 9.488
c. Fail to reject *Ho* if χ^2 is less than –2.706
d. Reject *Ho* if χ^2 is greater than 9.488
e. None of the above

11. The computed value of the test statistic is
    a. t_2 is equal to 4.92
    b. χ^2 is equal to +8.9
    c. χ^2 is equal to 48.2
    d. *H* is equal to 9.2
    e. None of the above
12. The correct decision for this problem is
    a. Reject the null hypothesis and accept the alternative hypothesis
    b. Fail to reject the null hypothesis
    c. Reject both null and alternative hypotheses
    d. All of the above

13.4 Glossary

binomial situation
A situation characterized by n independent trials, each having two outcomes with probabilities p_1 and p_2. These probabilities sum to one and remain the same on each trial.

contingency table
A table summarizing a population, according to two classifications (such as gender and college major).

expected values
Values calculated under the assumption that the null hypothesis is true.

goodness-of-fit test
An application of the chi-square statistic that can be used to test a specified set of binomial parameters, set of multinomial parameters, or distributional form.

multinomial situation
A situation characterized by n independent trials, each having k > 2 possible outcomes. The k probabilities corresponding to each outcome (p_1, p_2, AAA, p_k) sum to one and remain the same on each trial.

observed values
Values observed for each cell or category; these values are used, along with the corresponding expected values, to derive the chi-square test statistic.

test of homogeneity
A chi-square test using fixed row or column totals. The analysis procedure uses the same test statistic as the test of independence.

test of independence
An application of the chi-square statistic, used to test whether two classifications (such as gender and college major) are independent.

13. 5 Solution to Self-Test Problems

Solution to Self-Test Problem 13.3.1.

Step 1: H_0: The observed data comes from a Normal distribution with Mean = 30000 and standard deviation = 1000.

H_1: The observed data does not come from such a Normal distribution with Mean = 30000 and standard deviation = 1000.

Step 2: Test statistic is: The trick in this problem is to discretize the normal distribution into c categories and then apply the chi-square goodness of fit rules. The data provides a hint that is elaborated in the Step 4.

Step 3: If the calculated χ^2 > 11.0705 (look up in Table A.6 with degrees of freedom = 6-1, and in the column corresponding to right tail value of 0.05, which is the level of significance.) Reject H_0. Otherwise, Fail to Reject H_0.

Step 4: Calculation of Chi-Square values: The first step is to recognize that the categories used for the income are not random. Usually, you may be given raw data from which you can classify the data as shown in Table 13.3.1. In this case, the classification is done for you. You just need to recognize it, find the corresponding probabilities and use the total frequency times probability to find the expected frequency as shown in Table 13.5.1. Next, we conjoin categories to eliminate the low frequencies (< 5) to get the Table 13.5.2.

Normal distribution with Mean (μ) = 30000 and standard deviation (σ) = 1000	Income Category ($)	Probability	Expected Freq. = Probability x Total Frequency
$< \mu - 3\sigma$	< 27,000	0.0013	1.3
$\mu - 3\sigma$ to $\mu - 2\sigma$	27000-28000	0.0215	21.5
$\mu - 2\sigma$ to $\mu - 1\sigma$	28000-29000	0.1359	135.9
$\mu - 1\sigma$ to μ	29000-30000	0.3413	341.3
μ to $\mu + 1\sigma$	30000-31000	0.3413	341.3
$\mu + 1\sigma$ to $\mu + 2\sigma$	31000-32000	0.1359	135.9
$\mu + 2\sigma$ to $\mu + 3\sigma$	32000-33000	0.0215	21.5
$> \mu + 3\sigma$	> 33000	0.0013	1.3

Table 13.5.1. Expected frequencies.

Income Category	Obs. Freq	Exp.Freq	$(\text{Obs - Exp})^2/\text{Exp}$
< 28000	20	22.8	0.343
28000-29000	123	135.9	1.225
29000-30000	345	341.3	0.040
30000-31000	352	341.3	0.335
31000-32000	135	135.9	0.006
> 32000	25	22.8	0.212
		Chi-Square	2.162

Table 13.5.2. Chi-Square Calculations

The Chi-Square value = 2.16.

Step 5: Conclusion. We fail to reject the null hypothesis that the data comes from normal with mean = 30000 and standard deviation = 1000.

Solution to Self-test Problem 13.3.2.

Step 1: H_0: The observed data are random in the interval 0 to 9
H_1: The observed data are not random in the interval 0 to 9.

Step 2: Test statistic is: $\chi^2 = \sum_{i=1}^{c} \left(\frac{(O_i - E_i)^2}{E_i} \right)$ where c is the number of categories

Step 3: It is assumed that we are going to use 5 categories to classify the data. If the calculated χ^2 > 9.4877 (Found in Table A.6 with degrees of freedom = 5 - 1, and in the column corresponding to right-tail value of 0.05, which is the level of significance.) Reject H_0. Otherwise, Fail to Reject H_0.

Step 4: Calculation of Chi-Square values. We classify the data into 5 intervals.

Intervals	Obs. Freq.	Exp. Freq
0-1	17	20
2-3	14	20
4-5	20	20
6-7	16	20
8-9	33	20

Table 13.5.3. Data on expected and observed frequencies

Obs.	Exp.	$(O-E)^2$	$(O-E)^2/E$
17	20	9	0.45
14	20	36	1.8
20	20	0	0
16	20	16	0.8
33	20	169	8.45
			11.5

Table 13.5.4. Chi-Square Calculations

Chi-Square = 11.5

Critical value (degrees of freedom = 5-1) = 9.488

Step 5: Since the test statistic is more than the critical value, reject the null hypothesis. That is the data is not uniform, and hence not random

Solution to Self-Test Problem 13.3.3.

Step 1: H_0: The management level and concern level are independent.
H_1: The management level and concern level are not independent

Step 2: Test statistic is:

$$\chi^2 = \sum \frac{(O-E)^2}{E}$$ with (c-1) (r-1) degrees of freedom where c is the number of column and r is the number of rows.

Step 3: If the calculated $\chi^2 > 16.8119$, Reject H_0. Otherwise, Fail to Reject H_0. (Degrees of freedom = (c-1)(r-1) = (3-1)(4-1) = 6, where c is the number of columns of data (not counting the totals column) and r is the number of rows, not counting the totals column. Looking at the chi-square table, we get 16.8119.).

Step 4: Calculation of Chi-Square values. This involves several steps.
Assuming H_0 is true (a common assumption for all hypothesis testing, as you may recall)

- Calculate the row and column totals (Table 13.5.5.)
- Calculate the expected frequencies in the cells using the formula:
  Expected frequency = (row total)(column total)/(grand total). (Table 13.5.6.)
- Calculate the Chi-Square value using the $\chi^2 = \sum \frac{(O-E)^2}{E}$ (Table 13.5.7.)

	No concern	Some concern	Great concern	Totals
Top Mgmt.	15	13	12	40
Middle Mgmt.	20	19	21	60
Supervisor	7	7	6	20
Group Leader	28	21	31	80
Totals	70	60	70	200

Table 13.5.5. Observed Frequencies with Row and Column Totals

	No concern	Some concern	Great concern	Totals
Top Mgmt.	14	12	14	40
Middle Mgmt.	21	18	21	60
Supervisor	7	6	7	20
Group Leader	28	24	28	80
Totals	70	60	70	200

Table 13.5.6. Expected Frequencies with Row and Column Totals

Using 0.01 level of significance and degrees of freedom of 6, the critical value is 16.8119. (For degrees of freedom = (c-1)(r-1) = (3-1)(4-1) = 6, where c is the number of columns of data, not counting the totals column, and r is the number of rows, not counting the totals column. Looking at the chi-square table, we get 16.8119.)

	No concern	Some concern	Great concern	
Top Mgmt.	0.071	0.083	0.286	
Middle Mgmt.	0.048	0.056	0	
Supervisor	0	0.167	0.143	
Group Leader	0	0.375	0.321	
			Chi-Square	1.55

Table 13.5.7. Chi-square calculations Σ((Obs. freq.-Exp. Freq.)^2/Exp. Freq) = 1.55.

The test statistic value using the usual calculations is 1.55.

Step 5: Conclusion. Fail to reject the null hypothesis. There is not enough evidence to reject the independence of management level and concern.

Answers (with Discussion) to Multiple Choice Questions

Question #	Answer
1	Since the time interval is 8:00 to 6:00, that is 10 hours, and the total frequency is 100, the rate per hour is 100/10 = 10 per hour. Since uniform the expected frequency must be proportional to the length of the time interval. Based on this, the frequencies must be as given in (d).
2	First find the critical value in the chi-square table with degrees of freedom (# of rows -1) = (8-1) = 7; for 0.05 significance level of the value of chi-square that makes the right tail equal to 0.05 is, 20.2777. Hence none of the above.
3	(see table below)

Class interval	Freq	Exp Freq	(Obs Freq. - Exp. Freq)^2/Exp.Freq.
8:00 - 9:00	6	10	1.6
9:00 - 10:00	8	10	0.4
10:00 - 11:00	12	10	0.4
11:00 - 12:00	16	10	3.6
12:00 - 1:00	10	10	0
1:00 - 2:00	7	10	0.9
2:00 - 4:00	21	20	0.05
4:00 - 6:00	20	20	0
			6.95

Observed and expected frequencies
Calculated chi-square is 6.95 and hence (d).

4	Answer: When they match, Obs. Freq - Exp. Freq = 0, Hence the test statistic will be 0. (a).
5	Since the test statistic is always positive and as the absolute value of the (observed-expected) increases, the numerical value of the test statistic will increase, resulting in possible rejection of the null hypothesis. (d)
6	The critical value for 0.10 level for a given degrees of freedom will always be smaller than the critical value for 0.05 level. Hence, if we reject at 0.10 level, then at 0.05 level, we may reject the null hypothesis or we may not. So sometimes (a) is the answer.
7	This is just a straightforward process of dividing the normal distribution into 6 or 8 sections, finding the probability for each section using the Z table and the finding the expected frequency by multiplying the probability by total frequency.

Interval	Corresponding Z-value	Probability from the Table	Expected frequency
$-\infty$ to 260	$-\infty$ to (260-300)/20 = -2	0.5-0.4772 = 0.0228	1500(0.0228) = 34.2
260 to 280	(260-300)/20 = -2 to (280-300)/20 = -1	0.4772-0.3413 = .1359	1500(0.1359) = 203.86
280 to 300	(280-300)/20 = -1 to (300-300)/20 = 0	0.3413	1500(0.3413) = 511.95
300 to 320	(300-300)/20 = 0 to (320-300)/20 = 1	0.3413	1500(0.3413) = 511.95
320 to 340	((320-300)/20 = 1 to (340-300)/20 = 2	0.1359	1500(0.1359) = 203.86
340 to ∞	(340-300)/20 = 2 to ∞	0.0228	1500(0.0228) = 34.2

For 260 to 280, the expected frequency is 203.86 rounded to 204. (b) Expected frequencies corresponding to the normal distribution

8	a
9	c
10	d
11	b
12	b

CHAPTER 14 CORRELATION AND SIMPLE LINEAR REGRESSION

Chapter Overview and Learning Objectives

The concepts of linear regression and correlation are introduced in this chapter. Formulas are motivated and discussed for computing the sample correlation and least squares line. Hypothesis testing for a significant sample slope and/or correlation are described along with the assumptions behind the use of such tests. Confidence intervals for a mean value of the dependent variable and prediction intervals for individual values of the dependent variable are discussed. Procedures for detecting influential sample observations and observations that have unusually large or small values of the independent variable (*X*) or dependent variable (*Y*) are explained. At the completion of the material, the student should be able to:

1. Calculate the sample covariance and correlation.
2. Determine the least squares line through a set of sample bivariate data.
3. Measure and test the strength of the linear model.
4. Construct confidence and prediction intervals using a calculator or a computer package such as Excel, SPSS, or MINITAB.
5. Be able to identify influential observations and detect outlying observations that have an unusually large or small value of the dependent or independent variable.

Chapter Outline

14.1 Bivariate Data and Correlation
14.2 The Sample Linear Regression Model
14.3 Inferences on Slope of β
14.4 Measuring the Strength of the Model
14.5 Estimation and Prediction Using the Simple Linear Model
14.6 Examining the Residuals
14.7 Self-Test Problems
14.8 Glossary
14.9 Solution to Self-Test Problems

14.1 Bivariate Data and Correlation

Each observation has two data points, which are potentially related. Examples would include: Hours worked on a course and grade, Advertisement expenditure and sales, Price and demand, investor confidence and stock index values. By convention, one of the variables is called *X* and the other called *Y*.

- **Scatter Plot**: Just a plot of *X* and *Y* on a graph. It usually helps in visualizing possible relationship (**positive or direct** meaning: as *X* increases *Y* increase and as *X* decreases *Y* decreases: **Negative or indirect** meaning: as *X* increases *Y* decreases and as *X* decreases *Y* increases: **No Relationship:** as *X* increases *Y* unchanged and as *X* decreases *Y* unchanged) between *X* and *Y*.
- **Coefficient of Correlation:** This is a formal statistical measure to capture the strength and nature of the relationship described in the scatter plot. It is only measuring linear relations. Any set of pairs of data will have a correlation measure. We have statistical test to check the strength (statistical significance) of the correlation using the 5-step procedure. Sample correlation coefficient denoted by r is given by:

$$r = \frac{\Sigma(X-\overline{X})(Y-\overline{Y})}{\sqrt{\Sigma(X-\overline{X})^2}\sqrt{(Y-\overline{Y})^2}}$$

This formula can be rewritten as follows using sum of squares notation.

$$SS_X = \Sigma(X-\overline{X})^2 = \Sigma X^2 - \frac{(\Sigma X)^2}{n} \quad \text{(Sum of squares of } X\text{)}$$

$$SS_Y = \Sigma(Y-\overline{Y})^2 = \Sigma Y^2 - \frac{(\Sigma Y)^2}{n} \quad \text{(Sum of squares of } Y\text{)}$$

$$SCP_{XY} = \Sigma(X-\overline{X})(Y-\overline{Y}) = \Sigma XY - \frac{(\Sigma X)(\Sigma Y)}{n} \quad \text{(Sum of cross-products for } XY\text{)}$$

$$r = \frac{SCP_{XY}}{\sqrt{SS_X}\sqrt{SS_Y}}$$

	Properties of Sample Correlation Coefficient (r)
1	$-1 \leq r \leq 1$;
2	Larger the $\|r\|$ stronger the linear relationship; $\|r\|$ close to 0 means poor relationship
3	$r = 1$ perfect positive or direct relationship; $r = -1$ perfect negative or indirect relationship.
4	$r > 0$ implies positive slope (**cannot** tell the magnitude of the slope) for the line connecting points in the scatter diagram $r < 0$ implies negative slope (**cannot** tell the magnitude of the slope) for the line connecting points in the scatter diagram

Review Problem 14.1.1.

Data collected from a random set of 8 students on the number of hours they put in for a course and the score they obtained in the final exam of that course is shown in Table 14.1.1.

a. Find the sample correlation coefficient between the two variables.
b. If you calculate the regression line using X as the independent variable and Y as the dependent variable, what will be sign of the slope of the regression line?
c. What can you tell about the magnitude of the slope?

X (Hours worked)	Y (Score in the final exam)
10	20
20	58
34	100
12	22
6	15
18	60
7	20
18	50

Table 14.1.1. Data on Hours Worked and Final Exam Score

Solution

a. It is easiest to do the calculations systematically as displayed in Table 14.1.2. The last row are the totals, the additional columns are self-explanatory.

	X (Hours)	Y (Score)	X^2	Y^2	XY
	10	20	100	400	200
	20	58	400	3364	1160
	34	100	1156	10000	3400
	12	22	144	484	264
	6	15	36	225	90
	18	60	324	3600	1080
	7	20	49	400	140
	18	50	324	2500	900
Totals	125	345	2533	20973	7234

Table 14.1.2. Calculations of Sum of Squares

$$\text{SS}_X = \Sigma\left(X-\overline{X}\right)^2 = \Sigma X^2 - \frac{(\Sigma X)^2}{n} = 2533 - \frac{(125)^2}{8} = 579.875$$

$$\text{SS}_Y = \Sigma\left(Y-\overline{Y}\right)^2 = \Sigma Y^2 - \frac{(\Sigma Y)^2}{n} = 20973 - \frac{(345)^2}{8} = 6094.875$$

$$\text{SCP}_{XY} = \Sigma\left(X-\overline{X}\right)\left(Y-\overline{Y}\right) = \Sigma XY - \frac{(\Sigma X)(\Sigma Y)}{n} = 7234 - \frac{(125).(345)}{8} = 1843.375$$

$$r = \frac{\text{SCP}_{XY}}{\sqrt{\text{SS}_X}\sqrt{\text{SS}_Y}} = \frac{1843.375}{\sqrt{579.875}\sqrt{6094.875}} = 0.98$$

b. The slope will be positive, since the correlation coefficient is positive.
c. You cannot tell anything about the magnitude of the slope, based on R.

Covariance and Correlation

Sample covariance is a measure, similar to variance in some sense and is related to sample correlation coefficient. It is used more extensively in Finance.

$$Cov(X,Y) = \frac{\Sigma\left(X-\overline{X}\right)\left(Y-\overline{Y}\right)}{n-1} = \frac{\text{SCP}_{XY}}{n-1}$$

Using standard deviation definitions, we can relate Cov(X,Y) and standard deviations of X and Y as well as r.

$$r = \frac{\text{cov}(X,Y)}{s_X s_Y} \text{ where } s_X = \text{standard deviation of } X = \sqrt{\frac{\text{SS}_X}{n-1}}$$

$$\text{and } s_Y = \text{standard deviation of } Y = \sqrt{\frac{\text{SS}_Y}{n-1}}$$

Least Square Line:
Least square line is the heart of linear regression. If there is a set of points, exhibiting a linear relationship, what is the best way to capture the linear relationship? Define the vertical deviation of actual Y values from the Y value corresponding to the(constructed) line for a given X value. If we somehow add up all these deviations and make them as small as possible, we might get a good line. But there is one problem. The deviations could be positive or negative. They will cancel each other. The next best thing is to square the deviations (which makes all deviations positive) and then add them up and the make it as small as possible. This is the logic behind least square line. If we define the line as:

$$\hat{Y} = b_0 + b_1 X$$

If we let d_i stand for the deviation of the ith value, then

$$d_i = Y_i - \hat{Y}_i \text{ and } d_i^2 = (Y_i - \hat{Y}_i)^2 \text{ and } \sum d_i^2 = \sum (Y_i - \hat{Y}_i)^2$$

Least square line tries to make the above right hand side as small as possible. It is an optimal procedure, in the sense there is no other line which can make the sum of squared deviations any smaller. If we have formulas for b_0 and b_1, we are done.

$$b_1 = \frac{\text{SCP}_{XY}}{\text{SS}_X} \text{ and } b_0 = \overline{Y} - b_1 \overline{X}$$

The derivation involves simple calculus, not the focus of this guide.

Review Problem 14.1.2.

Find the least square regression line for the data of Table14.1.1.

Solution
(Data from Table 14.1.2. will be used)

$$b_1 = \frac{\text{SCP}_{XY}}{\text{SS}_X} = \frac{1843.375}{579.875} = 3.179 \text{ and } b_0 = \overline{Y} - b_1 \overline{X} = \frac{345}{8} - (3.179)\frac{125}{8} = -6.547$$

The regression line is: $\hat{Y} = -6.547 + 3.179X$

Review Problem 14.1.3.

a. List the residuals for Review Problem 14.1.2.
b. Show the sum of squared residuals.
c. Discuss the meaning of the sum of squared residuals.

Solution

a. Residual is simply the $(Y_i - \hat{Y}_i)$. All details are shown in Table 14.1.3.

X (Hours)	Y (Score)	$(Y_i - \hat{Y}_i)$ = -6.547 + 3.179 X	Residual $(Y_i - \hat{Y}_i)$	Squared residuals $(Y_i - \hat{Y}_i)^2$
10	20	25.243	-5.243	27.48905
20	58	57.033	0.967	0.935089
34	100	101.539	-1.539	2.368521
12	22	31.601	-9.601	92.1792
6	15	12.527	2.473	6.115729
18	60	50.675	9.325	86.95563
7	20	15.706	4.294	18.43844
18	50	50.675	-0.675	0.455625
		Sum of squared residuals		234.9373

Table 14.1.3. Residuals

b. Sum of squared residuals = 234.9373
c. Anybody can draw a line through the scatter diagram somewhat linking *X* and *Y*. But, the least square regression procedure is optimal. Hence, nobody can draw a line, which has lower sum of squared residuals than 234.9373.

14.2 The Sample Linear Regression Model

The model: If we have data on the entire population of all students regarding the hours spent and final exam score and if we construct a regression line that may be called the population regression line. It may be represented as follows.

$$Y = \beta_0 + \beta_1 X + e$$

e is the error component. β_0 and β_1 are the unknown population parameters. The regression makes estimates of this population parameter as shown by the methods of Section 14.1.

Assumptions:

a. Mean of each error component (error in *Y* for a particular value of *X*) is zero.
b. Each error component follows an approximate normal distribution.
c. The variance of the error component is the same for each value of *X*. (also called assumption of homoscedasticity)
d. Errors are independent of each other.

Sum of Squares of Error (SSE)

$$\text{SSE} = \Sigma\left(Y - \hat{Y}\right)^2 = \text{SS}_Y - \frac{\left(\text{SCP}_{XY}\right)^2}{\text{SS}_X}$$

SSE is the sum of squared deviations. If there are lot of pairs of point, there will naturally be more deviations and hence SSE may go up. So it is normalized to find an estimate of the variance of errors as follows.

$$s^2 = \frac{\text{SSE}}{n-2} \quad \text{and} \quad s = \sqrt{\frac{\text{SSE}}{n-2}}$$

And it is an estimate of the standard deviation of errors. This will allow us to put a confidence interval around the estimate made using the sample regression line.

Review Problem 14.2.1.

Calculate s, the estimate of the standard deviation of errors for the regression line of Review Problem 14.1.3.

Solution

In Review Problem 14.1.3., the sum of squared deviations (also known as sum of squared residuals) SSE was found to be 234.9373.

$$s^2 = \frac{\text{SSE}}{n-2} = \frac{234.9373}{8-2} = 39.15 \text{ and } s = \sqrt{\frac{\text{SSE}}{n-2}} = \sqrt{\frac{234.9373}{8-2}} = 6.25$$

14.3 Inference on the Slope of β_1

Like many statistical parameters we have studied, we can conduct hypothesis tests on β_1 and also put a confidence interval for it. Just like confidence interval for μ is a function of X-bar, confidence interval for β_1 will be a function of b_1. A problem will illustrate these.

Review Problem 14.2.2.

Using the data on Review Problem 14.1.3.

a. Test the hypothesis $\beta_1 = 0$ against the hypothesis $\beta_1 \neq 0$, at a significance level of 0.10.
b. Construct a 90% confidence interval for β_1.

Solution

a. We repeat salient data from the problem referred.
Y-hat = -6.547 + 3.149 X. That is, $b_1 = 3.149$; $s = 6.25$; and $SS_X = 579.875$

Five step procedure for checking the significance of β_1.

Step 1: H_0: $\beta_1 = 0$
H_1: $\beta_1 \neq 0$
Step 2: Test statistic

$$t = \frac{b_1}{s_{b_1}} \text{ where } s_{b_1} = \frac{s}{\sqrt{SS_X}} \text{ and } (n-2) \text{ degrees of freedom}$$

Step 3: For (8-2) degrees of freedom t-distribution, two-sided hypothesis test, at a level of significance of 0.10, the critical values are: +1.943 and -1.943. If the calculated t falls between -1.943 and +1.943, you fail to reject H_0. Otherwise, reject H_0.
Step 4: Calculate the value of the test statistic.

$$s_{b_1} = \frac{s}{\sqrt{SS_X}} = \frac{6.25}{\sqrt{579.875}} = 0.259$$

$$t = \frac{b_1}{s_{b_1}} = \frac{3.149}{0.259} = 12.15$$

Step 5: Since the calculated value of t falls in the reject H_0 region, we reject H_0 and conclude that there is enough evidence to show that the coefficient of X is significantly different from 0.

b. Confidence interval for β_1: $\left[b_1 - t_{\beta/2,n-2}\left(s_{b_1}\right),\ b_1 + t_{\beta/2,n-2}\left(s_{b_1}\right)\right]$

$t = 1.943$

Confidence interval $\left[3.149 - 1.943(0.259), 3.149 + 1.943(0.259)\right]$, or $[2.645, 3.652]$

14.4. Measuring the Strength of the Model

How good is a regression line?

1. Is β_1 significant? If yes, the model is strong.
2. Is sample correlation coefficient (r) sufficiently strong to reject the null hypothesis $\rho = 0$ significant? There is 5-step procedure using t-statistic

   $$t = \frac{r}{\sqrt{\frac{1-r^2}{n-2}}}$$

   with (n-2) degrees of freedom In this test, we check the underlying population correlation coefficient denote as ρ, using hypothesis: $\rho = 0$ against $\rho \neq 0$. If we reject the null hypothesis, then the line is significant.
3. If r^2, the coefficient of determination, which is also equal to square of correlation coefficient, is high, then the model is significant. r^2 is also measure of how much the variation in the dependent variable is explained by changes in the independent variable. $r^2 = 1 - (SSE/SS_Y)$.
4. Higher the SSE, other things remaining the same, lower will be r^2, and less powerful will be the model.

   Total Variation:

   SS(total) = SS(factor) + SS(Error)

   $$\Sigma\left(y-\bar{y}\right)^2 = \Sigma\left(\hat{y}-\bar{y}\right)^2 + \Sigma\left(y-\hat{y}\right)^2$$

The LHS of the above expression is interpreted as: Why is *y* different from average of *y*? A measure of this is the sum of squares is called SS(total). The first of the two RHS expressions is *Y*-hat is different from *y*-bar because of changes in *X* and the second expression says, *y* is different from *y*-hat because of errors.

Using new terminology, SS(total) = SS(factor) + SS(Error), may be written as:

$SS_Y = SSR + SSE$, thus giving alternate names for SS(total), SS(factor) and SS(error).

14.5 Estimation and Prediction Using the Simple Linear Model:

There are two types of confidence intervals that may be used. Using the Review Problem 14.1.2. "hours worked" and "final exam score" , two questions can be asked:

1. What is the confidence interval for the average final exam score for an effort level of $X = 30$ hours?
2. What is the confidence interval for the score of an individual who has put in $X = 30$ hours?

Clearly interval for (1) above will be narrower than interval for (2) above.

Confidence interval formulas:
What is the confidence interval for the average final exam score for an effort level of $X_0 = 30$ hours?

$$\hat{Y} - t_{\alpha/2,(n-2)} \cdot s \cdot \sqrt{\frac{1}{n} + \frac{\left(X_0 - \overline{X}\right)^2}{SS_X}} \text{ to } \hat{Y} + t_{\alpha/2,(n-2)} \cdot s \cdot \sqrt{\frac{1}{n} + \frac{\left(X_0 - \overline{X}\right)^2}{SS_X}}$$

What is the confidence interval for the score of an individual who has put in $X_0 = 30$ hours?

$$\hat{Y} - t_{\alpha/2,(n-2)} \cdot s \cdot \sqrt{1 + \frac{1}{n} + \frac{\left(X_0 - \overline{X}\right)^2}{SS_X}} \text{ to } \hat{Y} + t_{\alpha/2,(n-2)} \cdot s \cdot \sqrt{1 + \frac{1}{n} + \frac{\left(X_0 - \overline{X}\right)^2}{SS_X}}$$

Review Problem 14.5.1.

a. What is the 90 % confidence interval for the average final exam score for an effort level of $X_0 = 30$ hours?
b. What is the 90% confidence interval for the score of an individual who has put in $X_0 = 30$ hours?

Solution

a. First we find the Y-hat for $X_0 = 30$, using the regression equation:
   Y-hat = -6.547+3.179 X
   = -6.547 + 3.179(30)
   = 88.823
   $t = 1.943$ (.05 right tail and 6 degrees of freedom)
   $s = 6.25$ (from previous calculations in Review Problem 14.2.1.)
   $X_0 = 30$
   X-bar = (125/8) = 15.625
   $n = 8$
   $SS_X = 579.875$
   Now we are ready to substitute and find the confidence interval

$$88.823-1.943.(6.25).\sqrt{\frac{1}{8}+\frac{(30-15.625)^2}{579.875}} \text{ to } 88.823+1.943.(6.25).\sqrt{\frac{1}{8}+\frac{(30-15.625)^2}{579.875}}$$

simplifies to [80.39, 97.25]

b.

$$88.823-1.943.(6.25).\sqrt{1+\frac{1}{8}+\frac{(30-15.625)^2}{579.875}} \text{ to } 88.823+1.943.(6.25).\sqrt{1+\frac{1}{8}+\frac{(30-15.625)^2}{579.875}}$$

Simplifies to [74.04, 103.60]

14.6 Examining Residuals

The assumptions of the linear regression model namely:

a. Mean of each error component (error in *Y* for a particular value of *X*) is zero.
b. Each error component follows an approximate normal distribution.
c. The variance of the error component is the same for each value of *X*. (also called assumption of homoscedasticity)
d. Errors are independent of each other.

can all be examined to see whether a particular data set satisfies these assumptions. The usual; strategy is to plot graphs or use EXCEL features to plot graphs and then satisfy oneself that these assumptions hold.

14.7 Self-Test Problems

Self-test Problem 14.7.1.

a. In a regression line, can exactly half the points (assuming even number of points) be above and the other half below the line? Why or why not? Explain.
b. Can all the points be on one side (above or below) the line? Why or why not? Explain.
c. Can you use a sophisticated computer to draw a regression line with sum of squared deviations less than the one obtained using the algebraic formulas? Why or why not? Explain.

Self-Test Problem 14.7.2.

The relationship between interest rates as a percent (*X*) and housing starts (*Y*) is given by the linear equation $Y' = 4094 - 269X$.

a. What will be the number of housing starts if the interest rate is 8.25%?
b. What will be the number of housing starts if the interest rate rose to 16%?
c. At what interest rate will there be no permits for housing starts?
d. What happens to housing starts as interest rates fall?
e. For what interest rate will the maximum number of housing starts be achieved?

Self-Test Problem 14.7.3.

a. Using a regression equation of the form, Y-hat = $b_0 + b_1X$, I found that for $X = 5.0$, Y-hat was equal to 10.4. I know that $b_0 = 19.1$. Find the regression equation. Let n = 8, $\Sigma X = 39$, $\Sigma Y = 85$, $\Sigma X^2 = 211$, $\Sigma Y^2 = 983$, $\Sigma XY = 378$.
b. Let X represent price per unit and Y represent demand. Find expected demand when $X = 4$.
c. Determine a 98% confidence interval for average demand when $X = 4$.
d. What will the 98% confidence interval for demand be at a specific time, when $X = 4$?
e. For what value of X, will the confidence interval be the smallest? Why? (Assume that other things remain the same.)

Multiple Choice Questions:

1. Given the equation for a straight line, $Y = -6 + 7X$, we can say:
   a. The Y-intercept is -6
   b. The slope is -6
   c. The dependent variable is X
   d. None of the above
2. The estimating equation would be a perfect estimate of the dependent variable if:
   a. The standard error of estimate is zero
   b. The coefficient of determination is +l.
   c. All data points lie on the regression line
   d. All of the above
3. If the dependent variable, Y, decreases as X increases in an estimating equation, the value of the coefficient of correlation will be somewhere in the range:
   a. 0 to +1.0
   b. -1.0 to 0
   c. -1.0 to -2.0
   d. -0.5 to 0.5
4. Correlation coefficient for any set of pairs of data will ________ be between 0 and -1 both inclusive.
   a. sometimes
   b. always
   c. never
   d. None of the above

Data for Problems 5-7: Note that the last row gives the totals

X	Y	X^2	Y^2	XY
42	73	1764	5329	3066
41	53	1681	2809	2173
34	63	1156	3969	2142
28	73	784	5329	2044
30	52	900	2704	1560
32	72	1024	5184	2304
23	75	529	5625	1725
46	78	2116	6084	3588
276	539	9954	37033	18602

5. Based on the above data the SCP_{XY} will be
   a. 37033
   b. 9954
   c. 18606
   d. 6.5
   e. None of the above
6. Based on the above data the SS_X will be
   a. 276
   b. 9954
   c. 432
   d. -432
   e. None of the above
7. Correlation coefficient for *X* and *Y* will be
   a. -.9884
   b. 0.0116
   c. 0.9884
   d. -0.0116
   e. None of the above
8. Other things remaining the same, confidence interval will get wider as the confidence level required increases.
   a. True   b. False
9. Correlation coefficient for any set of pairs of data will ____________ be between 0 and 1 both inclusive.
   a. sometimes
   b. always
   c. never
   d. None of the above

Data for Questions 10-12

X	Y	X^2	Y^2	XY
10	20	100	400	200
20	58	400	3364	1160
34	100	1156	10000	3400
12	22	144	484	264
6	15	36	225	90
18	60	324	3600	1080
7	20	49	400	140
18	50	324	2500	900
125	345	2533	20973	7234

10. Based on the above data the SCP_{XY} will be
    a. 2533
    b. 345
    c. 20973
    d. 7234
    e. None of the above
11. Correlation coefficient for *X* and *Y* will be
    a. -.98
    b. -.02
    c. .98
    d. .02
    e. None of the above

12. If you calculate the regression line using *X* as the independent variable and *Y* as the dependent variable, slope of the regression line will be
    a. Positive
    b. Negative
    c. Almost 0
    d. Almost infinity
    e. None of the above

14.8 Glossary

autocorrelation
A term used to describe residuals in a regression analysis that are not independent, whereby neighboring residuals have roughly the same value (positive autocorrelation) or neighboring residuals are generally very unequal in size (negative autocorrelation).

coefficient of correlation (r)
A statistical measure of the strength of the linear relationship between two variables, calculated from a sample of bivariate data. It is an estimate of the population coefficient of correlation.

coefficient of determination (r^2)
The percentage of total variation in the sample *Y* values (measured by SS_Y) that has been explained using the independent variable, *X*.

Cook's distance measure
A statistic that is calculated for each sample observation in order to detect influential observations.

covariance
A measure of the joint variation between two variables, calculated from a sample of bivariate data. The covariance has the same sign as the corresponding coefficient of correlation, but ranges from - 4 to + 4.

dependent variable
In simple linear regression, the variable (*Y*) that is predicted or explained using a single independent variable (*X*).

deterministic portion of the model
In simple linear regression, the assumed line, $\beta_0 + \beta_1 X$, about which all points will fall.

heteroscedasticity
A violation of the assumptions behind the simple linear regression model; this violation occurs when the variance of the error component does <u>not</u> remain constant for all values of the independent variable.

homoscedasticity
An assumption behind the simple linear regression model; it states that the variance of the error component remains constant for all values of the independent variable.

independent variable
In simple linear regression, the variable (*X*) used to predict or explain values of the dependent variable (*Y*).

influential observation
An observation that has a large impact on the calculation of the least squares line. If such an observation were removed from the sample, there would be a dramatic shift in the least squares regression line. These observations can be detected using Cook's distance measure.

intercept (b_0)
The distance from the origin to the point where the least squares line crosses the vertical axis It is calculated from the sample of bivariate data and estimates the population intercept, β_0.

least squares line
The "best" line through a sample of bivariate data; it minimizes the sum of the squares of the vertical distances from each point to the line. This sum is denoted SSE.

leverage
A statistic that is computed to identify observations in the sample that have unusual values of the independent variable, *X*.

negative (inverse) relationship
A relationship between two variables, *X* and *Y*, in which large values of *X* are associated with small values of *Y*.

positive (direct) relationship
A relationship between two variables, *X* and *Y*, in which large values of *X* are associated with large values of *Y*.

random error component (e)
In simple linear regression, the error portion of the model, assumed to be independent, normally distributed random variables with zero mean and common variance.

residual
For each observation in the sample, the actual value of the dependent variable (*Y*) minus the estimated value (*Y*-hat); that is (*Y* – *Y*-hat).

scatter diagram
A two-dimensional graph on which each observation in the sample of bivariate data is represented by a point (dot).

simple linear regression
An analysis in which two variables are assumed to be approximately related by a straight line.

slope (b_1)
A value specifying the steepness (slant) of the least squares line. It is calculated from the sample of bivariate data and estimates the population slope, β_1.

standardized residual
A value that can be used to identify sample observations that have an unusually large or small value of the dependent variable, *Y*.

14.9 Solution to Self-Test Problems

Solution to Self-test Problem 14.7.1.

a. This is possible, but not likely in most cases. In fact, you can construct examples where only one point is above the line and all the rest are below the line or vice-versa. These will be pathological examples of one out of whack point balancing out the deviation squares from all other points.
b. This is not possible, since by moving the line towards the points, we can reduce the sum of squared deviations and hence improve the solution, violating the optimality of the linear regression method.
c. No. Algebraic formulas give you the optimum value (minimum value) of the sum of squares.. Nothing could reduce it any further.

Solution to Self-Test Problem 14.7.2.

a. *Y*-hat (at $X = 8.25$) is found by substituting the *X* value in the regresion equation. Thus *Y*-hat= 4094-269(8.25) = 125.55
b. *Y*-hat (at $X = 16$) = 4094-269(16) = -210. (the figure is meaningless, shows that regression can be useful only within broad ranges of values previously encountered. 16 is way too off for this data.)
c. 0 = 4094-269(*X*) = 15.21% (set the y-hat to 0 and solve for *X*)
d. Increases as shown by negative coefficient (b1) for *X*.
e. 0% (since negative interest rate is meaningless.)

Solution to Self-test Problem 14.7.3.

a. Using the general equation and the pair of known values, you can find the unknown as follows.
   Y-hat = $b_0 + b_1 X$
   $10.4 = 19.1 + b_1.5$, solve for $b_1 = -1.74$
   Y-hat = 19.1 - 1.74 *X*
b. *Y*-hat = 19.4 - 1.74(4) = 12.44

c. $t = 3.143$ (0.01 on the right tail and degrees of freedom = 6)

$$\text{SS}_X = \Sigma X^2 - \frac{(\Sigma X)^2}{n} = 211 - \frac{39^2}{8} = 20.875$$

$$\text{SS}_Y = \Sigma Y^2 - \frac{(\Sigma Y)^2}{n} = 983 - \frac{(85)^2}{8} = 79.875$$

$$\text{SCP}_{XY} = \Sigma XY - \frac{(\Sigma X)(\Sigma Y)}{n} = 378 - \frac{(39)85}{8} = -36.375$$

$$SSE = \sum\left(Y-\hat{Y}\right)^2 = 79.875 - \frac{(-36.375)^2}{20.875} = 16.49$$

s = sqrt(SSE/(n-2)) = sqrt(16.49/6) = 1.658

$$12.44 - 3.143.(1.658).\sqrt{\frac{1}{8}+\frac{(4-4.875)^2}{20.875}} \quad \text{to} \quad 12.44 + 3.143.(1.658).\sqrt{\frac{1}{8}+\frac{(4-4.875)^2}{20.875}}$$

in shortened form, [10.34, 14.53]

d.

$$12.44 - 3.143.(1.658).\sqrt{1+\frac{1}{8}+\frac{(4-4.875)^2}{20.875}} \quad \text{to} \quad 12.44 + 3.143.(1.658).\sqrt{1+\frac{1}{8}+\frac{(4-4.875)^2}{20.875}}$$

in shortened form, [6.82, 18.06]

e. When X_0 equals X-bar, the confidence interval will be smallest, because the term (X_0 - X-bar) drops off. That is, when the X value is around its mean, it is the "best" place to predict or estimate.

Solutions to Multiple Choice Questions

Question #	Answer	Question #	Answer	Question #	Answer
1	a	5	d	9	a
2	d	6	c	10	d
3	b	7	b	11	c
4	a	8	a	12	a

CHAPTER 15 MULTIPLE LINEAR REGRESSION

Chapter Overview and Learning Objectives

In this chapter, the concept of simple linear regression is extended to the case of two or more predictor (independent) variables. Computer solutions of the model coefficients are discussed using Excel, SPSS, and MINITAB. Hypothesis testing is introduced for a set of predictor variables (*F* test) or the predictive ability of individual predictors (*t* tests). Additional topics are discussed, including multicollinearity, dummy variables, stepwise procedures, an examination of the residuals, using the computer packages for prediction, and constructing a first and second order regression model. Upon completion of this chapter, the student should be able to:

1. Use a computer package to determine the model coefficients and carry out the resulting hypothesis tests.
2. Discuss and verify the assumptions behind the use of a multiple linear regression model.
3. Examine and discuss the possible existence of multicollinearity.
4. Use dummy variables and stepwise procedures to strengthen the regression analysis.
5. Identify influential and outlying observations.
6. Construct and evaluate a first and second order regression model.

Chapter Outline

15.1 Multiple Regression Model
15.2 Hypothesis Testing and Confidence Intervals for β Parameters
15.3 Determining Predictive Ability for Certain Independent Variables
15.4 The Problem of Multicollinearity
15.5 Dummy Variable sand Additional Topics in Multiple Regression
15.6 Model Building
15.7 Self-Test Problems
15.8 Glossary
15.9 Solution to Self-Test Problems

15.1 Multiple Regression Model

If one dependent variable depends on more than one independent variable, we use multiple regression. The general model for 3 independent variables and one dependent variable is:

$$\hat{Y} = \beta_0 + \beta_1 X_1 + \beta_2 X_2 + \beta_3 + e$$

We are given a set of values of Y, X_1, X_2, and X_3, and using the multiple regression model we can find the linear equation that minimizes the sum of squared deviations. Hand calculations are pretty messy and we seldom indulge in that. Excel is very easy to use for this problem (see your text for details).

The principle is still the same: Find that linear equation that minimizes $\text{SSE} = \sum\left(Y - \hat{Y}\right)^2$

The values calculated are b_0, b_1, b_2, and b_3. These are estimates for the corresponding population parameters: β_0, β_1, β_2, and β_3. The coefficient β_1 represents the estimated change in Y-hat per unit change X_1 while other independent variables are held constant. He same holds for β_2, and β_3. If the predictor variables X_1, X_2, X_3 are totally unrelated, the interpretation will hold well. Often, they are related and hence effect of changes in the predictor variables on the dependent variable are much harder to estimate and will be discussed later.

Model has assumptions regarding error term *e:* follows normal distribution, centered at 0, have common variance and are independent.

An estimate of the standard deviation of errors, denoted as s = sqrt((SSE/($n - k + 1$))), where n is the number of sets of data and k is the number of predictor (independent) variables.

15.2 Hypothesis Testing and Confidence Intervals for the β parameters.

Significance of the Overall Model: In single regression, if r is significant or β_1 is significant, then the model will be significant. In multiple regression, we need to do an ANOVA test to check the overall significance of the model, on the same lines as Chapter 14.

Source	Degrees of Freedom	SS.	MS	F
Regression	k	SSR	MSR	F = MSR/MSE
Error	n-k-1	SSE	MSE	
Total	n-1	SST		

Table 15.1.1. Analysis of Variance (ANOVA) for Multiple Regression

If we have the definitions for the entries in the Table 15.1.1., we can conduct the test for overall significance of the regression model.

$$\text{SST}=\text{SS}_Y = \Sigma\left(Y-\bar{Y}\right)^2 = \Sigma Y^2 - \frac{\left(\Sigma Y\right)^2}{n} \quad \text{(Sum of squares of total)}$$

$$\text{SSE} = \Sigma\left(Y-\hat{Y}\right)^2$$

$$\text{SSR} = \Sigma\left(\hat{Y}-\bar{Y}\right)^2 = \text{SST-SSE}$$

$$\text{MSR} = \frac{\text{SSR}}{k} \text{ and MSE} = \frac{\text{SSE}}{n-k-1}$$

Review Problem 15.2.1.

Study the data and the computer output that follows the data and then answer the questions. Data on heating costs and a set of related variables are given below.

Heading Cost (X1)	High for the Day (X2)	# of Trees around the House (X3)	South Facing? (Yes = 1; No = 0) (X4)
250	35	3	0
360	29	4	1
165	36	7	0
43	60	6	0
92	65	5	0
200	30	5	0
355	10	6	1
290	7	10	1
230	21	9	0
120	55	2	0

Table 15.1.2. Data on Heating Costs

The regression equation is Y-hat = 440 - 4.53 X_1 - 16.6 X_2 + 74.7 X_3

ANOVA				
	df	SS	MS	*F*
Regression	3	96226.56	32075.52	24.88423
Residual	6	7733.94	1288.99	
Total	9	103960.5		

Table 15.1.3. ANOVA Table

	Coefficients	Standard Error	*t* Stat	*P*-value
Intercept	440.2954	64.01847	6.877631	0.000466
High for the Day	-4.53247	0.946485	-4.78874	0.003036
# of Trees around the House	-16.5746	5.816671	-2.84951	0.0292
South Facing?	74.70008	33.94038	2.20092	0.070013

Table 15.1.4. Data for Tests of Significance for the Coefficients

a. What are the predicted heating costs for a home with outside average outside temperature of 32, insulation of 4 and has no garage?
b. Conduct a global test of hypothesis to determine if any of the regression line is significant at 0.05 level of significance.
c. Conduct a test to see whether the coefficients are significant at 0.05 level
d. Which independent variable, if any, would you omit and why?

Solution

a. The regression equation is Y-hat = 440 - 4.53 X_1 - 16.6 X_2 + 74.7 X_3

Predicted heating costs = 440 – 4.53(32) - 16.6(4) + 74.7(0) = 228.64

b.
Step 1: H_0: $\beta_1 = 0$; $\beta_2 = 0$; $\beta_3 = 0$.
H_1: Not all β's are 0.

Step2: Test statistic is F, with 3 (numerator. d.f.) and 6 (denominator. d.f.) and for a significance level of 0.05, the critical value is 4.76.

Step 3: If the test statistic > 4.76, reject H_0. Otherwise fail to reject H_0

Step 4: Calculate the test statistic value: F = 32076/1289 = 24.8.

Step 5: Conclusion, Reject H_0. At least one of the β's is significant.

c. Conduct a test to see whether the coefficients are significant at 0.05 levels. We just look at the *p*-value for each coefficient, (we ignore the constant). The first independent (predictor) variable is significant because the corresponding *p*-value is less than 0.05. The second independent (predictor) variable is significant because the corresponding *p*-value is less than 0.05. The third independent (predictor) variable is not significant because the corresponding *p*-value is greater than 0.05.

d. Which independent variable, if any, would you omit and why?
The third, (South facing?) because it is not significant statistically.

15.3 Determining Predictive Ability for Certain Independent Variables

R^2 = 1- (SSE/SST) is a useful measure of how good the line is. It tells you the amount of variation in the dependent variable that is explained by the regression line. It is always between 0 and 1. R^2 increases as you add more variables to the model. R^2 will be 1 if the number of sets of data equals number of predictor variables + 1. This means, we do not have enough data, and not a good regression line.

Adjusted R^2 = 1- ((SSE/(n-k-1))/(SST/(n-1))). This does not necessarily increase as you add variables. If it does, it means the variable is perhaps a good candidate to add.

In general, if the β for a variable is not significant, we may drop that variable. We have to drop one variable at a time to see what effect does it have on the remaining variables and the regression line. We do discuss this in greater detail in the next section.

15.4 The Problem of Multicollinearity.

In general, we would like to have the independent (predictor) variables highly correlated to the dependent variables. However, we would not like the independent (predictor) variables to be correlated among them. If they are, problem of multicollinearity arises. A multiple regression line may be significant overall, but the predictor variable t-test may show that all of them are not significant. This is because of the problem of multicollinearity. If we run a correlation analysis of all the variables, we can easily detect highly correlated independent variables and omit one or more of them suitably.
Step-wise regression, a procedure in which variables are added one at a time, mindful of how they are improving R^2. And removing a variable, if it did not improve R^2 significantly.

15.5 Dummy Variable sand Additional Topics in Multiple Regression

Dummy variables (binary variables) allow you to add qualitative variables or indicator variables to the model. (South facing or not?, Male or female, neighborhood 0,1, or 2 modeled with just two binary dummy variables etc.) by treating one of them as 1 and the other as 0.

Step-Wise Procedure:
Forward regression: Out of all independent variable, choose the one which will have highest R^2. Then add one variable from the rest, which together with the already added variables will make the R^2 highest. Proceed in this way till addition variables do not add significantly to R^2.
Backward Regression: Starts with the full set of variables and drops them one at a time in a meaningful fashion till the required set (in terms of significance) is reached.

Standardized Residual: Higher the residual, more the error. But the magnitude is deceptive in statistics, because ewe can change the scale to make it look big. The true measures in statistics are standardized measures (like Z value).

Standardized residual = $\dfrac{Y_i - \hat{Y}_i}{s\sqrt{1-h_i}}$ where s is the estimate of the standard deviation of errors and h_i is leverage, which is a function of how far the X value is from its average. If a point has more than 2 or less than –2 standardized residual, it may be omitted as being an outlier.

Confidence Interval:

(1-α)100% confidence interval for $\mu_{Y/X0}$ is:

$\hat{Y} - t_{\alpha/2.n-k-1} \cdot s_{\hat{Y}}$ to $\hat{Y} + t_{\alpha/2.n-k-1} \cdot s_{\hat{Y}}$

(1-α)100% confidence interval for Y_{X0}

$\hat{Y} - t_{\alpha/2.n-k-1}\sqrt{s^2 s_{\hat{Y}}^2}$ to $\hat{Y} + t_{\alpha/2.n-k-1}\sqrt{s^2 s_{\hat{Y}}^2}$

s is the estimate of the standard deviation of errors and $s_{\hat{Y}}$ is called standard error prediction and is available from EXCEL computer output.

15.6 Model Building

More flexible linear models which include the effect of interactive terms and quadratic terms are discussed in this section of the test. These advanced topics are not usually covered at the introductory level and it is not covered in this study guide.

15.7. Self-Test Problems

Review Self-Test Problem 15.7.1.

Suppose the output given below correspond to the regression line for the data given in the table, using advertising cost per page as the dependent variable.

Advertising Cost ($) Per Page (*Y*)	Circulation (*X*1)	Median Age Of Readers (*X*2)	Median Income ($) Of Readers (*X*3)
73820	8000	41	23241
35140	845	39	30884
23795	725	31	25982
28980	2250	28	22785
21886	1250	33	16505
62750	7450	42	21785
33760	2000	34	24337
25090	700	42	36783
30040	670	40	35204
24340	1800	27	21828

ANOVA				
	df	SS	MS	F
Regression	3	2.72E+09	9.06E+08	44.65639
Residual	6	1.22E+08	20287390	
Total	9	2.84E+09		

	Coefficients	Standard Error	*t* Stat	*P*-value
Intercept	-3368.6	9630.322	-0.34979	0.738446
Circulation (*X*1)	6.099642	0.889141	6.860153	0.000472
Median Age of readers (*X*2)	394.0439	454.2879	0.867388	0.419063
Median Income ($) of readers(*X*3)	0.369846	0.413479	0.894473	0.405518

a. Write down the Regression equation
b. What is the predicted advertising expenditure for a circulation of 7000, median age of 43 and median income of $25,000?
c. Is the overall regression line significant at the 0.10 level?
d. Is median age significant at the 0.10 level?
e. Which independent variable/s, if any, would you omit and why?

Self-Test Problem 15.7.2.

The total value of a baseball franchise is affected by several factors, including gate receipts and player costs. Typically high gate receipts make a franchise valuable, provided that its operating expenses are not excessive. High player costs affect a franchise's operating costs. However, to attract some of the best players, player costs may have to be high. The table below displays 10 baseball franchises along with gate receipts, player costs, and franchise value. All units are in millions of dollars.

Franchise	Gate Receipts	Player Costs	Franchise Value
New York Yankees	42.6	63.0	241
Baltimore Orioles	51.0	55.8	207
Atlanta Braves	40.1	55.4	199
Colorado Rockies	46.0	41.6	184
Los Angeles Dodgers	31.9	39.1	178
Cleveland Indians	48.0	51.4	175
Texas Rangers	35.5	42.8	174
Boston Red Sox	39.0	42.2	172
Chicago Cubs	28.3	32.2	165
Toronto Blue Jays	36.3	30.7	155

a. Interpret the following computer printout. Interpret the confidence interval for the regression coefficient of player costs.
b. What is the predicted franchise value for the Los Angeles Dodgers?

Regression Statistics	
Multiple *R*	0.906331
R Square	0.821435
Adjusted *R* Square	0.770417
Standard Error	11.90502
Observations	10

ANOVA					
	D.f.	SS	MS	*F*	Significance F
Regression	2	4563.894	2281.947	16.10073	0.002406
Residual	7	992.106	141.7294		
Total	9	5556			

	Coefficients	Standard Error	t Stat	*P*-value	Lower 95%	Upper 95%
Intercept	104.9207	22.52618	4.657723	0.002321	51.6548	158.1866
Gate Receipts	-0.7609	0.744637	-1.02184	0.340868	-2.52168	0.999889
Player Costs	2.431006	0.503938	4.824019	0.001913	1.239383	3.622629

Self-Test Problem 15.7.3.

The model $\hat{Y} = 3.2 + 6.1X_1 + 5.2\,X_2$ was calculated to fit 20 data points pertaining to the growth rate of a hog. The variable X_1 represents the daily food consumption of the hog and X_2 represents the age of the hog. If the standard deviation of the estimate of b_1 is 2.5, what is a 95% confidence interval for the parameter b_1?

Self-Test Problem 15.7.4.

The least squares equation $\hat{Y} = 3.4 + 1.2 X_1 + 4.3 X_2$ was obtained. The sample residuals of the 20 observations used in fitting the regression equation are:

4.1,	–3.2,	1.5,	6.7,	6.4,	3.8,	–4.2,	–2.4,	1.6,	–8.7,
–3.1,	1.2,	–5.1,	2.1,	0.6,	5.4,	3.4,	–7.1,	–6.2,	3.2

Given that the value of SST is 510, test the null hypothesis that the variables X_1 and X_2 do not contribute to predicting the variation in the dependent variable. Use a 5% significance level.

Self-Test Problem 15.7.5.

The following set of data was collected:

Y	X_1	X_2	Y	X_1	X_2
2.02	1.01	.97	4.20	1.61	2.62
7.95	2.34	5.50	2.62	1.19	1.42
2.61	1.21	1.49	.07	.07	.01
.31	.23	.05	1.53	.80	.67
1.63	.85	.72	6.19	2.03	4.17

a. Construct the correlation matrix for the variables. Does multicollinearity appear to be a problem?
b. Find the coefficient of determination for the model using only X_1. Then find it using only X_2.
c. The coefficient of determination for the complete model is .9996. Does it appear that both variables, X_1 and X_2, should stay in the model?

Multiple Choice Questions

1. A multiple regression equation defines the relationship between the dependent variable and the independent variables in the form of an equation.
   a. True
   b. False

2. It has been hypothesized that overall academic success for freshmen at college as measured by grade point average (GPA) is a function of IQ scores (X_1), hours spent studying each week (X_2), and one's high school average (X_3). Suppose the regression equation is:
   $Y' = -6.9 + 0.055 X_1 + 0.107 X_2 + 0.0083X_3$. and $R^2 = 0.826$.
   What effect on the GPA will there be if the numbers of hours spent studying per week increases from 32 to 36 (Other things held constant)?
   a. 0.107
   b. 0.0083
   c. 0.055
   d. 3.852
   e. 0.428

Questions 3-6 refer to the following problem. A random sample of homes was taken and data collected on the following variables:

y = COST = annual energy cost of the home ($100s)
x_1 = SIZE = size of the home (1000s of square feet), and
x_2 = INSUL = 1 if the home has a standard insulation package
0 if the home has an energy saving insulation package
A multiple regression was run in an attempt to explain variation in COST as a function of SIZE and INSUL. Here is a computer output ("?" appears where output has been deleted):

PREDICTOR	COEF	*p*-value
CONSTANT	0.963	
SIZE	5.7764	.002
INSUL	0.8230	.18

R-SQ = ?

ANALYSIS OF VARIANCE

SOURCE	d.f.	SS	MS	*F*-value
REGRESSION	2	92.767	? 46.3835 (SS/DF)	40.7946
ERROR	9	10.233	1.137	
TOTAL	11			

Hint: The table is similar to ANOVA: Use a .01 level of significance.
H_0: all regression coefficients are 0 ($\beta_1 = \beta_2 = 0$)
H_1: Not all βs are 0
(Hint: It is an *F*-distribution, see text for the hypothesis statement)

3. Computed *F*-value is:
   a. 92.767
   b. 46.3835
   c. 1.137
   d. 40.7946
   e. None of the above
4. Computed MS Regression value is
   a. 92.767
   b. 46.3835
   c. 1.137
   d. 40.7946
   e. None of the above
5. Computed MS Error value is
   a. 92.767
   b. 46.3835
   c. 1.137
   d. 40.7946
   e. None of the above
6. What is the decision rule?
   a. Reject H_0 if $F > 8.02$ (Look at *F*-table with numerator degrees of freedom = 2 and denominator degrees of freedom = 9 and a 0.01 significance level)
   b. Reject H_0 if $t > 3.250$
   c. Reject H_0 if $t < -3.250$ or if $t > 3.250$
   d. Reject H_0 if $t > 2.821$
   e. None of the above

Questions 7-11 refer to the following tables.

Price	Bedrooms	Size	Pool	Distance	Twnship	Garage	Baths
263.115	4	2349	0	17	5	1	2
182.385	4	2102	1	19	4	0	2
242.055	3	2271	1	12	3	0	2

Table 1: Data Snippet

SUMMARY OUTPUT					
Regression Statistics					
R Square	0.532805				
Standard Error	33.34207				
Observations	105				
ANOVA					
	Df	SS	MS	F	Significance F
Regression	7	122978	17568.28	15.80316	1.09E-13
Residual	97	107834.3	1111.694		
Total	104	230812.3			
	Coefficients	Standard Error	t Stat	*P*-value	Lower 95%
Intercept	43.92833	39.84805	1.102396	0.273017	-35.159
Bedrooms(X1)	7.340897	2.6039	2.819193	0.005837	2.172879
Size(X2)	0.038186	0.014792	2.581455	0.011335	0.008827
Pool(X3)	19.22957	7.128271	2.697649	0.008236	5.081933
Distance(X4)	-0.98081	0.742834	-1.32036	0.189821	-2.45513
Twnship(X5)	-1.65289	2.700024	-0.61218	0.541854	-7.01169
Garage(X6)	35.56384	7.683909	4.628353	1.14E-05	20.31342
Baths(X7)	22.69673	9.049927	2.507946	0.013803	4.735138

Table 2: Output with all variables

SUMMARY OUTPUT					
Regression Statistics					
Multiple *R*	0.723658				
R Square	0.523681				
Standard Error	33.32428				
Observations	105				
ANOVA					
	Df	SS	MS	F	Significance F
Regression	5	120872	24174.4	21.76878	1.2E-14
Residual	99	109940.3	1110.508		
Total	104	230812.3			
	Coefficients	Standard Error	t Stat	*P*-value	Lower 95%
Intercept	17.8991	35.03162	0.510941	0.61053	-51.6112
Bedrooms(X1)	7.116924	2.569791	2.769457	0.006705	2.017901
Size(X2)	0.039126	0.014718	2.658356	0.009158	0.009922

Pool(X3)	19.20538	6.988945	2.747965	0.007127	5.337793
Garage(X4)	38.8086	7.282415	5.329083	6.21E-07	24.3587
Baths(X5)	24.19785	8.978217	2.695173	0.008267	6.383111

Table 3: Output With Two Variables Eliminated Because They Were Not Significant

	Price	Bedrooms	Size	Pool	Distance	Twnship	Garage	Baths
Price	1							
Bedrooms(X1	0.467506	1						
Size(X2)	0.38006	0.397945	1					
Pool(X3)	0.294057	0.005301	0.196969	1				
Distance(X4)	-0.34697	-0.15336	-0.13402	-0.13938	1			
Twnship(X5)	0.128092	0.200127	0.178226	0.201095	-0.20859	1		
Garage(X6)	0.526273	0.234102	0.090172	0.114153	-0.35929	0.056668	1	
Baths(X7)	0.382168	0.32893	0.044435	0.054533	-0.19499	0.04967	0.221289	1

Table 4: Autocorrelation Matrix

7. Correct the regression equation using data of Table 2
   a. $Y' = 43.92 + 7.34\,X1 + 0.038\,X2 + 19.22\,X3 - 0.98\,X4 - 1.65\,X5 + 35.56\,X6 + 22.69\,X7$
   b. $Y' = 39.84 + 2.6\,X1 + .014X2 + 7.12X3 + .74X4 + 2.7X5 + 7.6X6 + 9.04X7$
   c. $Y' = 17.89 + 7.11X1 + .039X2 + 19.2X3 + 38.8X4 + 24.19X5$
   d. $Y' = 35.03 + 2.56X1 + .014X2 + 6.98X3 + 7.28X4 + 8.97X5$
   e. (a) or (c)
8. In Table 2, (at 0.01 significance level) exactly ______ independent variables are significant.
   a. Seven
   b. six
   c. Five
   d. four
   e. three
9. In Table 3, (at 0.01 significance level) exactly ______ independent variables are significant.
   a. Five
   b. four
   c. three
   d. two
   e. six
10. Using Table 2, the overall regression line is significant (level of significance 0.05) That is we reject H_0 all regression coefficients are 0 against H_1: Not all βs are 0, because:
    a. F-value is 15.8
    b. P-value corresponding to F is less than 0.05
    c. All p-values corresponding to the coefficients are less than 0.05
    d. None
11. The correlation matrix (Table 4) tells us that the regression will have multicollinearity problem with variables:
    a. $X1$ and $X2$
    b. $X3$ and $X5$
    c. $X1$ and $X5$
    d. None

15.8 Glossary

adjusted coefficient of variation [R^2(adj)]
A statistic similar to R^2, except SSE and SST are divided by their respective degrees of freedom The value of this statistic does not necessarily increase as variables are added to the model.

autocorrelation
The internal correlation between residuals when using multiple linear regression on time series data.

backward regression
A regression procedure that places all variables into the model, then removes them one at a time, until all variables remaining in the model produce a significant decrease in R^2 if removed.

coefficient of determination (R^2)
The percentage of total variation in the sample *Y* values (measured by SST) that has been explained using the independent variables. This value is computed using $R^2 = 1 - (SSE/SST)$.

Cook's distance measure
A statistic that is calculated for each sample observation in order to detect influential observations.

dependent variable
In multiple linear regression, the variable (*Y*) that is predicted or explained using the independent variables (X_1, X_2, AAA, X_k).

dummy variables
Variables used in regression models to represent the categories of a qualitative variable (such as, $X = 1$ if female and 0 if male).

Durbin-Watson statistic
A statistic used to detect residuals that are not independent; that is, correlated with each other (autocorrelated).

first order model
A regression model containing strictly a linear combination of the predictor variables.

forward regression
A regression procedure that introduces independent variables into the model, one at a time, until all remaining variables produce an insignificant increase in R^2 if entered.

independent (predictor) variables
In multiple linear regression, the variables used to predict or explain values of the dependent variable (*Y*).

influential observation
An observation that has a large impact on the calculation of the least squares equation If such an observation were removed from the sample, there would be a dramatic change in this equation. These observations can be detected using Cook's distance measure.

interaction term.
A regression variable that is the product of two individual predictor variables, e.g., X_2X_5.

leverage
A statistic that is computed to identify observations in the sample that have unusual values of one or more predictor variables.

multicollinearity
A condition that exists when the independent variables are not independent; in particular, when one independent variable is nearly a linear combination of one or more of the remaining independent variables.

multiple linear regression
An analysis in which a dependent variable (Y) is approximately explained using a linear combination of independent (predictor) variables.

partial F test
A statistical test used to determine the predictive contribution of a subset of independent variables.

polynomial regression
An application of multiple linear regression that uses a single predictor (X) and a model usually of the form $Y = \beta_0 + \beta_1 X + \beta_2 X^2 + e$. This model is useful when the relationship between X and Y is steadily increasing or steadily decreasing but is curvilinear.

quadratic term
A regression variable that is the square of one of the original predictor variables; e.g., X_3^2.

residual
For each observation in the sample, the actual value of the dependent variable (Y) minus the estimated value ($\hat{Y}$); that is, $Y - \hat{Y}$.

second order model
A regression model containing a linear combination of the predictor variables, interaction terms, and quadratic terms.

standardized residual
A value that can be used to identify sample observations that have an unusually large or small value of the dependent variable, Y.

stepwise regression
A regression procedure that is similar to forward regression, except has the option to remove a previously entered variable that has become redundant.

variance inflation factor (VIF)
A statistic computed for each predictor variable in a multiple regression model. The value of this statistic is large (say, > 10) whenever one predictor is nearly a linear combination of one or more other predictor variables and indicates that multicollinearity is present in the regression data.

15.9 Solution to Self-Test Problems

Solution to Self-Test Problem 15.7.1.

a. The regression equation is Y-hat = -3368.6 + 6.099642 X_1 + 394.0439 X_2 + 0.369846 X_3

b. Predicted heating costs = -3368.6 + 6.099642 (7000) + 394.0439 (43) + 0.369846 (25000)
= 65518.92

c. .
Step 1: H_0: $\beta_1 = 0;\ \beta_2 = 0;\ \beta_3 = 0$.
H_1: Not all β's are 0.

Step 2: Test statistic is F, with 3 (numerator. d.f.) and 6 (denominator. d.f.) and for a significanc level of 0.10, the critical value is 3.29.

Step 3: If the test statistic > 3.29, reject H_0. Otherwise fail to reject H_0

Step 4: Calculate the test statistic value: F = 44.65.

Step 5: Conclusion. Reject H_0. At least one of the βs is significant.

d. Conduct a test to see whether the coefficients are significant at 0.10 level. We just look at the p-value for each coefficient, (we ignore the constant). The first independent (predictor) variable is significant because the corresponding p-value is less than 0.10. The second independent (predictor) variable is not significant because the corresponding p-value is less than 0.10. The third independent (predictor) variable is not significant because the corresponding p-value is greater than 0.10.

e. Which independent variable, if any, would you omit and why?
One of the second and third variables may be dropped. Then run the regression and see what the significance of the remaining variables are, before proceeding further. We would not want to drop more than one variable at a time, because dropping one variable may affect all numbers in a regression analysis.

Solution to Self-Test Problem 15.7.2.

a. The p-value for the model with both independent variables is equal to .0024, indicating that the model is useful in predicting franchise value. We are 95% confident that the true value of regression coefficient of player costs is between 1.239 and 3.623.
b. Predicated value is 104.921 - 0.761(31.9) + 2.431(39.1) = 175.7.

Solution to Self-Test Problem 15.7.3.

Given $b_1 = 6.1$ $s_{b_1} = 2.5$ $n = 20$

95% confidence interval for β_1 is $b_1 \pm t_{.025,17}\, s_{b_1}$
$6.1 \pm 2.110(2.5)$ (i.e., 0.825 to 11.375)

Solution to Self-Test Problem 15.7.4.

$SSE = (4.1)^2 + (-3.2)^2 + (1.5)^2 + \ldots + (-6.2)^2 + (3.2)^2 = 412.88$

ANOVA TABLE

Source	df	SS	MS	F
Regression	2	97.12	48.56	1.9994
Residual	17	412.88	24.287	
Total	19	510		

H_0: $\beta_1 = \beta_2 = 0$ H_a: at least one β is $\neq 0$.

Since $F^* = 1.9994 < F_{.05,2,17} = 3.59$, fail to reject H_0 and thus conclude that the independent variables in the model do not significantly help predict the dependent variable.

Solution to Self-Test Problem 15.7.5.

a) Correlation matrix

	Y	X_1	X_2
Y	1	.975	.9965
X_1		1	.955
X_2			1

b. R^2 using $X_1 = .951$, R^2 using $X_2 = .993$

c. Although partial F tests for each variable are significant here, the high correlation between X_1 and X_2 dictates using one, but not both, of these variables. Since the R^2 using X_2 alone is larger, a preferred model would be to include only X_2 in the prediction equation.

Answers to Multiple Choice Questions

Question #	Answer	Question #	Answer	Question #	Answer
1	a	5	c	9	a
2	e	6	a	10	b
3	d	7	a	11	b
4	b	8	e		

CHAPTER 16 TIME SERIES ANALYSIS AND INDEX NUMBERS

Chapter Overview and Learning Objectives

This chapter presents an introduction to time series analysis with procedures to decompose a time series into the individual components. An actual monthly time series is examined containing definite effects of seasonality, trend and cyclical activity. Index numbers are discussed using both simple and aggregate price indexes. Having completed this material, the student should be able to:

1. Deseasonalize a time series by first calculating the seasonal indexes.
2. Discuss the nature of additive and multiplicative seasonality.
3. Estimate the trend and cyclical components.
4. Calculate price indexes, including the Laspeyres and Paasche index.

Chapter Outline

16.1 Components of a Time Series
16.2 Measuring Trend: No Seasonality
16.3 Measuring Cyclical Activity: No seasonality
16.4 Types of Seasonal Variation
16.5 Measuring Seasonality
16.6 Index Numbers
16.7 Self-Test Problems
16.8 Glossary
16.9 Solution to Self-Test Problems

16.1 Components of a Time Series

- **Time series** is variables observed over time, often at equal intervals. The time is months, days, quarters or years. The observed variables may be stock price, temperature, sales, production etc. Components of time series are: Trend (TR), seasonal variation (S), cyclical variation (C) and irregular activity (I).
- **Trend** is an increasing or decreasing or constant trend. Could be linear or non-linear.
- **Seasonality** is the periodic increase or decrease within a year, usually predictable (Christmas sales, power use in hot summer days, etc.)
- **Cyclical variation** is movement about the trend due to economic boom or slowdown.
- **Irregular activity** is what is left over, error, noise etc.
- These components may be combined using an additive or multiplicative model.

Review Problem 16.1.1.

Suppose that the sales of a retail store can best be described by a multiplicative structure with respect to trend, seasonality, cyclical variation, and irregular activity. Describe the seasonal effect on sales over time if the trend is increasing.

Solution

The seasonal effect increases according to the underlying trend. The amplitude of the seasonal effects becomes more dramatic after a long period of time.

Review Problem 16.1.2.

The following data set shows the percentage of disposable income (DPI) set aside as personal savings by people in the United States for the years 1983–1992.

Year	Percentage of DPI Set Aside as Savings
1983	5.4
1984	6.1
1985	4.4
1986	4.1
1987	3.2
1988	4.2
1989	4.6
1990	5.1
1991	4.7
1992	4.8

a. Plot the data against time.
b. Describe the trend.

Solution

a. Plot of time series:

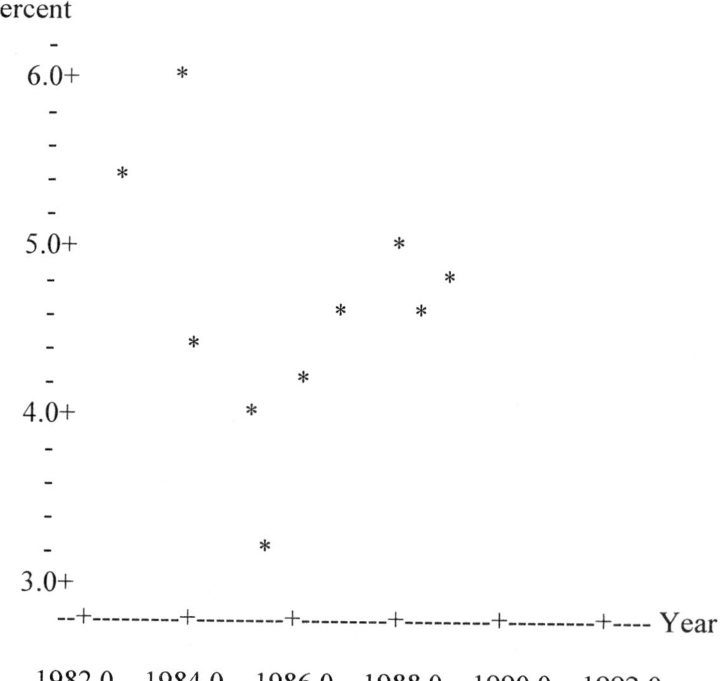

b. There is a decreasing trend from 1983 to 1987 and then an increasing trend from 1987 to 1992.

16.2 Measuring Trend: No Seasonality

If there is no seasonal variation, we can measure linear trend by simply using time, suitably numbered as the independent variable and the time series as the dependent variable and use linear regression to capture the trend. Some types of quadratic trend may be captured using multiple regression models.

Review Problem 16.2.1.

Broadcast TV still commands the lion's share of advertising dollars. However, by the year 2005, market researchers predict advertisers will spend $14.5 billion on cable. Average time spent weekly watching cable television per household has been steadily increasing since 1988. Find the least squares prediction equation that best describes this trend. What is your estimate for the average weekly time spent watching cable television per household in the year 2005?

Year	Average Weekly Time Spent Watching Cable Television per Household, in Hours
1988	9.4
1989	14.3
1990	16.1
1991	17.4
1992	17.5
1993	19.4
1994	19.0
1995	22.1
1996	22.9
1997	24.0

(Source: Adapted from *The Wall Street Journal,* " In Battle for TV Ads, Cable Is Now the Enemy," May 6, 1998, p. B1.)

Solution

$\Sigma t = 55, \quad \Sigma t^2 = 385, \quad \Sigma y_t = 182.1, \quad \Sigma t y_t = 1115.7$

$$b_1 = \frac{= 1115.7 - \dfrac{(55)(182.1)}{10}}{385 - \dfrac{55^2}{10}} = \frac{114.15}{82.5} = 1.3836$$

$$b_0 = 18.21 - (1.3836)(5.5) = 10.60$$

$$\hat{y}_t = 10.60 + 1.3836t$$

16.3 Measuring Cyclical Activity: No Seasonality

To examine a cyclical activity, we can describe each component as a percentage of the trend line and actual over estimate will be a measure of the cyclical component. A review problem will clarify the points.

Review Problem 16.3.1.

Recently sales among Japan's top shipbuilders reached a record six trillion yen ($48 billion dollars). Conventional wisdom in the 1980s had it that countries such as South Korea and Taiwan would overtake Japan in the shipbuilding industry, just as Japan had done to U.S. shipyards. For a while, that happened. Japan fell behind South Korea in 1993 in tonnage. Now Japan's shipbuilders rank among the world's most profitable shipbuilders. Consider the total sales of the top 10 Japanese shipbuilders, presented below in terms of billions of dollars.

Year	Total Sales in Billions of Dollars
1986	32.1
1987	30.2
1988	30.9
1989	33.5
1990	39.3
1991	42.0
1992	42.3
1993	43.0
1994	43.1
1995	45.3
1996	48.1

(Adapted from *The Wall Street Journal,* "Defying the Odds, Japan Shipbuilders Beat Back Their Hungry Competitors," Feb. 12, 1998, p. A19.)

a. Estimate the trend equation. How would you interpret the coefficients of the equation?
b. Estimate the cyclical components.
c. Construct a bar chart of the total sales using time as the horizontal axis and describe the pattern.

Solution

a. $\Sigma t = 66,\ \Sigma t^2 = 506,\ \Sigma y_t = 429.8,\ \Sigma t y_t = 2777.8$

Plotting the Total Sales (y_t) values versus Year, the trend appears to be nearly linear. Letting $t = 1$ for 1986, $t = 2$ for 1987, and so on, the linear trend equation is $\hat{y}_t = 28.218 + 1.8091t$. On the average, the total sales are increasing 1.8 billion dollars each year. The estimated sales for 1985 ($t = 0$) is $b_0 = 28.2$ billion dollars.

b.

Time	Sales	$\hat{y}_t$	$y_t / \hat{y}_t$
1	32.1	30.0273	1.06903
2	30.2	31.8364	0.94860
3	30.9	33.6455	0.91840
4	33.5	35.4545	0.94487
5	39.3	37.2636	1.05465
6	42.0	39.0727	1.07492
7	42.3	40.8818	1.03469
8	43.0	42.6909	1.00724
9	43.1	44.5000	0.96854
10	45.3	46.3091	0.97821
11	48.1	48.1182	0.99962

c. The sales are increasing, beginning in 1987.

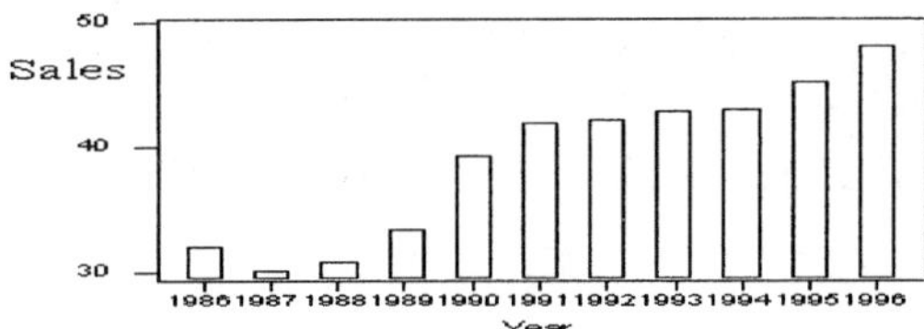

16.4. Types of Seasonal Variation

- **Additive Seasonal variation** occurs when the variation does not depend on the level of the sales, but just an amount over or under the estimate. Once you estimate the amount per season (quarter or month) you can add or subtract as the case may be.

- **Multiplicative Seasonal Variation:** Here the variation is proportional to the trend amount. You estimate the multiplier for each season and use it to multiply the trend value and get a seasonally adjusted forecast.

Review Problem 16.4.1

Year: Year from 1995 to 1998
Quarter: One through four for the four quarters of the year
Aluminum Prod: Number of metric tons of aluminum produced per quarter

The Aluminum Association records the number of metric tons in units of millions for each quarter. A strong economy typically increases the demand for aluminum. However, aluminum tends to be a cyclical commodity. Assume that the seasonal indexes are $S_1 = 1.041$, $S_2 = .953$, $S_3 = .994$, and $S_4 = 1.012$. If the production of aluminum is subject to multiplicative seasonal variation, what are the deseasonalized production figures per quarter from 1995 to 1998?

(Source: Adapted from *The Wall Street Journal,* " Aluminum Production," July 14, 1998, p. A1.)
For the sake of brevity, data and solution are given in the solution.

Solution

Year	Quarter	S_t	Deseasonalized Exchange Rate
1990	1	.993	85.17
	2	.997	85.70
	3	1.004	86.37
	4	1.006	85.62

1991	1	.993	87.13
	2	.997	87.31
	3	1.004	87.10
	4	1.006	87.61
1992	1	.993	85.56
	2	.997	83.99
	3	1.004	82.90
	4	1.006	78.78

16.5 Measuring Seasonality

Review Problem 16.5.1.

Year: Year from 1994 to 1999
Quarter: One through four for the four quarters of the year
CellularLines: Number of cellular telephone lines in Brazil

The state-owned telephone company of Brazil, Telecommunicacoes Brasileiros (Telebras), is fighting vast inefficiencies because they need to compete with foreign telecommunication companies offering digital technology. Suppose that a manager of the Telebras system is interested in the seasonal indexes for the number of cellular telephone lines in Brazil. Compute the seasonal indexes for these data (in units of millions). For which quarter is this index the smallest? The largest?

(Source: Adapted from *The Wall Street Journal,* " Telebras Wards Off Competition," July 15, 1998, p.A9.)
For the sake of brevity, data and solution is presented in the solution.

Solution
The calculations for determining the seasonal indexes are:

I	Y(I)	SUM	MOV.AVG.	RATIO
1	1.10			
2	1.50			
		6.10		
3	1.60		1.65	0.970
		7.10		
4	1.90		1.91	0.993
		8.20		
5	2.10		2.19	0.960
		9.30		
6	2.60		2.47	1.051
		10.50		
7	2.70		2.78	0.973
		11.70		
8	3.10		3.05	1.016
		12.70		
9	3.30		3.30	1.000

		13.70		
10	3.60		3.55	1.014
		14.70		
11	3.70		3.79	0.977
		15.60		
12	4.10		4.06	1.009
		16.90		
13	4.20		4.40	0.955
		18.30		
14	4.90		4.72	1.037
		19.50		
15	5.10		5.04	1.012
		20.80		
16	5.30		5.39	0.984
		22.30		
17	5.50		5.76	0.954
		23.80		
18	6.40		6.15	1.041
		25.40		
19	6.60		6.59	1.002
		27.30		
20	6.90		7.19	0.960
		30.20		
21	7.40		7.91	0.935
		33.10		
22	9.30		8.76	1.061
		37.00		
23	9.50			
24	10.80			

SUMMARY OF RATIOS

PERIOD	1	2	3	4
1			0.970	0.993
2	0.960	1.051	0.973	1.016
3	1.000	1.014	0.977	1.009
4	0.955	1.037	1.012	0.984
5	0.954	1.041	1.002	0.960
6	0.935	1.061		
AVERAGE	0.961	1.041	0.987	0.993
SEASONAL INDEX	0.965	1.046	0.992	0.997

Assuming multiplicative seasonality, the quarterly seasonal indexes are $S_1 = .965$, $S_2 = 1.046$, $S_3 = .992$, and $S_4 = .997$. The smallest index is S_1, which indicates that the number of Brazilian telephone lines in the first quarter is 96.5% of the yearly average. The largest index is S_2 and the number of lines in the second quarter is 104.6% of the yearly average. There is very little seasonality during the third and fourth quarters.

16.6 Time Series Containing Seasonality, Trend and Cycles

This problem becomes quite cumbersome and laborious to do by hand. The general principles are: First remove the effect of seasonal variation. Then estimate the cyclical components. Finally put together all of these in a forecasting context.

16.7 Index Numbers

We have all run into index numbers like Dow Jones Industrial Average, unemployment %, consumer price index, production index, etc. These are generally calculated to enable the listener or a reader to come to a quick understanding of how things are relative to how things were in the immediate past or at some fixed point of time with which we may be familiar.

Review Problem 16.7.1.

Resource-based industries are an important component of the Canadian economy. Consider the following short list on Canadian mineral production (in millions of kilograms) and price per kilogram (in Canadian dollars) for 1988 through 1990.

	Quantity			Price		
Mineral	**1998**	**1989**	**1990**	**1998**	**1989**	**1990**
Zinc	1370	1272	1285	1.65	2.15	1.92
Copper	758	704	779	3.16	3.39	3.20
Nickel	198	195	196	14.04	15.59	10.29

(Source: *Canada Year Book,* pp.408–409.)

a. Calculate the Laspeyres index for 1989 and 1990 using 1988 as the base year.
b. Calculate the Paasche index for 1989 and 1990 using 1988 as the base year.
c. Compare the two indexes.

Solution

a. $\Sigma P_0Q_0 = 7435.7$
For 1989, $\Sigma P_1Q_0 = 8601.94$ For 1990, $\Sigma P_1Q_0 = 7093.42$
Laspeyres Index:
For 1989, $(\Sigma P_1Q_0/\Sigma P_0Q_0)100 = (8601.94/7435.7)100 = 115.68$
For 1990, $(\Sigma P_1Q_0/\Sigma P_0Q_0)100 = (7093.42/7435.7)100 = 95.4$

b. For 1989, $\Sigma P_1Q_1 = 8161.41$ $\Sigma P_0Q_1 = 7061.24$
Paasche Index $= (\Sigma P_1Q_1/\Sigma P_0Q_1)100 = (8161.41/7061.24)100 = 115.58$
For 1990, $\Sigma P_1Q_1 = 6976.84$ $\Sigma P_0Q_1 = 7333.73$
Paasche Index $= (\Sigma P_1Q_1/\Sigma P_0Q_1)100 = (6976.84/7093.42)100 = 95.13$

c. For 1989, the Laspeyres and Paasche indexes are practically equal. For 1990, the Paasche index is slightly smaller than (or almost equal to) the Laspeyres index.

16.8 Self-Test Problems

Self-Test Problem 16.8.1.

From 1990 to 1997, the New York Stock Exchange has restricted program trading when the Dow Jones Industrial Average (DJIA) climbs or falls more than 50 points from its previous closing level. As the DJIA reached new records, it has been easier to activate the 50-point collar on program trading. The following data show the number of times that the 50-point collar has been activated since 1990.

Year	Percentage of Trading Days That the 50-Point Collar Was Activated
1990	23
1991	17
1992	15
1993	10
1994	17
1995	20
1996	30
1997	77

(Adapted from: *The Wall Street Journal,* "Big Board May Loosen Its 'Collar'," Mar. 23, 1998, p. C1.)

a. Estimate a linear trend and a quadratic trend for these data. Which do you think is a better fit?
b. What is your estimate of the percentage of trading days that the 50-point collar was activated in 1998?

Self-Test Problem 16.8.2.

[The money that many companies are spending on capital investment has gone heavily into cost-cutting technology, aided by tumbling computer prices, rather than new buildings and factories that add capacity. Therefore, the ratio of capital spending to cash flow has recently been near historic lows. The following table contains data on the ratio of capital spending to cash flow for the Standard & Poor's Industrials from 1977 to 1997 (displayed in units of percent).

Year	Ratio of Capital Spending to Cash Flow
1977	80.1
1978	89.3
1979	98.4
1980	103.9
1981	110.5
1982	116.3
1983	95.3
1984	94.3
1985	93.5
1986	91.8

1987	85.4
1988	83.1
1989	82.1
1990	81.8
1991	82.3
1992	78.4
1993	76.2
1994	70.1
1995	68.5
1996	66.4
1997	62.2

(Adapted from *The Wall Street Journal,* "With Dow 9000 Nearby, Stocks Get Boost As Corporate America Tightens Its Belt," Mar. 23, 1998, p. C1.)

a. Without performing any calculations, determine whether the ratio of capital spending to cash flow is trending upward, downward, or contains no trend.
b. Plot the data against time. Do you think there is a linear or quadratic trend present? Estimate the appropriate trend line.

Self-Test Problem 16.8.3

Year: Year, 1992 through 1998
Quarter: One through four for the four quarters of the year
Unemployment Rate: Unemployment rate in percentage for each quarter

The quarterly unemployment rate for the United States was recorded from 1992 through 1998. The unemployment rate was seasonally adjusted for students looking for work. This period of time was highly influenced by the spread of new technology and an increasingly strong economy. Therefore, the unemployment rate was in a sustained downward trend. Estimate the approximate period of the cycle for the unemployment rate between 1992 and 1998.

(Adapted from *The Wall Street Journal,* " Wages for Low-Paid Workers Rose in 1997," Mar. 23, 1998, p.A2.)
Data and some calculations:

Time	Rate(y_t)	$\hat{y}_t$	$y_t / \hat{y}_t$
1	12.1	11.8406	1.02190
2	11.8	11.6337	1.01430
3	11.5	11.4267	1.00642
4	11.4	11.2197	1.01607
5	10.7	11.0127	0.97160
6	10.1	10.8057	0.93469
7	10.3	10.5988	0.97181
8	10.5	10.3918	1.01041
9	10.8	10.1848	1.06040
10	10.6	9.9778	1.06235
11	10.3	9.7709	1.05416
12	9.2	9.5639	0.96195
13	8.4	9.3569	0.89773
14	8.1	9.1499	0.88525
15	8.7	8.9429	0.97283

16	8.9	8.7360	1.01878
17	9.4	8.5290	1.10212
18	9.1	8.3220	1.09349
19	8.5	8.1150	1.04744
20	8.2	7.9080	1.03692
21	7.2	7.7011	0.93494
22	6.4	7.4941	0.85401
23	6.9	7.2871	0.94688
24	7.1	7.0801	1.00281
25	7.4	6.8732	1.07665
26	7.0	6.6662	1.05008
27	6.5	6.4592	1.00632
28	6.2	6.2522	0.99165

Self-Test Problem 16.8.4

Enrollment data in a small college is given in the table below for 18 quarters from some arbitrary starting date. Make a seasonally adjusted forecast for enrollment projection for quarters 21, 22, 23, and 24.

Qtr	Enrollment
1	2033
2	1871
3	714
4	2318
5	2174
6	2069
7	840
8	2413
9	2370
10	2254
11	927
12	2704
13	2625
14	2478
15	1136
16	3001
17	2803
18	2668

Multiple Choice Questions

Use the following data for the firstt 5 questions.

Following are the seasonal factors for quarterly data on the number of crimes committed in Middletown. These are based on data from 1999 to 2001 (all quarters included. t= 1 for quarter 1 of 1999). The trend line is
Y' = 112 - 2 t. The final seasonal indices are given below:

Quarter	Seasonal Factor (S)
1	0.65
2	1.35
3	1.20
4	0.80

1. The trend line forecast for quarter 2 of year 2002 is:
   a. 112
   b. –28
   c. 86
   d. 84
   e. None of the above
2. The trend line forecast for crimes in quarter 4 of 2002 is 80. What is the seasonally adjusted forecast for that quarter.
   a. 64
   b. 100
   c. 80
   d. 96
3. For quarter 2 of 1999, the actual number of crimes was 135. The deseasonalized number of crimes for that quarter will be:
   a. 182.25
   b. 135
   c. 100
   d. 108
4. Number of crimes seemed to be
   a. Going down
   b. going up
   c. Staying the same
   d. Can not tell from the available information
5. Seasonally adjusted forecast for qtr 3 of year 2002 is
   a. 82
   b. 80
   c. 98.4
   d. 112
   e. None of the above

Questions 6-10 use the data below:

Following are the seasonal factors for quarterly data on the number of crimes committed in Middletown.

Quarter	Seasonal Factor (S_t)
1	.589
2	1.351
3	1.335
4	.726

6. If 35 crimes are committed in Middletown in quarter 3 of 1989, calculate the deseasonalized value.
   a. 26.217
   b. (b)36.335
   c. 46.725
   d. 59.423
7. Which quarter you expect the crime numbers to be highest?
   a. I b. II c. III d. IV
8. Which quarter you expect the crime numbers to be lowest?
   a. I b. II c. III d. IV
9. Which quarter the actual and seasonally adjusted figure will differ the most (in general)?
   a. I b. II c. III d. IV
10. Which quarter the actual and seasonally adjusted figure will differ the least (in general)?
   a. I b. II c. III d. IV
11. Laspeyres index is based on base year quantities and current prices
   a. True b. False
12. Paasche index is based on reference year quantities and current prices.
   a. True b. False

16.9 Glossary

additive structure
A time series structure where each observation can be described by a sum of its four components; that is $y_t = TR_t + S_t + C_t + I_t$.

aggregate price index
A price index that includes more than one item.

cyclical activity
Upward and downward movements of various lengths about the trend within time series observations.

deseasonalized value
A time series value that has been seasonally adjusted by dividing by the corresponding seasonal index.

index number
A value that measures the change in a particular item or collection of items between two time periods.

index time series
A time-related sequence of index numbers where all values are derived from the same base year.

irregular activity
The remaining activity (often called "noise") in time series observations after removal of the trend, seasonality, and cyclical activity components.

Laspeyres index
A weighted aggregate price index that is computed using the base year quantities (weights).

multiplicative structure
A time series structure where each observation can be described by a product of its four components; that is $y_t = TR_t \times S_t \times C_t \times I_t$.

Paasche index
A weighted aggregate price index that is computed using the reference year quantities (weights).

price index
An index number that measures the change in prices between two time periods.

seasonal index
A value specifying the average activity for this particular month or quarter. A value larger (smaller) than one implies that the observations for this month or quarter are typically larger (smaller) than the yearly average.

seasonality
Within-year recurrent fluctuations of time series observations.

simple aggregate price index
An aggregate price index that is computed by dividing the sum of sampled prices for the reference year by the corresponding sum for the base year.

time series
A set of measurements (observations) taken on a variable across successive points in time.

time series decomposition
The act of splitting a time series into its assumed components
These components typically are trend (TR), seasonality (S), cyclical activity (C) and irregular activity (I).

trend
A long term growth or decline in time series observations.

weighted aggregate price index
An aggregate price index that is computed by weighting the price of each sampled item by its corresponding quantity (measure of relative importance).

16.10 Solution to Self-Test Problems

Solution to Self-Test Problem 16.8.1.

a. By regressing y_t (percentage of trading days) on t (= 1, 2, 3, ..., 8), the resulting prediction equation is $\hat{y}_t$ = 1.21 + 5.536t. Here, $\Sigma t = 36$, $\Sigma t^2 = 204$, $\Sigma y_t = 209$, $\Sigma ty_t = 1173$. The quadratic trend line is obtained by regressing y_t on t and t^2. This equation is = 46.48 - 21.625t + 3.0179t^2. (This equation can also be obtained by using KGP Data Analysis > Time Series Analysis > Forecasting > Trend Only > Linear and Quadratic). The R^2 value using t is .402. The R^2 value using t and t^2 is .880. The quadratic trend model provides a better fit since the regression procedure wants to retain the t^2 term (p-value = .007) in the quadratic model.

b. $\hat{y}_9 = 46.48 - 21.625(9) + 3.0179(9)^2 = 96.3$.

Solution to Self-test Problem 16.8.2

a. For the first five years, the trend is increasing. For the remaining years, the trend is decreasing.
b. Based on the answer in part (a) and a plot of the time series values, the trend line appears to be quadratic. By regressing y_t on t and t^2, the resulting trend line is $\hat{y} = 92.998 + 1.567t - .153t^2$.

Solution to Self-Test Problem 16.8.3.

Examining the cyclical components reveals three very clear cycles, beginning towards the end of 1992 and ending towards the end of 1998.

Solution to Self-Test Problem 16.8.4.

Seasonal analysis has several steps. First is the estimation of the trend line by finding moving average (4-quarter moving average, since 4 quarters will make a year) and then centering the moving average and using the centered moving average to estimate the seasonal variation. Details are found in the following Table.

Qtr(1)	Enrollment (2)	Mov av1(3)	Centered Mov.av(4)	Specific Seasonal (5)=(2)/(4)
1	2033			
2	1871	1734		
3	714	1769.3	1751.63	0.407621494
4	2318	1818.8	1794	1.292084727
5	2174	1850.3	1834.5	1.18506405
6	2069	1874	1862.13	1.111096194
7	840	1923	1898.5	0.442454569
8	2413	1969.3	1946.13	1.239899801
9	2370	1991	1980.13	1.196894135

10	2254	2063.8	2027.38	1.111782477
11	927	2127.5	2095.63	0.442350134
12	2704	2183.5	2155.5	1.254465321
13	2625	2235.8	2209.63	1.187984386
14	2478	2310	2272.88	1.090249134
15	1136	2354.5	2332.25	0.487083289
16	3001	2402	2378.25	1.261852202
17	2803			
18	2668			

Table: Specific Seasonals

Next these specific seasonals are averaged out and normalized. Details are in the next table.

1	2	3	4	
		0.41	1.29	
1.19	1.11	0.44	1.24	
1.2	1.11	0.44	1.25	
1.19	1.09	0.49	1.26	
1.193333	1.1033333	0.445	1.26	4.001666667
1.192836	1.1028738	0.44481	1.25948	4

As you can see, the average seasonal index adds up to 4.00166666. All seasonal indices(numbers in row 6) are divided by 4.001666 and multiplied by 4.0, and thus normalized . They now add up to 4.

Next these seasonal indices are used to remove the effect of season (deseasonalized).

Qtr(1)	Enrollment (2)	Seasonal index (3)	Deseasonalized enrolment=(2)/(3)
1	2033	1.192	1705.536913
2	1871	1.102	1697.822142
3	714	0.444	1608.108108
4	2318	1.259	1841.143765
5	2174	1.192	1823.825503
6	2069	1.102	1877.495463
7	840	0.444	1891.891892
8	2413	1.259	1916.600477
9	2370	1.192	1988.255034
10	2254	1.102	2045.372051

11	927	0.444	2087.837838
12	2704	1.259	2147.736299
13	2625	1.192	2202.181208
14	2478	1.102	2248.638838
15	1136	0.444	2558.558559
16	3001	1.259	2383.637808
17	2803	1.192	2351.510067
18	2668	1.102	2421.052632
19			

A trend line is found using linear regression, independent variable is quarter number and the dependent variable is deseasonalized enrolment.
The trend line is:

Y-hat = 1574.79 + 49.42X

Qtr (1)	(2) Trend line forecast: 1574.79 + 49.42 × qtr# (col. 1)	Seas. Index(3)	Seas. adj. forecast=(2)*(3)
21	2611.4	1.192	3112.7888
22	2660.8	1.102	2932.2016
23	2710.2	0.444	1203.3288
24	2759.6	1.259	3474.3364

Answers to Multiple Choice Questions

Question #	Answer
1	d t = 14 for qtr2 yr 2002, counting from t = 1 for qtr 1 of 1999 is. trend line forecast = 112-2*14 = 84
2	a 80* 0.8 (seas. index for qtr 4 from the table above) = 64
3	c 135/1.35 = 100 (we are deseasonalizing, so divide by the seasonal index)
4	a Because the coefficient of t is –2 in the trend line.
5	c Trend line estimate= 112- 2* 15=82 seas. adj. forecast = 82* 1.2 = 98.4
6	a 35/1.335 = 26.217
7	b (because of highest seas. index value)
8	a (lowest seas. index)
9	a (because, of all four seasonal indices, it is most away from 1.0)
10	d (because, of all four seasonal indices its seas. index is closest to 1.0)
11	a

CHAPTER 17 QUANTITATIVE BUSINESS FORECASTING

Chapter Overview and Learning Objectives

In this chapter, the student is introduced to forecasting techniques using time series data. These procedures include the naive method, exponential smoothing (simple, Holt's and Winters' smoothing models) and autoregressive models. Linear regression procedures using time series data are discussed including using dummy variables to capture additive seasonality and lagged independent variables. Upon completion of this chapter, the student will be able to:

1. Construct and estimate the necessary parameters for a wide assortment of forecasting models.
2. Determine which of a variety of exponential smoothing models might be appropriate for forecasting a given time series.
3. Calculate the MSE, MAD and MAPE for a particular forecasting procedure.
4. Construct and evaluate linear regression models used for forecasting with time series data.

Chapter outline

17.1 Methods of Forecasting
17.2 The Naive Forecast
17.3 Projecting the Least Square trend Equation
17.4 Simple Exponential Smoothing
17.5 Exponential Smoothing for a Time Series Containing Trend
17.6 Exponential Smoothing Method for Trend and Seasonality
17.7 Choosing the appropriate Forecasting Procedure
17.8 Self-Test Problems
17.9 Glossary
17.10 Solution to Self-test Problems

17.1 Methods of Forecasting

Qualitative Forecasting: Using judgment, discussions, knowledge and intuition, guesses about unpredictable events and their impact on the forecast, make a forecast. Useful when no prior data is available. May also be very useful, if conditions have changed.
Quantitative Forecast: Using past data and some mathematical model, make a forecast. Regression is one approach and time series is another approach.

17.2 The Naive Forecast

This is simply: Tomorrow will be just like today and hence tomorrow's sales forecast will be the same as today's actual sales.

17.3 Projecting the Least Square trend Equation

One can use simple linear regression with sales as the dependent variable and time (month or quarter) as the independent variable and forecast sales. We can also use the seasonal variation based models discussed elaborately in Chapter 16.

17.4 Simple Exponential Smoothing

Moving average is a method of forecasting which averages the sales during the most recent set of periods to get a forecast. One way of looking at exponential smoothing is that it is a weighted average method of averaging past sales, where highest weightage is associated with the most recent period, and the decreasing weightages are associated with the previous periods as they go back in time. The formula is compact and it has a weight A, associated with the most recent actual data and a weight (1-A) associated with the most recent forecast (this forecast is a combination of previous actual sales and forecast). As you stretch this process long enough, you will see the method is indeed averaging out all actual sales of the past periods.
$S_t = AY_t + (1 - A)S_{t-1}$ where S_t the smoothed value for period t is indeed your forecast or estimate for period $t+1$, or $S_t = \hat{Y}_{t+1}$.

Using simple exponential smoothing

- One can only forecast for the immediate next period, not well into the future.
- This method will fail to catch up with increasing or deceasing trend quickly.

A problem will make things more clear.

Review Problem 17.4.1.

The trend in the price of Texas homes is up since 1992. However, the price of the average home in Texas is nowhere near as costly as during the 1980 boom. On an inflation-adjusted basis, the average price of a Texas home hit a 20-year low at $106,793 in 1991. During the 1998 and 1999 period, economists believe a four-and-a-half month supply of homes was on the Texas market, compared to a normal inventory of nine to 10 months.

Year	Average Home Sale Prices in Texas
1979	119,105
1980	120,500
1981	129,200
1982	130,350
1983	137,650
1984	141,100
1985	134,200
1986	131,700
1987	118,750
1988	112,425
1989	110,900
1990	108,300
1991	106,793
1992	108,450
1993	111,650
1994	113,210
1995	115,350
1996	118,900
1997	121,300
1998	122,100

a. Using simple exponential smoothing with $A = .25$, find the residuals for 1997 and 1998.
b. Repeat part (a) with $A = .5$ and compare the residuals for 1997 and 1998.

Solution

The output using KPK Data Analysis follows with A = .25:

Simple Exponential Smoothing (A = .25)				
T	Y(t)	SM(t)	Y-HAT	RESIDUAL
1	119105.	119105.000		
2	120500.	119453.750	119105.000	1395.000
3	129200.	121890.313	119453.750	9746.250
4	130350.	124005.234	121890.313	8459.688
5	137650.	127416.426	124005.234	13644.766
6	141100.	130837.319	127416.426	13683.574
7	134200.	131677.990	130837.319	3362.681
8	131700.	131683.492	131677.990	22.010
9	118750.	128450.119	131683.492	-12933.492
10	112425.	124443.839	128450.119	-16025.119
11	110900.	121057.879	124443.839	-13543.839
12	108300.	117868.410	121057.879	-12757.879
13	106793.	115099.557	117868.410	-11075.410
14	108450.	113437.168	115099.557	-6649.557
15	111650.	112990.376	113437.168	-1787.168
16	113210.	113045.282	112990.376	219.624
17	115350.	113621.461	113045.282	2304.718
18	118900.	114941.096	113621.461	5278.539
19	121300.	116530.822	114941.096	6358.904
20	122100.	117923.117	116530.822	5569.178

a. The residuals for 1997 and 1998 (highlighted) are 6,358.9 and 5,569.2, respectively.

b. Using $A = 0.5$:

Simple Exponential Smoothing (A = 0.5)				
T	Y(t)	SM(t)	Y-HAT	RESIDUAL
1	119105.	119105.000		
2	120500.	119802.500	119105.000	1395.000
3	129200.	124501.250	119802.500	9397.500
4	130350.	127425.625	124501.250	5848.750
5	137650.	132537.813	127425.625	10224.375
6	141100.	136818.906	132537.813	8562.188
7	134200.	135509.453	136818.906	-2618.906
8	131700.	133604.727	135509.453	-3809.453
9	118750.	126177.363	133604.727	-14854.727
10	112425.	119301.182	126177.363	-13752.363
11	110900.	115100.591	119301.182	-8401.182
12	108300.	111700.295	115100.591	-6800.591
13	106793.	109246.648	111700.295	-4907.295
14	108450.	108848.324	109246.648	-796.648
15	111650.	110249.162	108848.324	2801.676

16	113210.	111729.581	110249.162	2960.838
17	115350.	113539.790	111729.581	3620.419
18	118900.	116219.895	113539.790	5360.210
19	121300.	118759.948	116219.895	5080.105
20	122100.	120429.974	118759.948	3340.052

Using A = 0.5, the two residuals are 5080.1 and 3,340.1. The residuals are smaller using A = 0.5.

17.5 Exponential Smoothing for a Time Series Containing Trend

This method remedies some of the problems of exponential smoothing such as inability to forecast well into the future and inability to quickly capture rapidly changing trends. It keeps the basis philosophy of smoothing over a longer time.

$$S_t = AY_t + (1-A)(S_{t-1} + b_{t-1}) \text{ for } t = 2,3,4..$$

$$b_t = B(S_t - S_{t-1}) + (1-B)b_{t-1} \text{ for } t = 2,3,..$$

The smoothing constants A and B are usually < 0.3 and will always be between 0 and 1.0.

Review Problem 17.5.1.

The growth of the chip industry is vital to the tax base of many counties across the United States. For example, in Washington County, Oregon, Intel is the county's biggest property tax payer. In 1998, Intel paid about $10 million, about three times as much as the next-biggest property tax payer. Annual revenue for the computer chip industry is presented below in units of billions of dollars. Forecast the 1999 annual revenue using Holt's two-parameter linear exponential smoothing technique with an initial estimate of zero for the slope and with $A = .3$ and $B = .2$.

Year	Annual Revenue for Chip Industry	Year	Annual Revenue for Chip Industry
1988	46.3	1994	100.7
1989	48.6	1995	143.3
1990	50.5	1996	130.1
1991	62.3	1997	131.4
1992	69.5	1998	128.7
1993	75.8		

Solution

The output using KPK Data Analysis follows with A = .3, B =.2, and Procedure 1:

Holt's Exponential Smoothing (A=.3, B=.2)					
T	Y(t)	S(t)	B(t)	YHAT	RESIDUAL
1	46.3	46.300	0.000		
2	48.6	46.990	0.138	46.300	2.300
3	50.5	48.140	0.340	47.128	3.372
4	62.3	52.626	1.170	48.480	13.820
5	69.5	58.507	2.112	53.795	15.705

6	75.8	65.173	3.023	60.619	15.181
7	100.7	77.947	4.973	68.196	32.504
8	143.3	101.034	8.596	82.920	60.380
9	130.1	115.771	9.824	109.630	20.470
10	131.4	127.336	10.172	125.595	5.805
11	128.7	134.866	9.644	137.509	-8.809
Forecasts					
12	144.510				

The forecast for 1999 is $S_{11} + B_{11} = 134.866 + 9.644 = 144.51$.

17.6 Exponential Smoothing Method for Trend and Seasonality

This procedure gets quite cumbersome to do by hand. Many packages are available that use this method to obtain good forecasts. This is particularly useful for situations when you have a trend (upward or downward) and a seasonal component to your business.

17.7 Choosing Appropriate Forecasting Procedure

Three common classifications used in forecasting:

- Short term (1-3 months: Methods used: Exponential smoothing)
- Medium range forecast (3-24 months: Methods used: Projecting least square trend))
- Long range (more than 24 months: Methods Used: Many methods including qualitative)

Measures for Evaluating Forecasts

Mean absolute deviation (MAD) = $\dfrac{\sum|y_t - \hat{y}_t|}{n} = \dfrac{\sum e_t}{n}$, n is the number of predicted values, y_t and y_t-hat are actual and the corresponding predicted value for the same period.

(Predictive) Mean square error (MSE) = $\dfrac{\sum e_t^2}{n}$ where e_t is the forecast error in period t.

Mean absolute percentage error (MAPE) = $\dfrac{\sum\left|\dfrac{e_t}{y_t}\right|}{n}$ are some of the measures.

Review Problem 17.7.1.

Table 17.7.1. gives the actual and forecast for number of ice-cream cones sold by Jones, a street vendor taking a statistics class. Find MAD, MSE and MAPE for the forecasts made by Jones.

Day #	Actual	Forecast	Abs(Act-frcst)	Abs(act-frcst)^2	abs((Act-frst)/act)
1	23	40	17	289	0.73913
2	37	40	3	9	0.081081
3	35	25	10	100	0.285714

4	25	38	13	169	0.52
5	23	46	23	529	1
6	16	35	19	361	1.1875
7	10	42	32	1024	3.2
8	25	29	4	16	0.16
9	49	45	4	16	0.081633
10	23	24	1	1	0.043478
			12.6	251.4	72.98537

Table 17.7.1. Forecast and measures of forecast

Solution

MAD = 12.6
MSE = 251.4
MAPE = 72.98% or 0.7298 as a proportion.

Use for the forecasts and Measures:
For some products such as newspaper, fresh food, where you cannot carry forward, MAD may be a more important measure, where as for some products like paint, or groceries it may be enough if you had a good overall forecast. MSE may be useful if deviations are to be penalized at an increasing rate.

Smoothing constants:
Using the forecast evaluation measures, you can evaluate the forecasts made with as starting values of smoothing coefficients, change them gradually until you have searched the entire set of possible values and the choose that set of smoothing constants which produces the "best" forecast, the one with least amount of undesirable errors.

17.8 Self-Test Problems

Self-Test Problem 17.8.1.

The Purchasing Managers' Index tracks overall business activity at 300 industrial companies, in percent. A reading above 50% means the industrial economy is expanding. Using simple exponential smoothing with $A = 0.2$, predict the value of this index for February, March, and April 1997.

Year	Month	Purchasing Managers' Index
1996	May	49.5
	June	54.5
	July	50.2
	August	52.5
	September	50.3
	October	49.7
	November	54.5
	December	55.0
1997	January	52.3
	February	53.5
	March	54.7
	April	53.9

(Source: Adapted from *The Dallas Morning News,* "Incomes, Spending Creep Up Mere 0.1%," June 3, 1997, p.7D.)

Self-Test Problem 17.8.2.

More than 20% of the American population lives in households wired for e-mail. Though no one keeps track of the recipients of all the messages, communications analysts say inter-family e-mail accounts for a large percentage of the traffic. The estimated numbers of messages per day per person since 1989 are presented below.

Year	Estimated Messages per Day per Person	Year	Estimated Messages per Day per Person
1989	1.7	1994	2.2
1990	1.8	1995	2.4
1991	2.0	1996	2.5
1992	2.1	1997	2.7
1993	2.1	1998	3.1

(Adapted from *The Wall Street Journal,* "Getting the Message," June 7, 1997, p. R22.)

a. Using zero as an initial estimate of the slope, find the predicted value for the estimated number of messages received per day per person at households that are wired for e-mail. Let $A = 0.25$ and $B = 0.1$.
b. Using the least squares estimate from the first five years for the slope, redo part (a). Compare the predicted value from part (a) to the predicted value using this procedure.

Self-Test Problem 17.8.3.

Evaluate the forecasts given in the following Table using several measures such as MSE, MAD and MAPE. Comment on the usefulness of the measures if the product being forecasted is fresh food.

Day #	Actual	Forecast
1	32	65
2	44	68
3	62	67
4	94	65
5	46	74
6	97	67
7	36	73
8	92	73
9	75	65
10	83	68

Self-Test Problem 17.8.4.

The Purchasing Managers' Index tracks overall business activity at 300 industrial companies, in percent. A reading above 50% means the industrial economy is expanding. Using simple exponential smoothing with $A = 0.2$, predict the value of this index for February, March, and April 1997.

Year	Month	Purchasing Managers' Index
1996	May	49.5
	June	54.5
	July	50.2
	August	52.5
	September	50.3
	October	49.7
	November	54.5
	December	55.0
1997	January	52.3
	February	53.5
	March	54.7
	April	53.9

(Source: Adapted from *The Dallas Morning News,* "Incomes, Spending Creep Up Mere 0.1%," June 3, 1997, p.7D.)

Multiple Choice Questions

1. Qualitative forecasts may be useful
   a. for new products
   b. to accommodate unexpected events
   c. where 5 years of daily data is available
   d. where a new use has been found for an existing product
   e. a, b, and d
2. DELPHI method is a sophisticated computerized forecasting technique
   a. True b. False
3. Simple exponential smoothing uses only two terms and hence it should be using only the most recent actual sales to make the forecast.
   a. True b. False
4. Using simple exponential smoothing you can make monthly forecasts for the next year.
   a. True b. False
5. Stationary time series means, it does not change from year to year
   a. True b. False
6. The number of cups of water consumed in the U.S.A. per capita is most likely a stationary time series because its mean is not changing, but it has a variance.
   a. True b. False
7. Smoothing constants used in exponential smoothing must be between 0 and 1.0
   a. True b. False
8. Smoothing constants used in simple exponential smoothing tells you the weight given for the most recent period's actual demand.
   a. True b. False
9. Exponential smoothing with trend can be used to forecast monthly demand for the next 12 months.
   a. True b. False
10. Exponential smoothing with trend would be an appropriate method if the time series is stationary.
    a. True b. False

17.9 Glossary

autoregressive forecast model
A statistical forecasting model which uses a multiple regression equation with the lagged observations as predictor variables.

correlogram
A graphical representation of sample autocorrelations.

cross sectional data
Data for a linear regression model that is obtained at a single point in time, such as data from 20 different factories collected during May, 2002.

Delphi method
A qualitative forecasting procedure which uses a group of individuals in an attempt to arrive at a group opinion (forecast). Members of the group are informed of the responses of other group members and are asked to possibly revise their response in light of this information.

Durbin-Watson statistic
A statistic used to measure the degree of autocorrelation in the residuals when using a linear regression model with time series data.

dummy variable
A variable used in a regression model to represent a nominal variable (such as gender).

exponential smoothing
A smoothing or forecasting procedure which uses a weighted average of past time series values to arrive at a smoother (less noise) time series or forecasts for future time periods. These techniques include simple exponential smoothing (no trend or seasonality), Holt's linear exponential smoothing (trend, no seasonality), and Winters' linear and seasonal exponential smoothing (trend and seasonality).

lagged variable (lag = *k*)
A variable used in a regression model whose value during time period t is equal to the observed value in time period $t - k$.

mean absolute deviation (MAD)
A measure of forecast accuracy equal to the average of the absolute values of the residuals.

mean absolute percentage error (MAPE)
A measure of forecast accuracy equal to the average of the absolute values of the relative errors.

mean squared error (MSE)
A measure of forecast accuracy equal to the average of the squared residuals.

qualitative forecast
A forecast based on subjective opinion(s), rather than a quantitative technique.

quantitative forecast
A forecast based on a specific quantitative procedure, such as exponential smoothing or linear regression.

smoothing constant
A value to be specified for exponential smoothing which determines the relative weights when using a smoothing equation.

stationary time series
A time series which exhibits no trend and has constant variance about the mean.

time series data
Data on one or more variables that are collected across successive periods of time.

17.10 Solution to Self-Test Problems

Solution to Self-Test Problem 17.8.1

The output using KPK Data Analysis follows with A = 0.2:

Simple Exponential Smoothing (A = 0.2)				
t	Y(t)	SM(t)	YHAT	RESIDUAL
1	49.5	49.500		
2	54.5	50.500	49.500	5.000
3	50.2	50.440	50.500	-0.300
4	52.5	50.852	50.440	2.060
5	50.3	50.742	50.852	-0.552
6	49.7	50.533	50.742	-1.042

Solution to Self-Test Problem 17.8.2

The output using KPK Data Analysis follows with A = 0.25, B = 0.1, and Procedure 1:

Holt's Exponential Smoothing (A = 0.25, B = 0.1)					
t	Y(t)	S(t)	B(t)	YHAT	RESIDUAL
1	1.7	1.700	0.000		
2	1.8	1.725	0.002	1.700	0.100
3	2.	1.796	0.009	1.728	0.272
4	2.1	1.879	0.017	1.805	0.295
5	2.1	1.947	0.022	1.895	0.205
6	2.2	2.026	0.028	1.968	0.232
7	2.4	2.140	0.036	2.054	0.346
8	2.5	2.257	0.044	2.177	0.323
9	2.7	2.401	0.054	2.302	0.398
10	3.1	2.617	0.070	2.456	0.644
Forecasts					
11	2.687				

The forecast for 1999 is $S_{10} + B_{10} = 2.617 + 0.070 = 2.687$. The output using KPK Data Analysis follows with A = 0.25, B = 0.1, and Procedure 2:

Holt's Exponential Smoothing (A = 0.25, B = 0.1)					
T	Y(t)	S(t)	B(t)	YHAT	RESIDUAL
1	1.7	1.700	0.110		
2	1.8	1.808	0.110	1.810	-0.010
3	2.	1.938	0.112	1.917	0.083
4	2.1	2.062	0.113	2.050	0.050
5	2.1	2.157	0.111	2.175	-0.075
6	2.2	2.251	0.109	2.268	-0.068
7	2.4	2.370	0.110	2.360	0.040
8	2.5	2.486	0.111	2.481	0.019
9	2.7	2.622	0.114	2.597	0.103
10	3.1	2.827	0.123	2.736	0.364
Forecasts					
11	2.950				

The forecast for 1999 is $S_{10} + B_{10} = 2.827 + 0.123 = 2.950$. The predicted value has increased using Procedure 2 and appears to be a better forecast based on the residuals for the 10 periods.

Solution to Self-Test Problem 17.8.3.

Day #	Actual	Forecast	Abs(Act-frcst)	abs(act-frcst)^2	abs(act-frcst)/act
1	32	65	33	1089	1.03125
2	44	68	24	576	0.545455
3	62	67	5	25	0.080645
4	94	65	29	841	0.308511
5	46	74	28	784	0.608696
6	97	67	30	900	0.309278
7	36	73	37	1369	1.027778
8	92	73	19	361	0.206522
9	75	65	10	100	0.133333
10	83	68	15	225	0.180723
		Totals	230	6270	4.43219
		Averages	23	627	0.443219

MAD = 23
MSE = 627
MAPE = 0.44 (or 44%)
The forecast is not very good, and you will be looking closely at MAD for this application. It is quite high, so is MAPE, which is also relevant for this application.

Solution to Self-Test Problem 17.8.4.

The output using KPK Data Analysis follows with A = 0.2:

Simple Exponential Smoothing (A = 0.2)				
t	Y(t)	SM(t)	YHAT	RESIDUAL
1	49.5	49.500		
2	54.5	50.500	49.500	5.000
3	50.2	50.440	50.500	-0.300
4	52.5	50.852	50.440	2.060
5	50.3	50.742	50.852	-0.552
6	49.7	50.533	50.742	-1.042
7	54.5	51.327	50.533	3.967
8	55.	52.061	51.327	3.673
9	52.3	52.109	52.061	0.239
10	53.5	52.387	**52.109**	1.391
11	54.7	52.850	**52.387**	2.313
12	53.9	53.060	**52.850**	1.050

The predicted values for February, March, and April 1997 (highlighted) are 52.11, 52.39, and 52.85, respectively.

Answers to Multiple Choice Questions

Question #	Answer	Question #	Answer	Question #	Answer
1	e	5	b	9	a
2	b	6	a	10	b
3	b	7	a		
4	b	8	a		

CHAPTER 18 NONPARAMETRIC STATISTICS

Chapter Overview and Learning Objectives

The use of nonparametric statistics is introduced in this chapter. Nonparametric procedures include the runs test for randomness, Mann-Whitney test for two independent samples, Wilcoxon test for paired samples, the Kruskal-Wallis test for comparing more than two populations using independent samples and the Friedman test for dependent samples. The Spearman rank correlation as a measure of association between two variables is presented. Having completed this chapter, the student should be able to:

1. Discuss under what conditions a nonparametric test would be appropriate.
2. Perform the calculation and/or use a computer package to carry out any of the above nonparametric tests.
3. Measure the association between two variables using the Spearman rank correlation and test the significance of this value.
4. Construct a regression line through the medians as an alternative to the least squares line from Chapter 14 (a regression line through the means).

Chapter Outline

18.1 A Test for Randomness: The Runs Test
18.2 Nonparametric Tests for Central Tendency: Two Populations
18.3 Comparing More Than Two Populations: Kruskal-Wallis Test and Friedman Test
18.4 Self-Test Problems
18.5 Glossary
18.6 Solution to Self-Test Problems

18.1: Tests for Randomness (Runs Test)

Nonparametric statistics deals with tests that do not require the assumption that the underlying population is normal or approximately normal. It is also used when interval measurements, (that is, a numerical value associated with a measurement) of the data is not available or difficult to get. For example what would be your answer to the question "How do you like your Statistics class as compared to Organizational Behavior?" You may like statistics better, about the same or worse than organizational behavior but you may not be able to put down a number corresponding to your liking.

Almost all nonparametric tests use ranking of data to execute the test. Sometimes, you may have actual numerical values, which you convert to ranks. At other times, you may just have rank values given to you.

Runs Test For Small Sample Sizes ($n_1 \leq 20$ and $n_2 \leq 20$):
If two items such as H (Head) and T (Tail) are generated by a coin tossing, how could you tell that the series of outcomes (H and T) are truly random, That is, the series does not exhibit any dependence on history, or cycling tendency, etc. This is a little different from the question of whether the coin is fair, which will be studied in a later test. Similar scenarios present themselves when: (a) a Financial analyst studies the movement of stock prices, (b) a computer generates a

series of random numbers, or (c) a statistician uses some method for generating random samples (a very important statistical activity).

In the coin tossing experiment, a run is defined as consecutive stream of H or T. For example, the following outcome of an experiment, which consists of tossing a coin 16 times and having obtained 8 H and 8 T, as the outcome, with specific values being: HH TTTT H TT H T HH T H. This sequence has 9 runs, starting with the first (HH), second (TTTT),... ending with the 9th (H). In this test, we first ask the question: how many different arrangements of 16 objects out of which 8 are (H) and 8 are (T) are theoretically possible? The answer is $\frac{n!}{n_1!n_2!} = \frac{16!}{8!.8!} = 12870$, where n is the total number of objects, and n_1 and n_2 are number of identical objects of each type. In many of these arrangements number of runs would be the same. If the objects are not arranged in random order, the number of runs would be very small or very large. This test uses "this" property of randomly arranged objects to determine whether or not we should reject the null hypothesis. In general:

Step 1: Null and alternate hypotheses
H_0: The sequence was generated in a random manner
H_a: The sequence was not generated in a random manner.

Step 2: Test Statistic. In this case R the number of runs is the test statistic.

Step 3: Critical values for a given significance level
If H_0 is true, as mentioned before, the number of runs will be neither too few, nor too many. Hence, we pick that number k_1 and k_2 such that R the number of runs satisfies: $P(R \leq k_1) \leq \alpha/2$ and $P(R \geq k_2) \leq \alpha/2$, where α is the level of significance of the test. And k_1 and k_2 become the critical values for the test.

Step 4: Calculate the test statistic value, which is to count the number of runs.

Step 5: (Reject or fail to reject H_0): If the number of runs is less than or equal to k_1 or more than or equal to k_2 reject H_0, otherwise fail to reject H_0.

Review Problem 18.1.1

According to random walk theory of stock market movements, the movement of any leading stock market index, that is, closing up or closing down compared to the previous day's closing figure is random. In this test, we are only testing the randomness of the event and not anything about the probability of going up or going down. Closing figures of Jamestown Industrial average (JIA) for 13 consecutive days is presented in Table 18.1. (It is assumed that the index is measured to sufficient accuracy that no two consecutive days will close at the same exact value.)

Test at 0.05 level of significance whether random walk theory of stock index movements holds for this data.

Day #	1	2	3	4	5	6	7	8	9	10	11	12	13
Closing JIA	123	128	107	123	128	120	133	114	130	129	114	116	119

Table 18.1.1 Closing value of JIA

The 13 days will produce 12 data points corresponding to increase or decrease as compared to the previous day. For example, from Day 1 to Day 2, there was an increase denoted by I. Table 18.2 gives the values of I and D (decrease).

I	D	I	I	D	I	D	I	D	D	I	I

Table 18.1.2: Changes in the JIA, captured as I (increase from previous closing) or D (decrease).

Solution

Step 1. Null Hypothesis: I and D occur randomly.
Alternate hypothesis: I and D are not occurring randomly.

Step 2. The number of runs is the test statistic.

Step 3. $n_1 = 7$ and $n_2 = 5$. From Appendix Table A.15 in the text, $k_1 = 3$ and $k_2 = 11$. According to the test, if $R \leq 3$ or if $R \geq 11$, reject H_0. Otherwise, Fail to reject H_0.

Step 4. From the data in Table 18.2, $R = 9$.

Step 5. Hence, we fail to reject H_0. That is, the increases and decreases appear to be random.

Runs Test For Large Sample Sizes ($n_1 > 20$ and $n_2 > 20$)
The distribution of R, the number of runs if the generating process is random is approximately normal with

$$\mu_R = 1 + \frac{2\, n_1 n_2}{n_1 + n_2} \text{ and } \sigma_R = \sqrt{\frac{2\, n_1 n_2 (2\, n_1 n_2 - n_1 - n_2)}{(n_1 + n_2)^2 (n_1 + n_2 - 1)}}.$$

Using this information, the following 5-step solution procedure is developed for the Review Problem 18.1.2.

Review Problem 18.1.2

JCI Universal Com a universe-wide telecom company recently got into trouble with the earth based securities and exchange commission (SEC) for misclassifying transactions involving expenditures into capital (C) or operating (O) expenditures. An auditor from SEC requested an internal auditor of JCI Universal Com to randomly pick 60 transactions involving expenditure for scrutiny. The internal auditor picked the following sequence of transactions coded as C or O:
CCOOCCCOOO OOCCCCOCOC OCOCCOCOOC COCCOOCCCO COCOCOCOCO COCOCOCOCC

Test, using nonparametric methods, whether the internal auditor picked the transactions (classified as C or O) at random at a significance level of 0.10.

Solution

Step 1. Null Hypothesis: C and O occur randomly.
Alternate hypothesis: C and O are not occurring randomly.

Step 2. The test statistic is $Z = \dfrac{R - \mu_R}{\sigma_R}$.

Step 3. For a two-tailed test, using Z, with a significance level of 0.10, the critical values are -1.645 and +1.645. Reject H_0 if the computed $|Z| \geq 1.645$. Otherwise, Fail to reject H_0.

Step 4. From the given data, n_1 (number of C's) = 33 and n_2 (number of O's) = 27. $R = 41$.

$$\mu_R = 1 + \frac{2.33.27}{33+27} = 30.7 \text{ and } \sigma_R = \sqrt{\frac{2.33.27(2.33.27 - 33 - 27)}{(33+27)^2(33+27-1)}} = 3.747$$

$$\text{and } Z = \frac{41 - 30.7}{3.747} = 2.748$$

Step 5. Since Z falls in the reject H_0 region, reject H_0. The appearance of C and O does not look like a random stream.

One-tailed Runs Test:
It is possible to have a one-tailed runs test in situations where we will reject H_0 only in cases where there are too few runs resulting in a left-tailed test with a critical region to the left. For example, when examining the residuals of a linear regression as to being positive or negative in a random manner.

18.2 Nonparametric Tests for Central Tendency: Two Populations

Mann-Whitney Test for Independent Samples:
Used for small sample sizes, i.e. $n_1 \leq 10$ and $n_2 \leq 10$, and populations need not be normal. To be used under the assumptions:

a. Samples are independent
b. Sample data are at least ordinal
c. Populations if they differ, differ only in location, but they have same variation and shape.
d. $n_1 \leq n_2$.

Review Problem 18.2.1

There are two processes to make a tension rod of certain strength. The strength measured in pounds per square inch (psi) of the population of rods is not considered normally distributed. Samples from each process with its strength are given below. Test using Mann-Whitney test whether the location parameters of both populations have the same strength. Use significance level of 0.05.

Process I		Process II	
1.4		1.2	1.6
1.6		1.5	1.8
1.4		1.5	1.5
1.75		1.45	1.9
2.0		1.4	
1.9		2.05	
		1.5	

Table 18.2.1. Data for Problem 18.2.1

Solution

Step 1. H_0: The two populations have identical distributions
H_a: The two populations differ in location.

Step 2. The test statistic is Mann-Whitney's $U = \text{Min.}(U_1, U_2)$. The probability values corresponding to the U is given in a series of tables in Appendix Table A10.

Step 3. For a two-tailed test, using a significance level of 0.05, the critical values are: If the probability value corresponding to the U value is less than 0.05/2 = 0.025, reject H_0. Otherwise, fail to reject H_0

Step 4. Calculate the test statistic. First step is to group the data and rank them. Recall that as per assumption 4, $n_1 \le n_2$. In case of tied values, average rank is assigned. For example, there are three tie values 1.4, each of which is assigned a rank equal to the average rank of the three values, ((2+3+4)/3) = 3.

Rank	Sample from Process I	Sample from Process II	Ranks for Process I	Ranks for Process II
1		1.2		1
2		1.4		3
3	1.4		3	
4	1.4		3	
5		1.45		5
6		1.5		7
7		1.5		7
8		1.5		7
9	1.6		9.5	
10		1.6		9.5
11	1.75		11	
12		1.8		12
13		1.9		13
14	1.9		14	
15	2.0		15	
16		2.05		16
		Sum of ranks:	55.5 (T_1)	80.5 (T_2)

Table 18.2.2. Ranking of data of Problem 18.2.1.

$$U_1 = n_1 n_2 + \frac{n_1(n_1+1)}{2} - T_1 = 6\times 10 + \frac{6(6+1)}{2} - 55.5 = 25.5$$

$$U_2 = n_1 n_2 + \frac{n_2(n_2+1)}{2} - T_2 = 6\times 10 + \frac{10(10+1)}{2} - 80.5 = 34.5$$

Intuitive meaning behind U_1 and U_2: The first portion of U_1 may be considered as the total rank of all elements of sample 1, if all items of sample 1 are larger than all items of sample 2. When T_1 is subtracted from this value, you get a measure of how much is this over the actual total. If U_1 is small (can never be negative), it implies that the location of population 1 is higher than that of 2 and vice-versa. U_2 may be interpreted in a similar manner.

$U = \text{Min}(U_1, U_2) = \text{Min}(25.5, 34.5) = 25.5$. (Round it up to 26.) $n_2 = 10$.

U	n1		
		6	
26		0.3564	

Table 18.2.3: Distribution function of the Mann-Whitney *U* statistic (Appendix Table A10)

Step 5. Since the significance level is 0.05, and the corresponding probability value 0.3564 is higher than 0.05/2 = 0.025, we fail to reject H_0. We conclude that there is no evidence to believe that the locations of the two distributions are any different.

One-sided Mann-Whitney Tests for Small Samples:

Step 1. H_0: The two populations have identical distributions

a. H_a: Population 1 is shifted to the right of Population 2.
b. H_a: Population 1 is shifted to the left of Population 2.

Step 2. The test statistic is Mann-Whitney's *U*.

a. $U = U_1$. The probability values corresponding to the *U* is given in a series of Tables in Appendix 10.
b. $U = U_2$. The probability values corresponding to the *U* is given in a series of Tables in Appendix 10

Step 3. For a one-tailed test, using a significance level of 0.05, the critical values are: If the probability value corresponding to the *U* value is less than 0.05, reject H_0. Otherwise, fail to reject H_0.

Step 4. Calculate the test statistic: Same as the two-tailed test procedure with the modification in Step 2.

Step 5. Conclude: Same as for two-tailed procedure taking into account Sep 3 above.

Mann-Whitney Test for Independent Samples:

Requires large sample sizes ($n_1 > 10$ and $n_2 > 10$). Populations need not be normal.

Assumptions:

a. Samples are independent
b. Sample data are at least ordinal
c. Populations if they differ, differed only in location, but they have same variation and shape.
d. $n_1 \leq n_2$

Procedure (for two-tailed test):

Step 1. H_0: The two populations have identical distributions
H_a: The two populations differ in location.

Step 2. The test statistic is Mann-Whitney's $U = U_2$. Distribution of the test statistic is *Z*.

$$Z = \frac{U_2 - \mu_{U2}}{\sigma_{U2}}$$

$$where\, \mu_{U_2} = \frac{n_1 n_2}{2} \text{ and } \sigma_{U_2} = \sqrt{\frac{n_1 n_2 (n_1 + n_2 + 1)}{12}}$$

Step 3. For a two-tailed test, using a significance level of 0.05, the critical values: If $|Z| > 1.96$, reject H_0. Otherwise, fail to reject H_0.

Step 4. Calculate the test statistic: Calculation of U_2 uses the same procedure as in Problem 18.2.1.

Step 5. Conclude: Same as for any other test.

Procedure (for one-tailed test):

Step 1. H_0: The two populations have identical distributions
   a. H_a: Population 1 is shifted to the right of Population 2.
   b. H_a: Population 1 is shifted to the left of Population 2.

Step 2. The test statistic is Mann-Whitney's $U = U_2$. Distribution of the test statistic is Z. The formulas are the same as those shown above for the two-tailed procedure.

Step 3. For a one-tailed test, using a significance level of 0.05:
   a. The critical value: If $Z > 1.645$, reject H_0. Otherwise, fail to reject H_0.
   b. The critical value: If $Z < -1.645$, reject H_0. Otherwise, fail to reject H_0.

Step 4. Calculate the test statistic: Calculation of U_2 uses the same procedure as in Problem 18.2.1.

Step 5. Conclude: Same as for any other test.

Wilcoxon Signed Rank Test:

Used for paired dependent samples; with small samples ($n_1 = n_2 = n \leq 15$). Populations need not be normal. To be used under the assumptions:

a. Samples are dependent, paired (e.g. husband and wives, siblings, before and after training, before and after a sales promotion) and randomly selected.
b. Absolute value of the differences can be ranked.

Review Problem 18.2.2

Jamesville Clothing wanted to investigate a proposal to allow employees to use employee discounts for purchases of their entire family. A random selection of 10 employees' purchase patterns were recorded to studied to see everybody and his increase the discounts to its employees for their purchases. Test whether the dollar value of purchases have changed.

Employee #	After the new discount policy	Before the new discount policy	After-before	Rank Positive	Rank Negative
1	125	200	-75		8(-)
2	375	188	187	9	
3	45	67	-22		4.5 (-) (average ranks 4 and 5)
4	98	76	22	4.5 (average of ranks 4 and 5)	
5	23	57	-34		6
6	72	72	0	Omit since both are equal	
7	99	100	-1		1 (-)
8	123	110	13	2	
9	104	124	-20		3 (-)
10	110	49	61	7	
			Total rank	22.5	22.5

Table 18.2.5.

Solution

Procedure (two-sided test):

Step 1. H_0: The two population differences are centered at 0.
H_a: The two population differences are not centered at 0

Step 2. The test statistic is Wilcoxon's T = Min. (T_+, T_-). The critical value corresponding to the T is given in a series of tables in Appendix Table A11.

Step 3. For a two-tailed test, using a significance level of 0.05, the critical value (for n = 9) = 6. Reject H_0 if $T \leq 6$. Otherwise, fail to reject H_0.

Step 4. Calculate the test statistic:

a. Determine n differences using each sample pair (sample1 - sample2).
b. Rank the absolute value of differences and mark negative differences with a (-) after the rank; T_+ = Sum of the ranks of the positive values; T_- = Sum of the ranks of the (-) marked values.
c. T = Min. (T_+, T_-)
d. For this problem: T = (min (22.5,22.5) = 22.5

Step 5. Conclude: Fail to reject H_0. There is not much difference.

Procedure (One-sided test):

Step 1. H_0: The two population differences are centered at 0.

a. H_a: The two population differences are centered at a value > 0.
b. H_a: The two population differences are centered at a value < 0.

Step 2. The test statistic is Wilcoxson's

a. $T = T_-$
b. $T = T_+$

Step 3. For a one-tailed test, using a significance level of 0.05, the critical value (look up in Tale A.11 corresponding to sample size n). If $T \leq$ critical value, reject H_0. Otherwise, fail to reject H_0.

Step 4. Calculate the test statistic:

a. Determine n differences using each sample pair (sample1- sample2).

b. Rank the absolute value of differences and mark negative differences with a (-) after the rank; T_+ = Sum of the ranks of the positive values; T_- = Sum of the ranks of the (-) marked values.

c. $T = T_+$ or T_- as the case may be.

Step 5. Conclude.

Wilcoxon Signed Rank Test

Used for paired dependent samples; with large samples ($n_1 = n_2 = n > 15$). Populations need not be normal. To be used under the assumptions:

a. Samples are dependent, paired (e.g. husband and wives, siblings, before and after training, before and after a sales promotion) and randomly selected.

b. Absolute value of the differences can be ranked.

Review Problem 18.2.3

Popularity of air travel before and after 9/11/2001 by members of an association of retirees is measured by the number of times per year members indulged in air travel. Data for a random sample of 20 retirees is given in Table 18.2.7. Test whether air travel has gone down in this population at a significance level of 0.10.

Sample #	# of trips/year Preceding 9/11/2002	# of trips/year Following 9/11/2002	Sample #	# of trips/year Preceding 9/11/2002	# of trips/year Following 9/11/2002
1	3	2	11	4	2
2	4	4	12	6	8
3	7	3	13	7	3
4	3	5	14	5	5
5	4	1	15	7	6
6	3	4	16	2	5
7	4	5	17	5	1
8	10	9	18	11	9
9	6	3	19	5	2
10	9	11	20	7	9

Solution

Step 1. H_0: The two population differences (after-before) are centered at 0.
H_a: The two population differences (after-before) are centered at a value < 0.

Step 2. To determine the test statistic, first we need to calculate the ranks:

Sample #	# of trips/year preceding 9/11/2002	# of trips/year following 9/11/2002	After-Before	Rank (Positive)	Rank (negative)
1	3	2	-1		3(-)
2	4	4	0	Omit because after = before	
3	7	3	-4		17(-)
4	3	5	2	8.5	
5	4	1	-3		13.5(-)
6	3	4	1		3(-)
7	4	5	1		3(-)
8	10	9	-1		3(-)
9	6	3	-3		13.5(-)
10	9	11	2	8.5	
11	4	2	-2		8.5(-)
12	6	8	2	8.5	
13	7	3	-4		17(-)
14	5	5	0	Omit because after = before	
15	7	6	-1		3(-)
16	2	5	3	13.5	
17	5	1	-4		17(-)
18	11	9	-2		8.5(-)
19	5	2	-3		13.5(-)
20	7	9	2	8.5	
			Total	47.5	123.5

$$Z = \frac{T_{+} - \mu_{T_{+}}}{\sigma_{T_{+}}} = \frac{47.5 - 85.5}{22.96} = -1.655$$

where $\mu_{T_{+}} = \frac{n(n+1)}{4} = \frac{18(18+1)}{4} = 85.5$ and $\sigma_{T_{+}} = \sqrt{\frac{18(18+1)(36+1)}{24}} = 22.96$

Step 3. For this problem, a one-tailed (left-tailed) test, using a significance level of 0.10, the critical value is -1.28. If $Z \leq -1.28$, reject H_0. Otherwise, fail to reject H_0. Since -1.655 is in the reject H_0 region, we reject H_0.

Step 4. Calculate the test statistic: Done

Step 5. Conclusion: Travel has probably gone down among this group.

18.3 Comparing 3 or More Populations -- Kruskal-Wallis (*KW*) Test

Used to test for 3 or more independent samples from respective populations. Samples maybe of all sizes. To be used under the assumptions:

a. Populations need not be normal
b. Samples are independent
c. Sample data are at least ordinal
d. Populations if they differ, differed only in location, but they have same variation and shape.

Problem 18.3.1

Jamesville Advertising agency has just released three different types of advertisements to entice car buyers to purchase cars. An independent agency selected a random set of consumers to rate the effectiveness of the advertisement on a 0 to 100 scale. Use a suitable non-parametric test, (since normality of the population can not be assumed) to check whether all populations have identical distributions at a significance level of 0.05.

Ad 1's score	Ad 1's rank	Ad 2's score	Ad 2's rank	Ad 3's score	Ad 3's rank
87	11	66	4	94	12
67	5.5	95	13	68	7
85	10	67	5.5	73	8
43	1	76	9	45	2
		58	3		
	27.5		34.5		29

Table 18.3.1 Data for Problem 18.3.1.

Solution

Step 1. H_0: The three populations have identical probability distributions
H_a: At least two of the populations differ in location.

Step 2. The test statistic is

$$KW = \frac{12}{n(n+1)}\sum_{i=1}^{k}\frac{T_i^2}{n_i} - 3(n+1) = \frac{12}{13(13+1)}\left[\frac{(27.5)^2}{4} + \frac{(34.5)^2}{5} + \frac{29^2}{4}\right] - 3(13+1) = 0.0239$$

where n is the total population size, T_i is the total rank of sample from population i, where the ranks are obtained by pooling all the data and ranking the data in ascending order, n_i is the sample size of the sample from the ith population, k is the total number of populations under study. KW approximately follows Chi-square distribution with k-1 degrees of freedom even for small samples.

Step 3. For this test, (there is no one- or two-tailed versions), using a significance level of 0.05, the critical value is (looking up in Appendix 6) 5.9915. If the calculated $KW < 5.9915$, we fail to reject H_0. Otherwise, we reject H_0.

Step 4. Calculate the test statistic. Since test statistic value is 0.0239 < CV of 5.9915, we fail to reject H_0. Calculations done in Step 2.

Step 5. We conclude that there is no evidence to believe that the locations differ.

Friedman Test for Comparing 3 or More Populations:
Uses dependent samples (of all sizes) from respective populations. To be used under the assumptions:

a. Populations are not normal.
b. The sample data are ordinal.
c. Populations if they differ, differed only in location, but they have same variation and shape.

Problem 18.3.2 (Friedman test)

Jamesville Consumer Digest is a firm engaged in rating automobiles. They have recently got an assignment to rate Honda-CRV, Toyota Rav4 and Saturn VUE. They selected a random set of 10 customers and had them test drive all three cars and rank them according to overall desirability of the three cars. The rankings are given below. Use Friedman test to determine whether the three populations have identical distributions against the hypothesis that at least two of them differ in location, at a significance level of 0.05.

Honda-CRV	Toyota-Rav4	Saturn VUE
3	1	2
2	3	1
1	2	3
2	1	3
2	3	1
3	1	2
1	2	3
1	2.5	2.5
2	1	3
3	2	1
Total of ranks = 20	Total of ranks = 18.5	Total of ranks = 21.5

Solution

Step 1. H_0: The three populations have identical probability distributions
H_a: At least two of the populations differ in location.

Step 2. The test statistic is

$$FR = \frac{12}{bk(k+1)}\sum_{i=1}^{k} T_i^2 - 3b(k+1) = \left[\frac{12}{10\times 3(3+1)}\right]\left[20^2 + (18.5)^2 + 21^2\right] - 3.10(3+1) = 0.45$$

where T_i is the total rank of sample from population i, where the ranks are obtained by ranking of the product by each consumer, b is the number of blocks of data (i.e. number customers who ranked all three) k is the total number of populations under study. FR approximately follows Chi-square distribution with k-1 degrees of freedom even for small samples.

Step 3. For this test, (there is no one- or two-tailed versions), using a significance level of 0.05, the critical value (looking up in Appendix Table A6) is 5.9915. If the calculated $FR <$ 5.9915, we fail to reject H_0. Otherwise, we reject H_0.

Step 4. Calculate the test statistic: Since test statistic value is 0.45 < critical value of 5.9915, we fail to reject H_0. Calculations done in Step 2.

Step 5. We conclude that there is no evidence to believe that the locations differ.

18.4 Self-Test Problems

Self-test Problem 18.4.1.
Viewers of a TV station are encouraged to call in at the end of a new show to vote yes/no on the show. We want to test the hypothesis that the stream of Y and N are random. The following stream of 25 calls was observed. YYNNNYYNYNYNNNYYYNNYYNNNN. Test for randomness using the runs test.

Self-test Problem 18.4.2

Global Blue-Green Tours Inc. conducts promotional presentations of its time-share for groups of 70 individual customers at a time. At the end, they sequentially ask them to buy a time-share. They want to test whether the sequence of Yes/No answers they were getting from the attendees is random at a significance level of 0.08. The following is the result of one such promotional meeting.
NNNNNYNYNY NNNNNYYYYY NNYNYNNYNY NNYNNYNYNN
NYNNYYNNNY NYNYYYNNYN YNYNYNYNNY
Use the runs test for large samples to answer this question.

Self-Test Problem 18.4.3

Two auditors of Jamesville LLC are given a score on a 100 point scale, for their integrity as perceived by their clients and the scores are presented in Table 18.2.4. These scores are not considered normally distributed. Using Mann-Whitney, test whether the location parameters of population of scores of the auditors are same or different, using 0.10 significance level.

Auditor I	Auditor II
96	85
78	89
92	80
67	87
72	84
81	90
89	92
	87

Table 18.4.1: Data for Self-test Problem 18.4.3

Self-test Problem 18.4.4.

Mr. Jim Jones, Vice-President of student Affairs at The University of Jamesville wanted to evaluate the impact of a policy of allowing students in Spring 2003, to take any credits from 12-15 for the same flat fee of $5400.00 on number of hours taken. The current policy is $400 per credit hour. Students are classified as full-time if they take 12 or more hours. He took a random sample of 12 students and checked the number of hours taken by them in Fall 2002 and Spring 2003. He wanted to check whether the hours taken has increased at a significance level of 0.05. Data is given in Table 18.4.2.

Name	Hours in Fall 2002	Hours in Spring 2003
Kathy	12	15
Devaki	14	12
Nicole	13	15
Alisha	17	19
John	14	15
Sundar	12	14
James	16	15

Kathy	13	13
Susan	14	13
Tanya	18	15
Ming	13	15
Wong	12	15

Table 18.4.2.

Self-test Problem 18.4.5.

Number of finance related arguments among couples in the 6 months preceding and following their marriage is documented for a sample of 26 couples. Using non-parametric methods, test whether there is a difference at a significance level of 0.05.

Sample #	# of finance-related arguments before marriage	# of finance-related arguments after marriage.	Sample #	# of finance-related arguments before marriage	# of finance-related arguments after marriage.
1	8	5	14	4	2
2	4	6	15	6	8
3	5	8	16	7	3
4	7	5	17	5	5
5	2	3	18	7	6
6	4	5	19	2	5
7	5	7	20	5	1
8	8	4	21	11	9
9	4	12	22	5	2
10	9	8	23	7	9
11	5	5	24	8	4
12	2	3	25	5	8
13	4	7	26	7	4

Self-test Problem 18.4.6.

There are three professors (Johnson, Smith and Peterson), each claiming to be as strict as the others in grading the final exam for their Introduction to Business Statistics course. They agreed to let an unbiased colleague test their claim. A random selection of final exam scores from each Professor's most recent course offering is shown in Table 8.3.2. Test using Kruskal-Wallis (*KW*) whether all three populations have identical probability distributions, at a significance level of 0.10.

Professor Johnson	Professor Smith	Professor Peterson
98	86	48
79	76	79
46	94	92
88	80	87
23	47	
	38	

Table 18.4.3. Data for Self-Test Problem 18.4.6.

Multiple Choice Questions

1. Dependent samples are obtained when
   a. Two populations are dependent on each other for some aspect of performance
   b. Observations in Sample 1 are related is some way to observations in Sample2
   c. Every observation in Sample 1 is matched with exactly one observation in Sample 2, and every observation in Sample 2 is exactly matched with one observation in Sample 1
   d. Observation 1 in Sample 1 matched with Observation 1 in Sample 2, Observation 2 in Sample 1 matched with Observation 2 in Sample 2, etc
   e. c and d
2. Independent samples
   a. Must have same sample size from each population
   b. Need not have same sample size from each population
   c. Are such that sample observations from one population is selected independent of the sample observations from the other population
   d. b and c
   e. None of the above
3. Non-parametric tests
   a. Do not assume normality of the underlying population
   b. Can be used in many instances where only ordinal data is available
   c. Can be used in many instances where only nominal data is available
   d. a and b
   e. None of the above
4. Runs test
   a. Can be used to test for randomness of two outcomes
   b. Can be used to test for independence of data
   c. Requires equal number of two outcomes in the sample
   d. a and c
   e. None of the above
5. Friedman test is used for
   a. Testing equality of variance in three or more populations
   b. Whether three or more populations have identical distributions when samples from the population are dependent
   c. An alternative to randomized block design
   d. b and c
   e. None of the above
6. Mann-Whitney *U* test
   a. Can only be used as a two-sided test
   b. Tests whether two populations differ in location using independent samples
   c. Tests whether three or more populations differ in location using two independent samples
   d. Tests whether two populations differ in location using dependent samples
   e. None of the above
7. Wilcoxon signed rank test
   a. Can only be used as a two-sided test
   b. Tests whether two populations differ in location using independent samples
   c. Tests whether three or more populations differ in location using two independent samples
   d. Tests whether two population differences are centered at 0 using dependent (paired) samples
   e. None of the above
8. Kruskal-Wallis test
   a. Tests whether three or more populations differ in location using two dependent samples

b. Tests whether two populations differ in location using independent samples
c. Tests whether two or more populations differ in location using independent samples
d. Tests whether two population differences are centered at 0 using dependent (paired) samples
e. None of the above

9. Kruskal Wallis test for large samples uses a test statistic which follows
   a. Normal distribution
   b. Chi-square distribution
   c. Does not follow any distribution and hence must be looked up in table form
   d. Poisson distribution
   e. None of the above
10. Mann-Whitney *U* test for large samples uses a test statistic which follows
    a. Normal distribution
    b. Chi-square distribution
    c. Does not follow any distribution and hence must be looked up in table form
    d. Poisson distribution
    e. None of the above

18.4 Glossary

dependent samples
Samples where observation 1 in sample 1 is matched-up (paired) with observation 1 in sample 2, observation 2 in sample 1 with observation 2 in sample 2, and so on.

independent samples
Samples from two or more populations where the observations in each sample are selected independently of the observations in the other sample(s).

Friedman test
A nonparametric procedure which is an alternative to the randomized block technique.

Kruskal-Wallis test
A nonparametric procedure for determining if two or more populations differ in location using independent samples (an alternative to one-factor ANOVA).

Spearman rank correlation
A nonparametric measure of the association between sample values on two variables that consist of ordinal data.

Mann-Whitney *U* test
A nonparametric procedure for determining if two populations differ in location using two independent samples.

Nonparametric methods
A collection of statistical procedures that require very few, if any, assumptions about the underlying population(s). They can be used when the sample contains ordinal (rank-order) data.

Runs test
A nonparametric procedure for determining if an arrangement of two symbols was generated in a random manner.

Wilcoxon signed rank test
A nonparametric procedure for determining if the population differences are centered at zero when dealing with two dependent (paired) samples.

18.6 Solution to Self-test Problems

Solution to Self-test Problem 18.4.1

Step 1. Null Hypothesis: Y and N occur randomly.
Alternate hypothesis: Y and N are not occurring randomly.

Step 2. The number of runs is the test statistic:

Step 3. n_1 (number of Y's in the stream) = 11 and n_2 (number of N's) = 14. From Appendix Table A.15, $k_1 = 8$ and $k_2 = 19$. According to the test, if $R \leq 8$ or if $R \geq 19$, reject H_0. Otherwise, Fail to reject H_0.

Step 4. From the data: YY NNN YY N Y N Y NNN YYY NN YY NNNN, $R = 12$.

Step 5. Hence, we fail to reject H_0. That is, the Y and N appear to be random.

Solution to Self-test Problem 18.4.2

Step 1. Null Hypothesis: Y and N occur randomly.
Alternate hypothesis: Y and N are not occurring randomly.

Step 2. The test statistic is $Z = \frac{R - \mu_R}{\sigma_R}$.

Step 3. For a two-tailed test, using Z, with a significance level of 0.08, the critical values are: -1.75 and +1.75. Reject H_0 if the computed $|Z| \geq 1.75$. Otherwise, Fail to reject H_0

Step 4. From the given data, n_1 (number of Y's) = 29 and n_2 (number of N's) = 41. $R = 44$.

$$\mu_R = 1 + \frac{(2)(29)(41)}{29+41} = 34.97 \text{ and } \sigma_R = \sqrt{\frac{[(2)(29)(41)][(2)(29)(41) - 29 - 41]}{(29+41)^2\,(29+41-1)}} = 4.029$$

$$\text{and } Z = \frac{44 - 34.97}{4.029} = 2.2412$$

Step 5. Since Z falls in the reject H_0 region, reject H_0 meaning the appearance of Y and N does not look like a random stream.

Solution to Self-test Problem 18.4.3.

Step 1. H_0: The two populations have identical distributions
H_a: The two populations differ in location.

Step 2. The test statistic is Mann-Whitney's U = Min. (U_1, U_2). The probability values corresponding to the U is given in a series of Tables in Appendix 10.

Step 3. For a two-tailed test, using a significance level of 0.10, the critical values is 0.05. If the probability value corresponding to the U value is less than 0.10/2 = 0.05, reject H_0. Otherwise, fail to reject H_0

Step 4. Calculate the test statistic: First step is to group the data and rank them. Recall that as per assumption 4, $n_1 \leq n_2$. (In case of tied values, average rank is assigned)*

Rank	Sample scores for Auditor I	Sample scores for Auditor II	Ranks for Auditor I	Ranks for Auditor II
1	67		1	
2	72		2	
3	78		3	
4		80		4
5	81		5	
6		84		6
7		85		7
8		87		8.5
9		87		8,5
10	89		10.5	
11		89		10.5
12		90		12
13	92		13.5	
14		92		13.5
15	96		15	
		Sum of Ranks	50 (T1)	70 (T2)

Table 18.2.5. Ranking of Data of Problem 18.2.1.

$$U_1 = n_1 n_2 + \frac{n_1(n_1+1)}{2} - T_1 = 7 \times 8 + \frac{7(7+1)}{2} - 50 = 34$$

$$U_2 = n_1 n_2 + \frac{n_2(n_2+1)}{2} - T_2 = 7 \times 8 + \frac{8(8+1)}{2} - 70 = 20$$

U = Min (U_1, U_2) = Min (34,20) = 20. $n_2 = 8$

U		n_1	
		7	
20		0.1984	

Table 18.2.6: Distribution function of the Mann-Whitney U Statistic (Appendix Table A.10)

Step 5. Since the significance level is 0.10, and the corresponding probability value 0.1984 is higher 0.10/2 = 0.05, we fail to reject H_0. We conclude that there is no evidence to believe that the locations of the two distributions are any different.

Solution to Self-test Problem 18.4.4.

Step 1. H_0: The two population differences (after-before) are centered at 0.
H_a: The two population differences (after-before) are centered at a value > 0.

Step 2. The test statistic is Wilcoxson's. $T = T_-$

Step 3. For a one-tailed test, using a significance level of 0.05, the critical value (Appendix Table A.11 corresponding to sample size $n = 11$, since one pair with same before and after value had to be omitted.) = 14. If $T \leq$ critical value, reject H_0. Otherwise, fail to reject H_0.

Step 4. Calculate the test statistic:

Name	Cr. Hrs. Fall 2002 (Before)	Cr. Hrs. Spring 2003 (After)	After-Before	Rank (positive)	Rank (Negative)
Kathy	12	15	3	10 ((9+10+11)/3)	
Devaki	14	12	-2		6(-)((4+5+6+7+8)/5)
Nicole	13	15	2	6((4+5+6+7+8)/5)	
Alisha	17	19	2	6((4+5+6+7+8)/5)	
John	14	15	1	2 ((1+2+3)/3)	
Sundar	12	14	2	6((4+5+6+7+8)/5)	
James	16	15	-1		2(-)((1+2+3)/3)
Kathy	13	13	0	Omit since both are equal	
Susan	14	13	-1		2(-)((1+2+3)/3)
Tanya	18	15	-3		10(-)((9+10+11)/3)
Ming	13	15	2	6((4+5+6+7+8)/5)	
Wong	12	15	3	10((9+10+11)/3)	
			Total	46	20

$T = 20$

Step 5. Since T (20) is not $\leq$ 14, we Fail to reject H_0. There is not enough evidence to support H_a.

Solution to Self-test Problem 18.4.5.

Step 1. H_0: The two population differences (after-before) are centered at 0.
H_a: The two population differences (after-before) are not centered at 0.

Step 2. To determine the test statistic, first we need to calculate the ranks:

Sample #	# of Finance-Related Arguments 6 Months Before Marriage	# of Finance-Related Arguments 6 Months After Marriage.	After - Before	Rank (Positive)	Rank (Negative)
1	8	5	-3		16(-)
2	4	6	2	9	
3	5	8	3	16	
4	7	5	-2		9(-)
5	2	3	1	3	
6	4	5	1	3	
7	5	7	2	9	
8	8	4	-4		21.5(-)
9	4	12	8	24	
10	9	8	-1		3(-)
11	5	5	0	Omit because after = before	
12	2	3	1	3	
13	4	7	3	16	
14	4	2	-2		9(-)
15	6	8	2	9	
16	7	3	-4		21.5(-)
17	5	5	0	Omit because after = before	
18	7	6	-1		3(-)
19	2	5	3	16	
20	5	1	-4		21.5(-)
21	11	9	-2		9(-)
22	5	2	-3		16(-)
23	7	9	2	9	
24	8	4	-4		21.5(-)
25	5	8	3	16	
26	7	4	-3		16(-)
			Total	133	167

$$Z = \frac{133 - 150}{35} = -0.485$$

where $\mu_{T_+} = \dfrac{24(24+1)}{4} = 150$ and $\sigma_{T_+} = \sqrt{\dfrac{24(24+1)(48+1)}{24}} = 35$

Step 3. For this problem, it is a two-tailed test, using a significance level of 0.05, the critical value is $|Z| > 1.96$, reject H_0. Otherwise, fail to reject H_0. -0.485 is in the Fail to reject H_0 region.

Step 4. Calculate the test statistic: Done

Step 5. Conclusion: Probably, there is not much difference between the numbers of finance-related arguments 6 months before and after marriage in the population studied.

Solution to Self-test Problem 18.4.6.

Data table and the corresponding ranks:

Professor Johnson		Professor Smith		Professor Peterson	
98	15	86	10	48	5
79	7.5	76	6	79	7.5
46	3	94	14	92	13
88	12	80	9	87	11
23	1	47	4		
		38	2		
Total	38.5	Total	45	Total	36.5

Step 1. H_0: The three populations have identical probability distributions
H_a: At least two of the populations differ in location.

Step 2. The test statistic is

$$KW = \left[\frac{12}{15(15+1)}\right]\left[\frac{(38.5)^2}{5} + \frac{45^2}{6} + \frac{(36.5)^2}{4}\right] - 3(15+1) = 0.3506$$

KW approximately follows Chi-square distribution with k - 1 = 3 - 1 = 2 degrees of freedom even for small samples.

Step 3. For this test, (there is no one- or two-tailed versions), and using a significance level of 0.05, the critical value (looking up in Appendix Table A6) is 4.6052 If the calculated $KW < 4.6052$, we fail to reject H_0. Otherwise, we reject H_0.

Step 4. Calculate the test statistic: Calculations done in Step 2.

Step 5. Since test statistic value is 0.3506 < critical value of 4.6052, we fail to reject H_0. We conclude that there is no evidence to believe that the locations differ.

Answers to Self-Test Multiple Choice Questions

Question #	Answer	Question #	Answer	Question#	Answer
1	e	5	d	9	b
2	d	6	b	10	a
3	d	7	d		
4	a	8	c		